Mike McGrath

R for Data Analysis

In easy steps is an imprint of In Easy Steps Limited
16 Hamilton Terrace · Holly Walk · Leamington Spa
Warwickshire · United Kingdom · CV32 4LY
www.ineasysteps.com

In Easy Steps Limited supports The Forest Stewardship Council (FSC), the leading international forest certification organization. All our titles that are printed on Greenpeace approved FSC certified paper carry the FSC logo.

Printed and bound in the United Kingdom

ISBN 978-1-84078-795-5

Contents

Preface

The creation of this book has been for me, Mike McGrath, an exciting personal journey in discovering how the R programming language can be used today for data analysis and the production of beautiful data visualizations. Example code listed in this book describes how to produce R Scripts in easy steps – and the screenshots illustrate the actual results. I sincerely hope you enjoy discovering the exciting possibilities of R programming and have as much fun with it as I did in writing this book.

In order to clarify the code listed in the steps given in each example I have adopted certain colorization conventions. Components and keywords of the R programming language are colored blue, programmer-specified names are colored red, literal numeric values and literal character string values are colored black, and comments are colored green, like this:

```
# Write the traditional greeting.
greeting = "Hello World!"
print( greeting )
```

Additionally, non-literal values are colored gray like this: **color="Red"**

In order to readily identify each source code file described in the steps a file icon and file name appears in the margin alongside the steps:

Script.R

For convenience I have placed source code files from the examples featured in this book into a single ZIP archive. You can obtain the complete archive by following these easy steps:

1. Browse to **www.ineasysteps.com** then navigate to Free Resources and choose the Downloads section

2. Find R for Data Analysis in easy steps in the list, then click on the hyperlink entitled All Code Examples to download the archive

3. Next, extract the "MyRScripts" folder to a convenient location on your system

4. Now, follow the steps to call upon the R program interpreter and see the output

1 Getting started

Welcome to the exciting world of R programming. This chapter describes how to set up an R environment and demonstrates how to create a first R program.

Understanding data

The term "data" refers to items of information that describe a (qualitative) status or a (quantitative) measure of magnitude. Various types of data is collected from a huge range of sources and reported for analysis to reveal pattern and trend insights:

This illustration depicts only some of the many data types that can be reported for analysis.

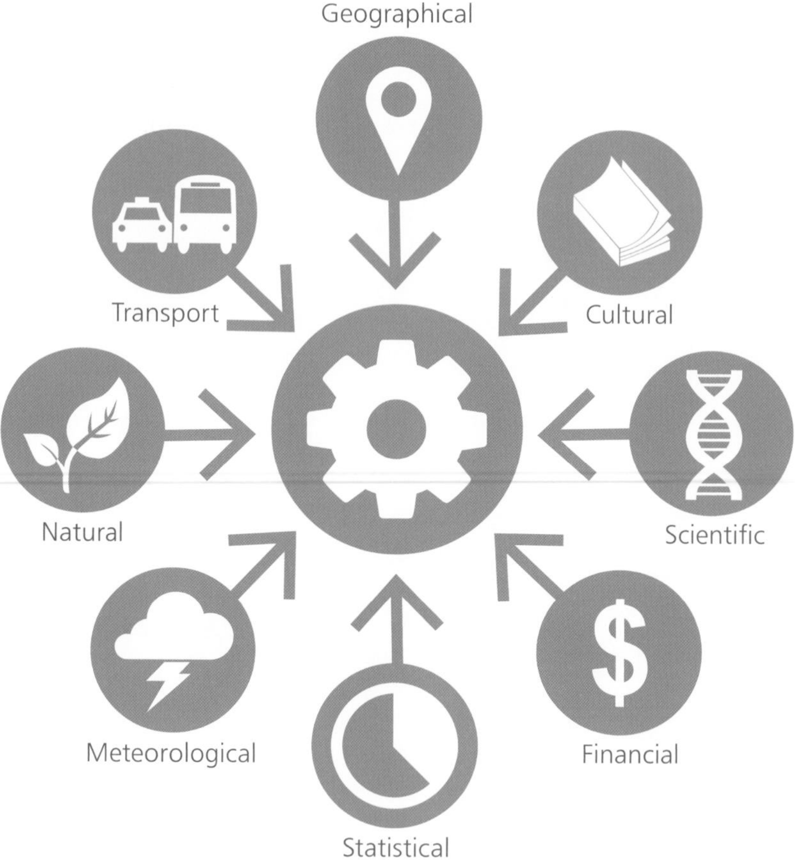

Around 13 billion devices are connected to the internet today. This is predicted to grow to 50 billion by 2020.

Data is increasingly being collected by devices that are able to report measurements for analysis via the internet ("The Cloud"). For example, devices that have temperature and humidity sensors can report measurements for instant analysis of climate conditions. The recent rapid decline in the cost of device sensors has given rise to the "Internet of Things" (IoT) that can easily and cheaply report vast amounts of data – this is often referred to as "big data". Big data consists of extremely large data sets that can best be analyzed by computer to reveal pattern and trend insights.

Data analysis (a.k.a. "data analytics") is the practice of converting collected data into information that is useful for decision-making. The collected "raw" data will, however, typically undergo two initial procedures before it can be explored for insights:

- **Data processing** – the raw data must be organized into a structured format. For example, it may be arranged into rows and columns in a table format for use in a spreadsheet.
- **Data cleaning** – the organized data must be stripped of incomplete, duplicated, and erroneous items. For, example, by the removal of duplicated rows in a spreadsheet.

"Data Science" is the study of how data can be turned into a valuable resource.

After the data has been processed and cleaned it can be explored to discover its main characteristics. This may require further data cleaning to refine the data to specific areas of interest, or may require additional data to better understand its messages. Descriptive statistics, such as average values, might be calculated to understand the data. Algorithms might be used to identify associations within the data. Data visualization might also be used to produce a graphical representation of the data for examination.

"Data Mining" is the process of searching large data sets to identify patterns.

After the data has been analyzed, the results can be communicated using data visualization to present tables, plots, or charts that clearly and efficiently convey the key messages within the data. Tables provide information in which the user can look up a specific number, whereas plots and charts provide information in a way that encourages the eye to make comparisons.

"R" is an interpreted programming language and software environment that is widely used for data analysis and visualization. The "RStudio" Integrated Development Environment (IDE) is often used with R, as RStudio provides a code editor, debugging features, and visualization tools that make R easier to use. The popularity of R has grown rapidly in recent years as the increase in big data has made data analysis more important than ever.

"Data Product" is digital information that can be purchased.

The R programming software and RStudio IDE are both available for Windows, Linux, and macOS operating systems, and both are used throughout this book to demonstrate R for data analysis.

Installing R

The R programming language and software environment is freely available open source software that you can install onto your computer from the Comprehensive R Archive Network (CRAN):

If you are having difficulty downloading R click the CRAN **Mirrors** link at **cran.r-project.org** then choose a server near to your location.

1. Open a web browser and visit **cran.r-project.org**

2. Select the link appropriate for your computer operating system. For example, click **Download R for Windows**

Download and Install R

Precompiled binary distributions of the base system and contributed packages, **Windows and Mac** users most likely want one of these versions of R:

- Download R for Linux
- Download R for (Mac) OS X
- Download R for Windows

R is part of many Linux distributions, you should check with your Linux package management system in addition to the link above.

3. Next, select the link for the **base** R distribution

R for Windows

Subdirectories:

base   Binaries for base distribution. This is what you want to **install R for the first time**.

4. Now, select the link to **download** the R installer

R-3.5.1 for Windows (32/64 bit)

Download R 3.5.1 for Windows (62 megabytes, 32/64 bit)
Installation and other instructions
New features in this version

You can click the link for **Installation and other instructions** for more help with installation.

5. When the download has completed, run the installer to open the **R Setup Wizard** and click the **Next** button

6. Read the **License** information, then click the **Next** button to continue

7. Accept the suggested installation location, then click the **Next** button to continue

8. Choose to install **Core Files** and **32-bit Files** for a 32-bit machine, or choose to install **Core Files** and **64-bit Files** for a 64-bit machine, then click the **Next** button to continue

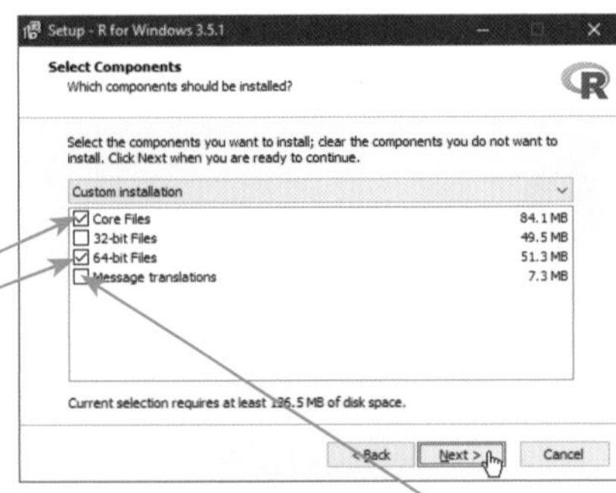

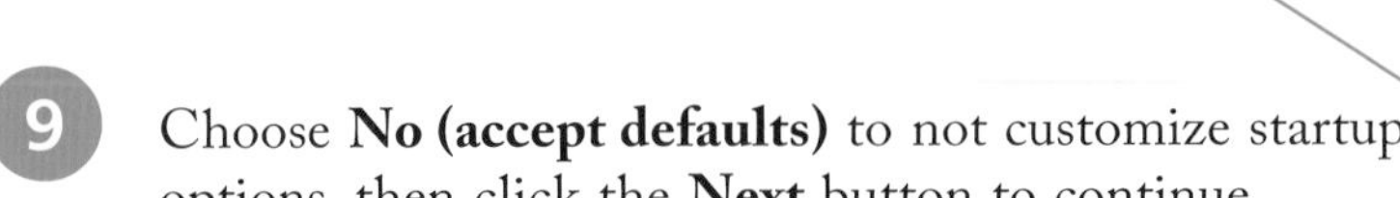

9. Choose **No (accept defaults)** to not customize startup options, then click the **Next** button to continue

10. Enter a name for a Start Menu folder (such as "R"), then click the **Next** button to continue

11. Choose additional tasks (such as **Create a desktop icon**), then click the **Next** button to begin the installation

12. When installation has completed, launch the **R** environment from the Start Menu folder you named

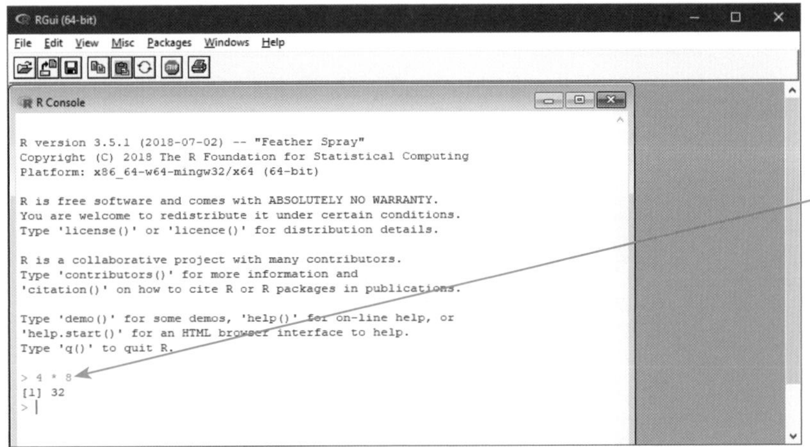

You can find the System Type on Windows by pressing **WinKey** + **R** then entering **msinfo32**.

You can install **Message translations** for error messages, warning messages, and menu labels in languages other than English.

You can type expressions in the R Console to see their result – but the RStudio IDE is a much more effective programming environment.

Installing RStudio

R Studio

The RStudio software is available in Desktop and Server versions with Open Source Licenses and Commercial Licenses for each version – be sure to download the Desktop version with the Open Source License to try the examples in this book for free.

The RStudio IDE has a freely available open source edition that you can install onto your computer from the RStudio website:

1. Open a web browser and visit the RStudio downloads page at **rstudio.com/products/rstudio/download**

2. Scroll down the page and select the **Installer** download link appropriate for your computer operating system. For example, click the edition for **Windows Vista/7/8/10**

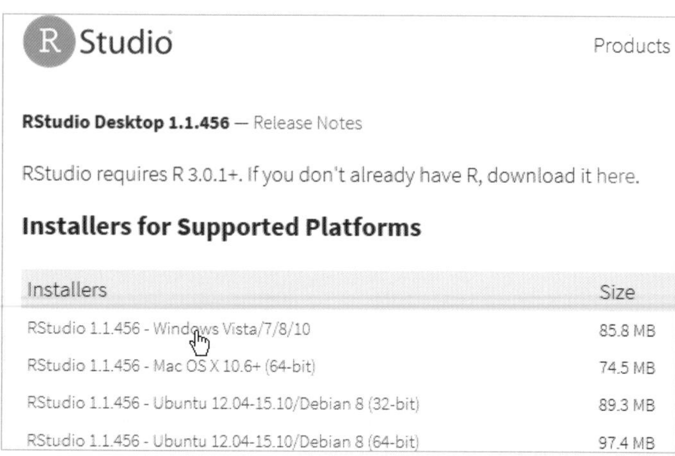

You must have R installed before you install RStudio. See pages 10-11 for the R software installation procedure.

3. When the download has completed, run the installer to open the **RStudio Setup Wizard** – then click **Next**

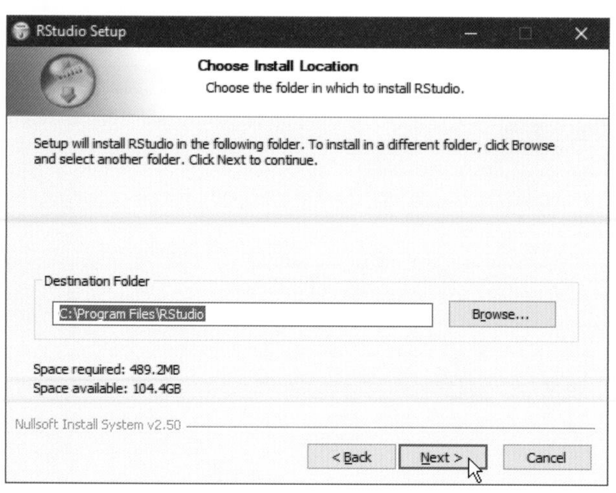

4. Accept the suggested installation location and click the **Next** button to continue

5. Accept the suggested Start Menu folder name "RStudio" and click the **Install** button to continue

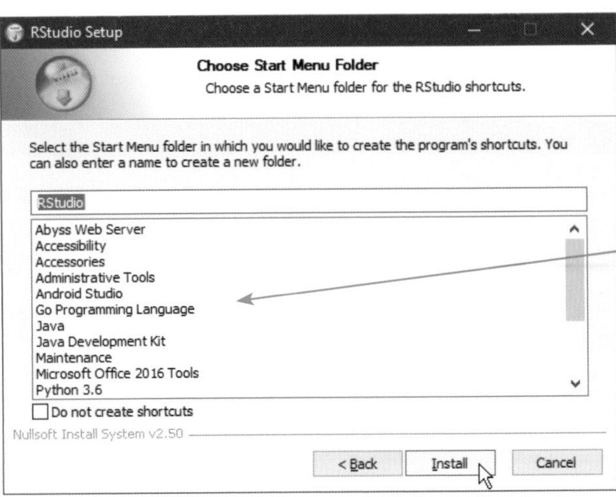

The items listed in this dialog box are the names of your existing Start Menu folders and will vary according to what you have installed on your computer.

6. When the installation has completed, click the **Finish** button to close the Setup Wizard

7. Launch the **RStudio** IDE from the Start Menu folder created by the Setup Wizard

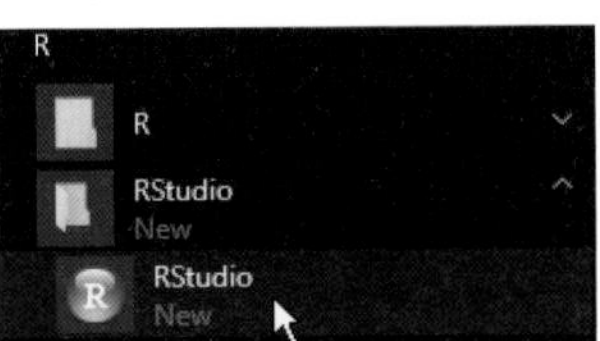

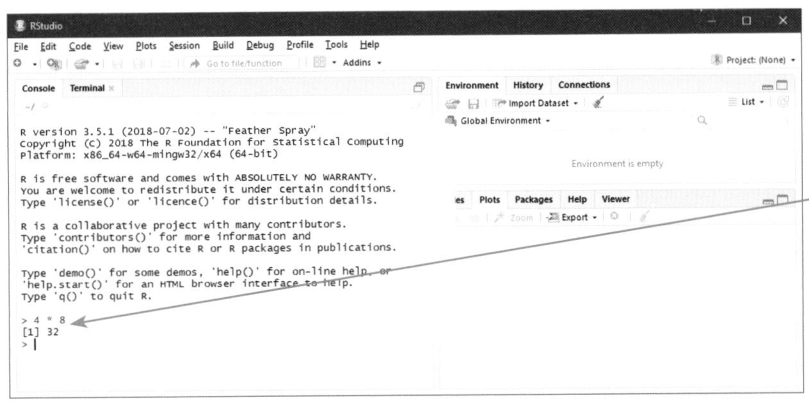

You can type expressions in the RStudio Console to see their result, just as you can in the R Console – but the RStudio IDE can do so much more.

Exploring RStudio

The RStudio interface consists of a menu bar and toolbar positioned at the top of the window, and four main panes whose position can be adjusted to suit your preference. When you launch RStudio only three panes may be visible until you select **File**, **New File**, **RScript** on the menu bar to open the "Code Editor" pane. The default layout positions the four panes as shown below:

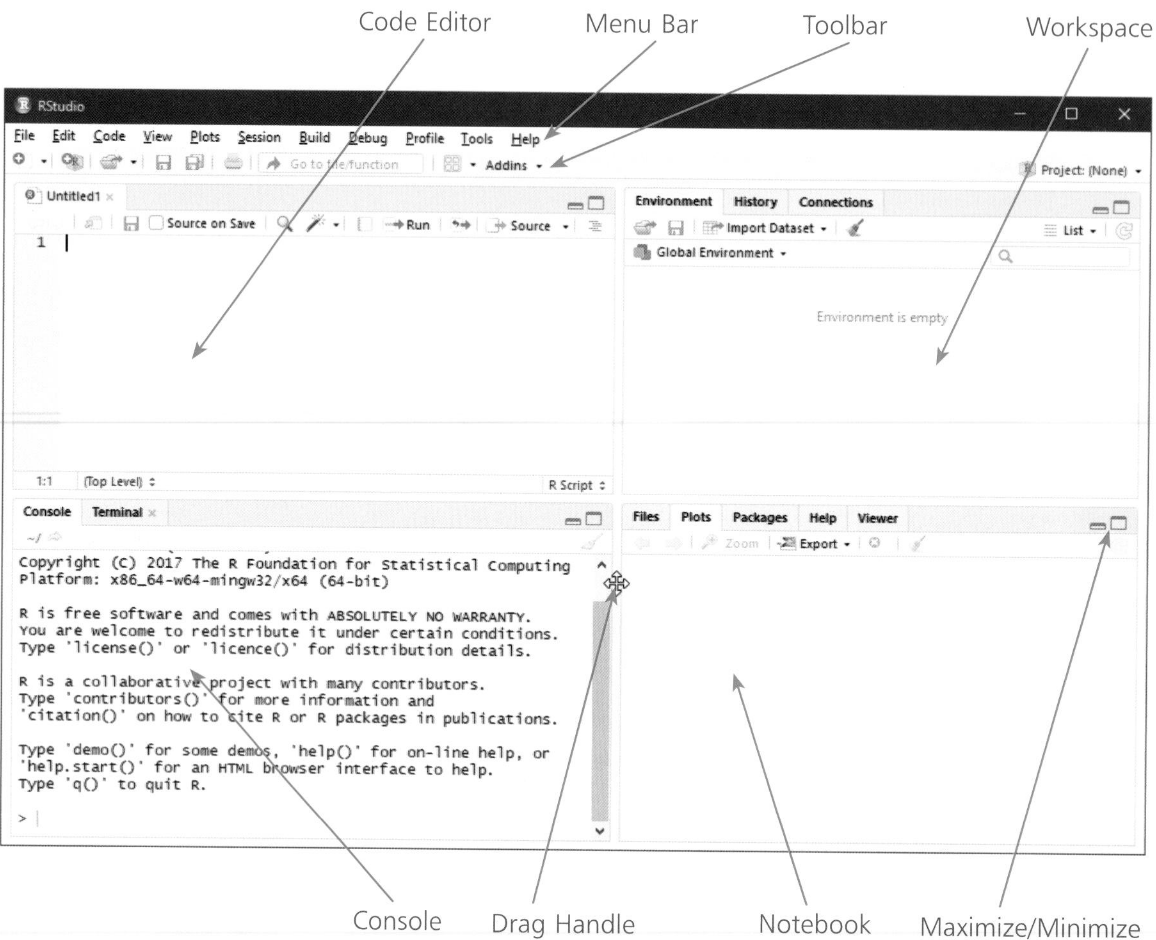

When the mouse pointer is placed on the border between any two panes, the pointer changes to a four-pointed "Drag Handle". This allows you to drag the vertical border to adjust the width of the left and right panes, and to drag the horizontal border to adjust the height of the top and bottom panes. The size of each pane can also be adjusted by clicking the Maximize and Minimize buttons.

Each RStudio pane can contain multiple tabs, and it is useful to initially explore each RStudio pane to understand its purpose:

Code Editor pane

The Code Editor is where you type or edit R Script code, and you see it automatically colored to highlight syntax – click this pane's Run button to see the script output appear in the Console pane.

R Script code can be saved as a file for later use, and multiple R Script files can be open on separate tabs in the Code Editor pane.

Console pane

- **Console tab** – This is where you can directly enter commands for immediate execution by the R interpreter.
- **Terminal tab** – This is where you can directly enter commands for execution by the operating system shell.

Workspace pane

- **Environment tab** – This is where you will see available objects such as variables and datasets.
- **History tab** – This is a list of your past commands executed by the R interpreter in the Console pane.
- **Connections tab** – This tab enables you to connect to databases to explore the objects and data inside the connection.

You can click on a data set listed in the Environment tab to open a spreadsheet of that data in the Code Editor pane.

Notebook pane

- **Files tab** – This is a file browser, which by default lists all the files in your working directory.
- **Plots tab** – This exciting tab is where your plots, graphs, and charts will appear as output from an R Script.
- **Packages tab** – This tab lists available packages that you can install to extend RStudio's functionality.
- **Help tab** – This is where you can seek assistance on the R language and RStudio IDE.
- **Viewer tab** – This is where you can see local HTML content that has been written to the session temporary directory.

You can click on an R Script file in the Files tab to open that file in the Code Editor pane.

Setting preferences

RStudio is highly customizable and it is worth setting up its features to better enjoy your R programming environment:

1. Create a new directory on your computer in which to save the R Scripts you will write. For example, on Windows you might create a directory of **C:\MyRScripts**

2. Launch RStudio then select **Tools**, **Global Options** on the menu bar – to open the "Options" dialog

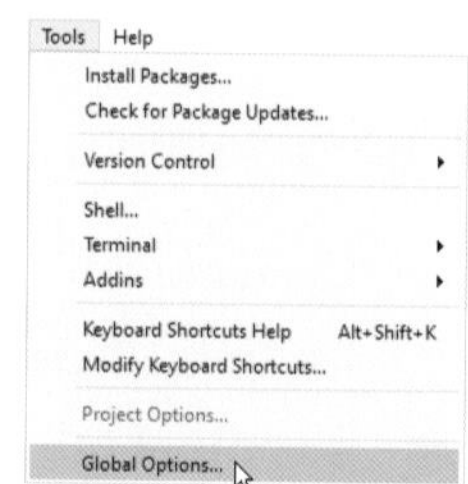

3. Select **General** in the left panel of the "Options" dialog, then enter the path to the directory you created into the **Default working directory** box

Don't forget

Your home directory is set as the default working directory until you specify an alternative.

Themes with dark backgrounds, such as the "Cobalt" theme shown here, are often considered to be more restful on your eyes than those with white backgrounds.

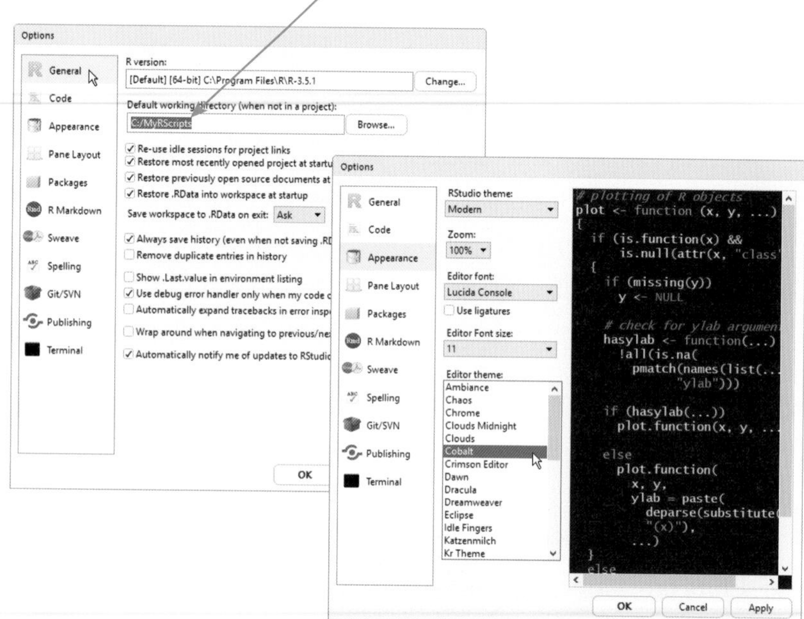

4. Next, select **Appearance** in the left panel, then click items in the **Editor theme** box to preview possible color themes

5. Use the **Editor font** and **Editor font size** drop-down menus to choose your font preferences

6. Click the **Apply** button to change the RStudio settings

7. Click the **OK** button to close the "Options" dialog and see your preferences have been applied – the working directory path appears on the Console title bar

```
Console C:/MyRScripts/

R version 3.5.1 (2018-07-02) -- "Feather Spray"
Copyright (C) 2018 The R Foundation for Statistical Computing
Platform: x86_64-w64-mingw32/x64 (64-bit)

R is free software and comes with ABSOLUTELY NO WARRANTY.
You are welcome to redistribute it under certain conditions.
Type 'license()' or 'licence()' for distribution details.

R is a collaborative project with many contributors.
Type 'contributors()' for more information and
'citation()' on how to cite R or R packages in publications.

Type 'demo()' for some demos, 'help()' for on-line help, or
'help.start()' for an HTML browser interface to help.
Type 'q()' to quit R.

> |
```

You can click the arrow button on the Console pane title bar to reveal the working directory's files in the Files pane.

8. You next need to select a pane to work with in RStudio – click on the Console pane to select it

9. Click the brush button on the Console pane's title bar, or press **Ctrl** + **L** keys, to clear existing Console content

10. Now, type **version** at the Console prompt, then hit **Enter** to run the command – see the R interpreter output version details in the Console window

```
Console C:/MyRScripts/
> version

platform       x86_64-w64-mingw32
arch           x86_64
os             mingw32
system         x86_64, mingw32
status
major          3
minor          5.1
year           2018
month          07
day            02
svn rev        74947
language       R
version.string R version 3.5.1 (2018-07-02)
nickname       Feather Spray
> |
```

Commands typed at the Console prompt must be entered again to run the command once more – whereas commands typed in the Code Editor can be run repeatedly.

Dark background themes are great for on-screen viewing but all ensuing screenshots throughout this book use a white background theme (TextMate) for better on-page clarity.

Creating an R Script

Unless you simply want to test a snippet of code directly at a Console prompt, you should always create an R Script using the Code Editor – so that your code can be run whenever required:

Hello.R

1. Launch RStudio, then click **File**, **New File**, **R Script** on the menu bar to open the Code Editor pane

2. Click on the Code Editor pane to select it and see a blinking cursor appear – here, type the command **print( )**

3. Type a " double-quote character between the command's parentheses and see RStudio automatically add a second character after the cursor – so you cannot forget the final double-quote that is required to enclose a text string

The command here is calling the built-in R **print( )** function. The R language is case-sensitive, so typing the command as **Print( )** or **PRINT( )** will simply produce an error.

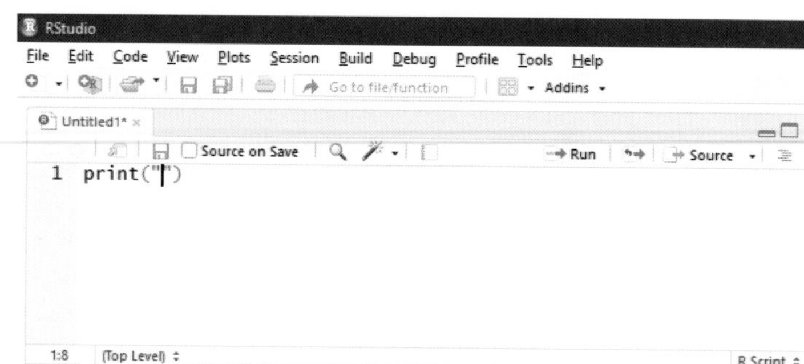

4. Next, type the traditional program greeting **Hello World!** text string between the double-quotes

The R interpreter will only run code on the line containing the cursor or multiple lines that you have selected (highlighted) by dragging the cursor over them.

5. IMPORTANT: Ensure that the cursor is now positioned on the same line as your code

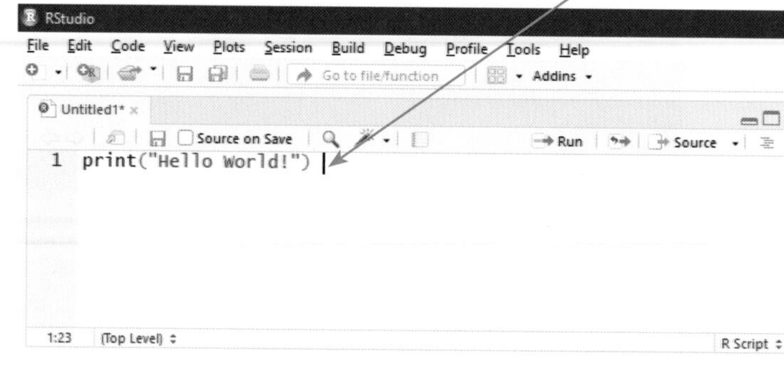

6 Click the Run button in the Code Editor, or press the **Ctrl** + **Enter** keys, to run the code – see the R interpreter repeat the code and display its output in the Console pane

7 Click the Save button in the Code Editor, or press the **Ctrl** + **S** keys, to open the "Save File" dialog

8 Save the R Script as a file named "Hello.R" in the current working directory

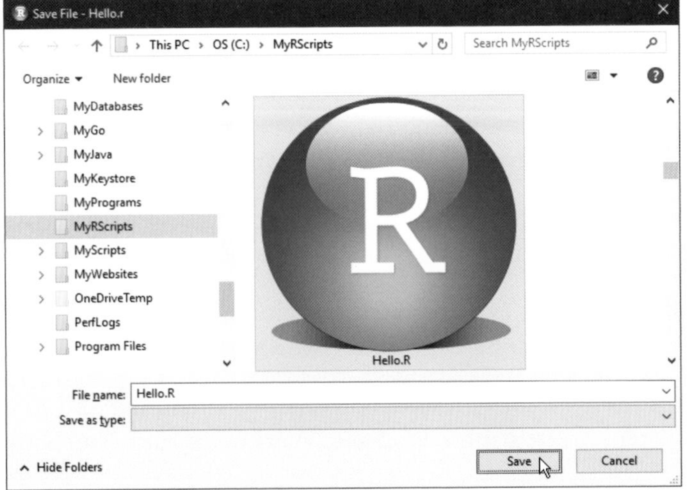

9 Edit the command in the Code Editor by adding a second argument between the parentheses to become **print("Hello World!", quote=FALSE)**

10 Run the code again – see the R interpreter repeat the code and display its output with quotes now suppressed

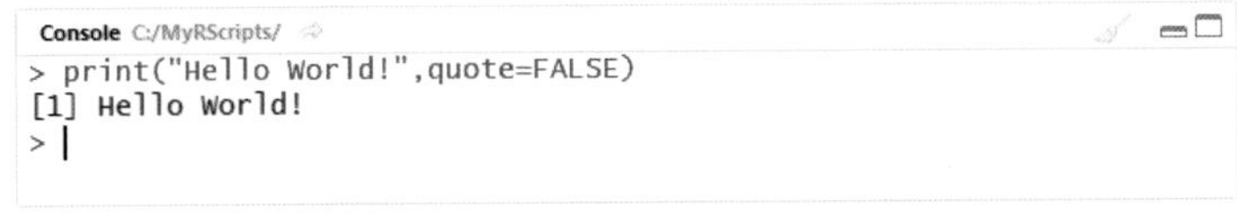

The bracketed number [1] that appears before the output indicates that the line begins with the first value of the result. Some results may have multiple values that fill several lines, so this indicator is occasionally useful but can generally be ignored.

Click the Open button in the Code Editor, or press the **Ctrl** + **O** keys to open the "Open File" dialog then choose a saved R Script file to reopen in the Code Editor. Click the arrow button beside the Open button to see a list of recently opened files that you can select to quickly reopen.

Summary

- Data is items of information that describe a qualitative status or a quantitative measure of magnitude.
- Devices that are connected to the internet are able to report sensor measurements for analysis in The Cloud.
- The decline in the cost of device sensors has given rise to the Internet of Things that can report on vast amounts of data.
- Big data consists of large data sets that can best be analyzed by computer to reveal pattern and trend insights.
- Data analysis is the practice of converting collected raw data into information that is useful for decision-making.
- Before analysis, raw data must be organized into a structured format and cleaned to remove incomplete, duplicated, and erroneous items.
- After data has been analyzed, the results can be communicated using data visualization to present tables, plots, or charts that efficiently convey the messages within the data.
- R is an interpreted programming language and software environment for data analysis and data visualization.
- RStudio is an Integrated Development Environment for R that provides a code editor, debugger, and visualization tools.
- The RStudio interface consists of a menu bar and toolbar, plus Code Editor, Console, Workspace, and Notebook panes.
- R Script code typed into the Code Editor can be run to see its output appear in the Console.
- Code snippets can be typed at the Console prompt for immediate execution by the R interpreter.
- RStudio's Global Options let you choose colorization themes, font settings, and default working directory.
- R Script in the Code Editor can be saved as a file with a **.R** file extension so the code can be re-run whenever required.

2 Storing values

This chapter demonstrates how to store data values in R Script programs and how to output stored data values in a simple plotted graph.

Storing a single value

In R programming a "variable" is simply a useful container in which a value may be stored for subsequent use by the program. The stored value may be changed (vary) as the R Script program executes its instructions – hence the term "variable".

A variable is created in R Script by writing a unique identifier name of your choice in the Code Editor, then assigning an initial value to be stored within the variable. The stored value can subsequently be retrieved using the given variable name.

Values can also be assigned using the = assignment operator, but this is best used only to assign default values to function parameters – see page 86.

The value can be assigned to a variable in R programming using the **<-** assignment operator. For example, to assign a number to a variable named "dozen", like this:

```
dozen <- 12
```

Variable names are chosen by the programmer but must adhere to certain naming conventions. The variable name may only begin with a letter, or a period followed by a letter, and may subsequently contain only letters, digits, periods, or underscore characters. Names are case-sensitive, so "var" and "Var" are distinctly different names, and spaces are not allowed in names.

Variable names should also avoid the reserved words, listed in the table below, as these have special meaning in the R language.

if	**else**	**repeat**	**while**
function	**for**	**in**	**next**
break	**TRUE**	**FALSE**	**NULL**
Inf	**NaN**	**NA**	**NA_integer**
NA_real	**NA_complex**	**NA_character**	**return**

Enter the **?reserved** command in the Console at any time to see the list of reserved words appear on the Help tab in the Notebook pane.

It is good practice to name variables with words that readily describe that variable's purpose. For example, **revenue** and **expenses** to describe income and costs. Lowercase letters are preferred by many R programmers, and variable names that consist of multiple words can separate each word with a period character. For example, a variable named **net.profit** to describe profit after costs deducted from income.

1. Open RStudio then click **File**, **New File**, **R Script**, or press **Ctrl** + **Shift** + **N**, to open a new Code Editor pane

FirstVariable.R

2. In the Code Editor, type **name** as the variable name

3. Type <- or press **Alt** + - to add the assignment operator

The **Alt** + **-** keyboard shortcut adds the **<-** assignment operator and a space at each side.

4. Next, press the " key to add two double quotes, then type **Username** between the quotes

5. Ensure that the cursor is positioned on the same line as your code, then click **Run**, or press **Ctrl** + **Enter** – see the variable and its value now appear on the Environment tab

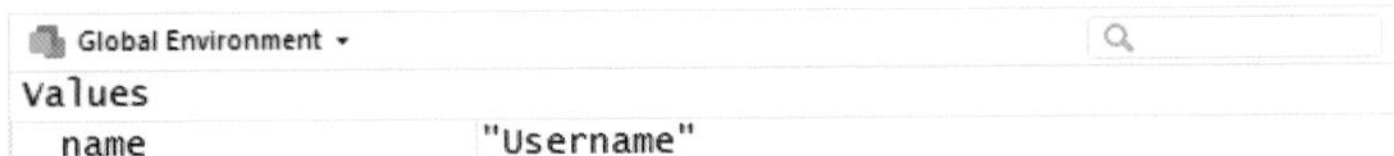

6. Back in the Code Editor, move to the next line and write **name <- ""**

7. Insert your own name between the quotes, then click **Run** to assign a new value to the variable – see the value change instantly on the Environment tab

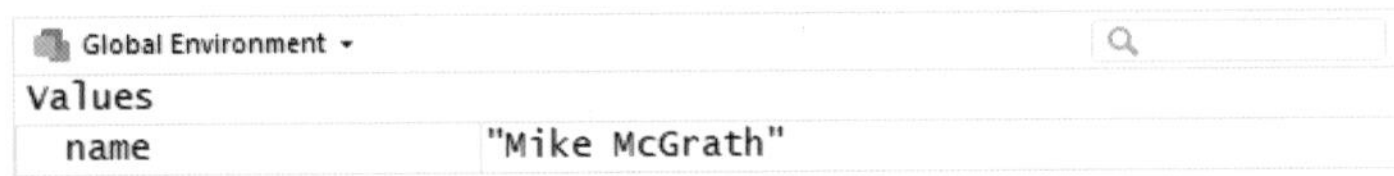

8. Move to the next line and write **print(name)**, then click **Run** to output the variable value in the Console

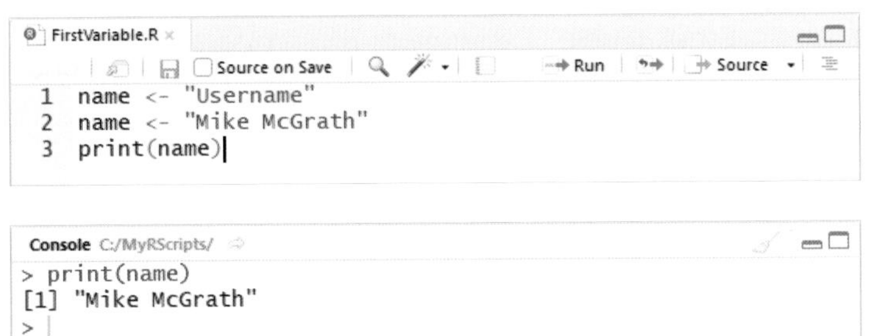

You can click the **Save** button to save the R Script for later use.

Adding comments

When programming, in any language, it is good practice to add comments to program code to explain each particular section. This makes the code more easily understood by others, and by yourself when revisiting a piece of code after a period of absence.

In R Script programming, comments can be added by beginning a line with the **#** hash character. All subsequent characters on that line will be completely ignored by the R interpreter. Unlike other programming languages there is no support for multi-line comments between /* and */ . RStudio does, however, provide a handy **Ctrl** + **Shift** + **C** keyboard shortcut that enables you to easily insert a # hash character on multiple lines in a single action.

Hot tip

The R interpreter also ignores tabs and spaces (whitespace) in R Script code, so you can safely space your code to your preferred coding style.

If your R Script will be shared with others, it is a great idea to document the code by including a header comment. This should include such details as:

- The name of the script
- The date the script was created
- The author of the script
- The purpose of the script
- The history of revisions made to the script

The header might also include any special instruction as to how the script should be executed. For example, an R Script that requests user input will need to wait until the user has entered the input before proceeding. In RStudio, this requires the entire script be sent to the Console rather than running it as usual. This technique is called "sourcing the script" and a notice to this effect could be included in the script header as a special instruction:

Comment.R

1. In the RStudio Code Editor, begin an R Script by typing lines of header information

```
Script name:    Comment.R
Created on:     March 1, 2019
Author:         Mike McGrath
Purpose:        Echo user input
Version:        1.0
Execution:      Must be run as Source to await user input.
```

2. Drag the cursor across the entire header to select it, then press **Ctrl** + **Shift** + **C** to comment-out all selected lines

3. Next, add a comment and instruction to request user input

```
# Request user input.
name <- readline( "Please enter your name: " )
```

4. Now, add a comment and instruction to paste the user input into a string

```
# Concatenate input and strings.
greeting <- paste( "Welcome", name, "!" )
```

5. Finally, add a comment and instruction to print out the entire string

```
# Output concatenated string.
print( greeting )
```

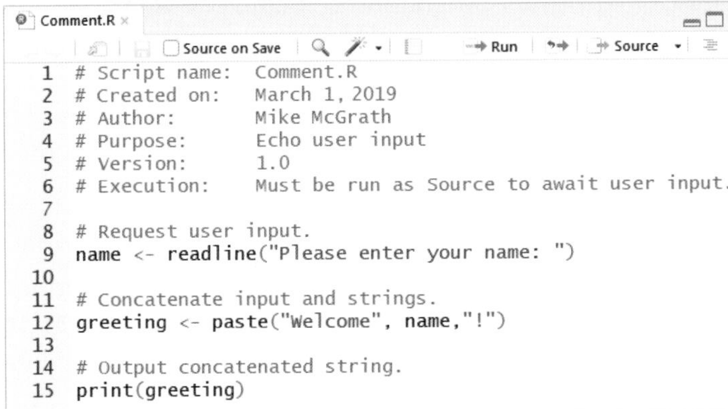

Comment.R
Source on Save
Run
Source
# Script name: Comment.R
# Created on: March 1, 2019
# Author: Mike McGrath
# Purpose: Echo user input
# Version: 1.0
# Execution: Must be run as Source to await user input.
# Request user input.
name <- readline("Please enter your name: ")
# Concatenate input and strings.
greeting <- paste("Welcome", name,"!")
# Output concatenated string.
print(greeting)

6. Following the header instruction, click the Source button in the Code Editor, or press **Ctrl** + **Shift** + **S**, to execute the script, then enter input when requested

Console C:/MyRScripts/
> source('C:/MyRScripts/Comment.R')
Please enter your name: Mike
[1] "Welcome Mike !"
Global Environment
Values
greeting "Welcome Mike !"
name "Mike"

Hot tip

The built-in **readline( )** function accepts a string argument within its parentheses to output as a prompt, then it awaits user input for assignment to a variable.

Hot tip

The built-in **paste( )** function accepts a comma-separated list of strings within its parentheses to join (concatenate) into a single string for assignment to a variable.

Don't forget

You can see the variables and their current values on the **Environment** tab in the Workspace pane.

Recognizing data types

Variables in R can contain data of various types. The most frequently used data types of variables in R programming are listed in the table below, together with a brief description:

Data type:	Description:	Example:
Character	A text character or string	"R" "R string"
Double	A decimal number	3.14
Integer	A whole number	5
Boolean	A logical value	TRUE

These four data types are sometimes referred to as the "atomic" or "primitive" data types as they represent the lowest level of data detail.

Unlike many other programming languages, which require the programmer to explicitly specify the data type when creating a variable, R automatically determines the variable data type according to the value it contains. The data type of a variable can be revealed by specifying its name as the argument to the built-in **typeof( )** function.

It is important to recognize that numeric variables are, by default, always created as a double data type unless an assigned integer value is suffixed by a letter **L**. For example, **number = 5L** creates an integer data type, but **number = 5** creates a double data type. More memory is allocated for the double data type, so integer values can be stored more efficiently if they are explicitly assigned to the integer data type.

Note that in R the Boolean values must appear in uppercase.

R provides several built-in functions to test the data type of a variable. The name of a variable can be specified as the argument to the **is.character( )** function, which will return a Boolean value of **TRUE** or **FALSE** according to the data type of the variable. There are also **is.double( )**, **is.integer( )**, and **is.logical( )** functions that can be used in a similar manner to test the data type of a variable.

Boolean values can be assigned to a variable using either the keywords **TRUE** and **FALSE**, or simply by using the letters **T** and **F**.

R

DataType.R

1. Open the RStudio Code Editor and create a variable that contains a text string value
title <- "R for Data Analysis"

2. Assign a string and data type to a second variable
result <- paste("Type of title:", typeof(title))

3. Output the combined string to see the variable's data type
print(result)

4. Next, create a variable containing a double value and a variable containing an integer value
pi <- 3.14159265
dozen <- 12L

Hot tip

Notice how this example includes function calls as arguments to other functions. The innermost function calls are executed first, passing their result to the outer function as their argument value.

5. Output the data type of each variable in the previous step
print(paste("Type of pi:", typeof(pi)))
print(paste("Type of dozen:", typeof(dozen)))

6. Now, create a variable containing a logical value and output the result of a data type test on this variable
flag <- T
print(paste("Is flag logical:", is.logical(flag)))

7. Click the Source button in the Code Editor, or press **Ctrl** + **Shift** + **S**, to execute the script

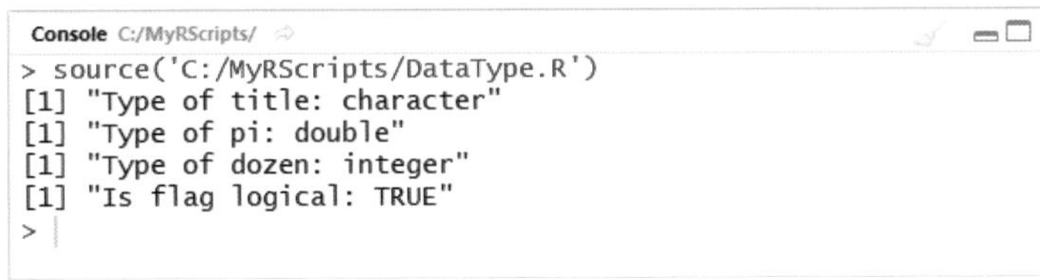
Console C:/MyRScripts/
> source('C:/MyRScripts/DataType.R')
[1] "Type of title: character"
[1] "Type of pi: double"
[1] "Type of dozen: integer"
[1] "Is flag logical: TRUE"
>

Environment | History | Connections

Import Dataset · List

Global Environment

Values	
dozen	12L
flag	TRUE
pi	3.14159265
result	"Type of title: character"
title	"R for Data Analysis"

Don't forget

The Environment tab lists the variables in alphabetical order, not in the order in which they are created.

Storing multiple values

Hot tip

A vector structure in R is similar to the "array" structure found in other programming languages.

As the R programming language is designed to handle sets of data, a variable is actually a "vector" that can contain multiple values. Each value is contained within an "element" of the vector.

Multiple values are assigned to a variable using the built-in combine function **c( )** that accepts a comma-separated list of values to be assigned to the vector elements. For example, to assign three values with **month = c("Jan", "Feb", "Mar").**

Vectors in R are indexed starting at one, so the first value stored in a vector is contained in element one, the second value is contained in element two, and so on. In code, the vector elements are addressed by placing the desired index number in **[ ]** square brackets after the variable name. For example, **month[1]** would retrieve the value contained in the first element of the **month** variable – the character string value **"Jan"** in this case.

You can retrieve all values except a specified element by prefixing a minus sign to an index number. For example, **month[-3]** retrieves all values except that in the third element.

New values can be assigned to individual elements using the variable name and index number. For example, to replace the value contained in the third element with **month[3] = "March".**

The length of a vector can be found by specifying the variable name as the argument to the built-in **length( )** function. For example, **length(month)** would reveal a length of three elements.

Vectors are flexible so are able to automatically expand when a value is assigned to an index number beyond the vector's current length. For example, the assignment **month[4] = "Apr"** would automatically expand the vector, and **length(month)** would now reveal a length of four elements.

A vector cannot contain mixed data types – the numeric value **5** will be converted to a character value **"5"** if mixed with character data types in the same vector variable.

It is important to recognize that each vector can only contain values of the same data type. If you assign a mixture of integers and doubles, all elements will contain doubles (integers converted). If you assign a mixture of numbers and characters, all elements will contain characters (numbers converted). The built-in **typeof( )** function can be used to establish the data type of all elements.

R provides several other structures in which data can be stored in addition to the vector variable, so it is sometimes useful to establish if a particular object is a vector. The name of the object can be specified as the argument to the **is.vector( )** function, which will return a Boolean value of **TRUE** or **FALSE** according to the whether the object is indeed a vector variable or not.

Multiple.R

1. Open the RStudio Code Editor and create a variable that contains multiple text string values

```
alphabet <- c( "Alpha", "Bravo", "Charlie" )
```

2. Output the entire content of all elements of the variable

```
print( alphabet )
```

3. Output a string and the value contained in one element

```
print( paste( "2nd Element: ", alphabet[ 2 ] ) )
```

4. Output a string and the number of elements in the vector

```
print( paste( "Vector Length: ", length( alphabet ) ) )
```

5. Assign another value to expand the vector, then output its entire content and length once more

```
alphabet[ 5 ] <- "Echo"
print( alphabet )
print( paste( "Vector Length Now: ", length( alphabet ) ) )
```

6. Output the result of a data type test on the variable

```
print( paste( "Is alphabet a Vector: ", is.vector( alphabet ) ) )
```

7. Click the Source button in the Code Editor, or press **Ctrl** + **Shift** + **S**, to execute the script

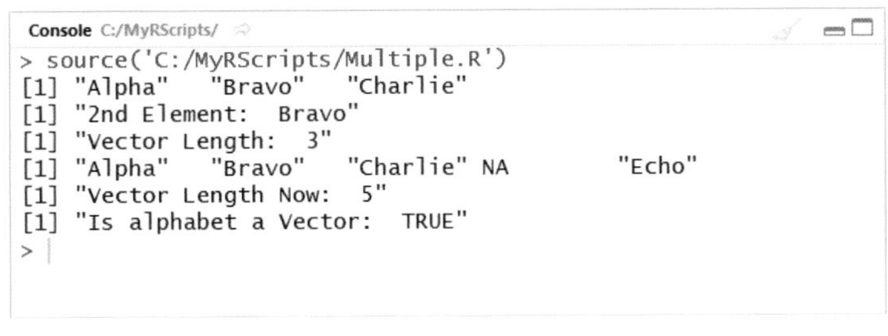

Console C:/MyRScripts/
> source('C:/MyRScripts/Multiple.R')
[1] "Alpha"   "Bravo"   "Charlie"
[1] "2nd Element: Bravo"
[1] "Vector Length: 3"
[1] "Alpha"   "Bravo"   "Charlie" NA   "Echo"
[1] "Vector Length Now: 5"
[1] "Is alphabet a Vector: TRUE"
>

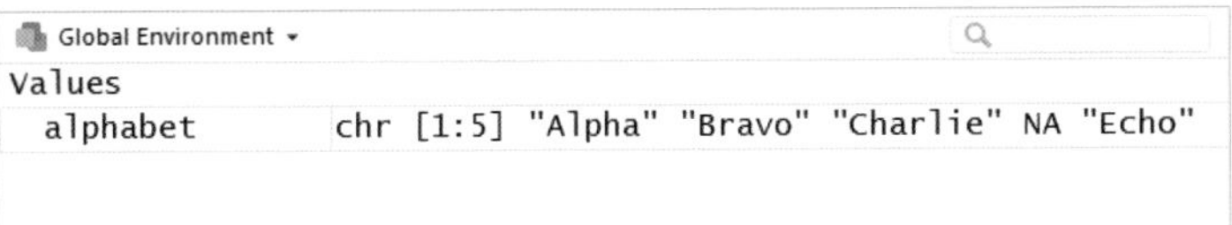

Notice here that the empty fourth element is represented by the **NA** keyword to indicate the value is Not Available.

Storing mixed data types

As items of different data types cannot be stored in a single vector, R provides a useful alternative "list" structure, whose elements can each contain values of any data type.

Lists are indexed starting at one, just like vectors, and values are assigned to list elements by specifying them as a comma-separated list of arguments to the built-in **list( )** function. For example, you can create a list containing values of each main data type, like this:

```
data <- list( 12, 3.14, "Mike", TRUE )
```

Hot tip

A list structure in R is similar to the "associative array" (dictionary) structure found in other programming languages.

The list length and structure type can be revealed using the **length( )** function and **typeof( )** function as with vectors, and there is an **is.list( )** function to establish whether an object is a list.

Like vectors, you can address each individual list element by specifying its index number within **[ ]** square brackets. For example, **data[3]** to retrieve the string in the list created above.

Unlike vectors, lists are not flexible, which means you cannot assign a value to an index number beyond the list's current length. You can, however, use the **c( )** function to combine an existing list with additional values, or other list, to extend the list length.

Most importantly, you may optionally name each element in a list by specifying key=value pairs as a comma-separated list of arguments to the built-in **list( )** function, like this:

```
data <- list( dozen=12, pi= 3.14, user="Mike", flag=TRUE )
```

With a named element you can retrieve its value by specifying the list name and element name separated by the **$** dollar operator. For example, **data$user** to retrieve the string in the list above.

Named elements can also be addressed using their index number or their element name within square brackets, such as **data[3]** and **data["user"]** – but remember that this will retrieve both the key and value, not just the value.

R provides two built-in functions especially for lists that contain key=value pairs. The **names( )** function retrieves all the keys in the order they appear in the list. The **unlist( )** function returns a vector of all keys and values in order, but the names can be explicitly ignored by including a **use.names=FALSE** argument.

The **sum( )** function can be used to total up the numeric values contained in a vector, and the **mean( )** function can be used to calculate an average of the numeric values contained in a vector.

FirstList.R

1. Open the RStudio Code Editor and create a list that contains multiple key=value pairs

```
sales <- list( Jan=1500, Feb=1300, Mar=2400 )
```

2. Combine the list with an additional key=value pair list to extend the length of the original list, then output all pairs

```
sales <- c( sales, list( Apr=1800 ) )
print( unlist( sales ) )
```

3. Assign the list values only to a vector variable

```
monthly.sales <- unlist( sales, use.names=FALSE )
```

4. Next, assign the calculated total of the list values to a variable, then output the total value

```
total.sales <- sum( monthly.sales )
print( paste( "Total Sales: ", total.sales ) )
```

5. Now, assign the calculated average of the list values to a variable, then output the average value

```
average.per.month <- mean( monthly.sales )
print( paste( "Monthly Average: ", average.per.month ) )
```

6. Output the result of a data type test on the list

```
print( paste( "Is sales a List: ", is.list( sales ) ) )
```

7. Click the Source button in the Code Editor, or press **Ctrl** + **Shift** + **S**, to execute the script

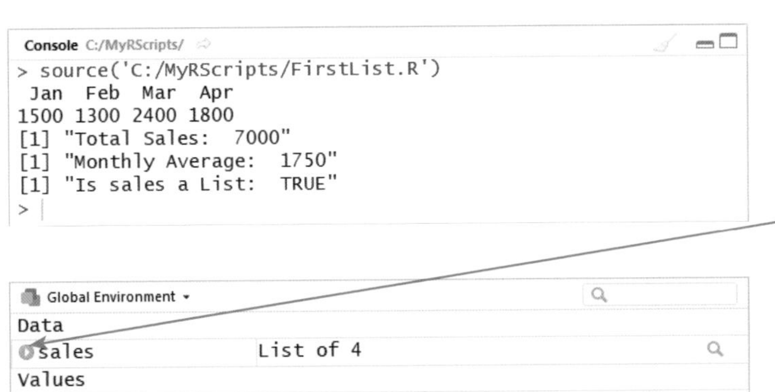

Click this button to expand the sales object and see its key=value pairs. Click the button once more to collapse the sales object.

Plotting stored values

The power of R programming lies in its ability to easily provide graphic depictions of the data stored within R Script structures. You can specify a vector argument to the built-in **plot( )** function to produce a scatter plot depicting data magnitude versus index. More typically, you can specify two vector arguments to the **plot( )** function to be represented on the plot's X and Y axes, and a third argument **type="o"** can be included to overplot points and lines:

FirstPlot.R

1. Open the RStudio Code Editor and create two vectors

```
x <- c( 1, 3, 5, 7, 9 )
y <- c( 8, 0, 4, 6, 2 )
```

2. Next, add an instruction to depict the vector values, then select all three lines in the Code Editor

```
plot( x, y, type="o" )
```

3. Click the Source button, or press **Ctrl** + **Shift** + **S** to execute the script – see a graph appear on the Plots tab

Other possible values for the type argument include "p" points only, "l" lines only, "b" both points and lines, "s" steps, "h" histogram-like vertical lines.

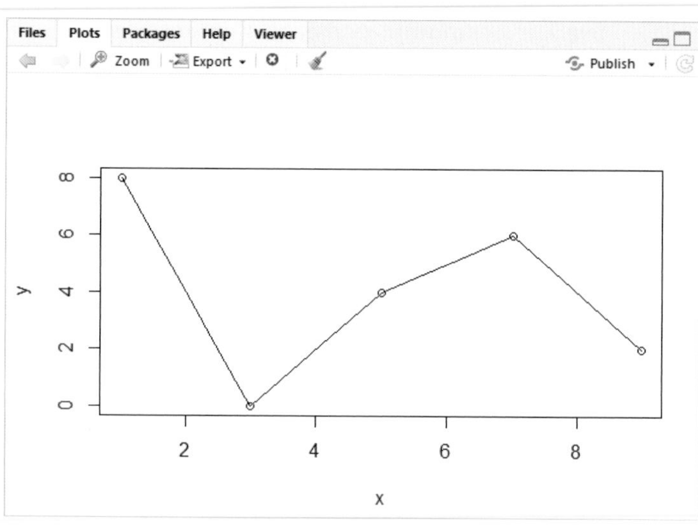

A box is drawn around the graph by default, but if you turn off annotations the box will not be drawn unless you call the built-in **box( )** function.

The graph depicts annotations based upon the range of the vector values, and the axes labels are simply the variable identifier names. But you can do better than this by taking control of annotation, axes labels, title, point character, and colors. Further arguments can be added to the **plot( )** function to specify the line color and point character, and built-in **title( )** and **axis( )** functions can be used to specify a main title, annotation, and axes labels.

1. Open the RStudio Code Editor and create four lists

```
qtr.1 <- list( Jan=1500, Feb=1300, Mar=2400 )
qtr.2 <- list( Apr=1800, May=1700, Jun=2800 )
qtr.3 <- list( Jul=3100, Aug=3800, Sep=3200 )
qtr.4 <- list( Oct=2600, Nov=2200, Dec=2400 )
```

CustomPlot.R

2. Combine the four lists above into a single vector

```
year <- unlist( c( qtr.1, qtr.2, qtr.3, qtr.4 ) )
```

3. Plot the vector specifying type, color, and point character, and turn off automatic annotation and axes labels

```
plot( year, type="o", col="Blue", pch=15,
        ann=FALSE, axes=FALSE )
```

Experiment with the point character by specifying a numeric value in the range 0-25 in the **pch** argument.

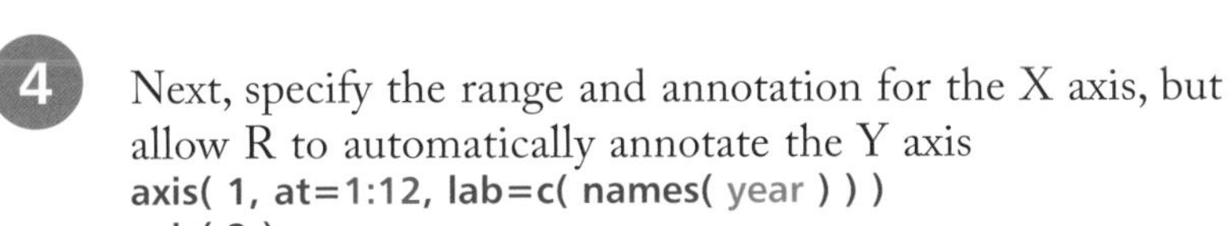

4. Next, specify the range and annotation for the X axis, but allow R to automatically annotate the Y axis

```
axis( 1, at=1:12, lab=c( names( year ) ) )
axis( 2 )
```

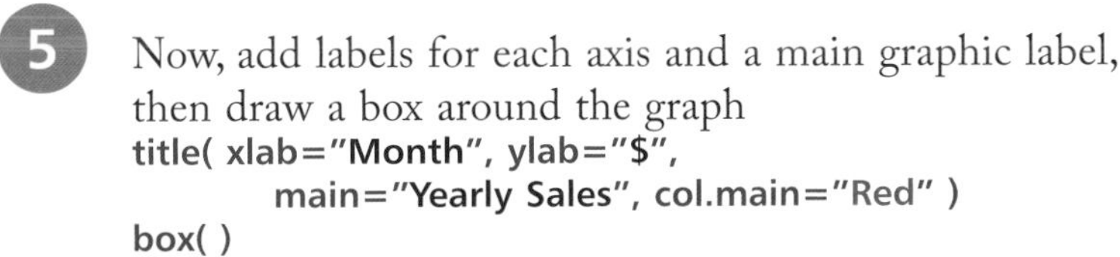

5. Now, add labels for each axis and a main graphic label, then draw a box around the graph

```
title( xlab="Month", ylab="$",
        main="Yearly Sales", col.main="Red" )
box( )
```

6. Click the Source button in the Code Editor, or press **Ctrl** + **Shift** + **S**, to execute the script and see the graph

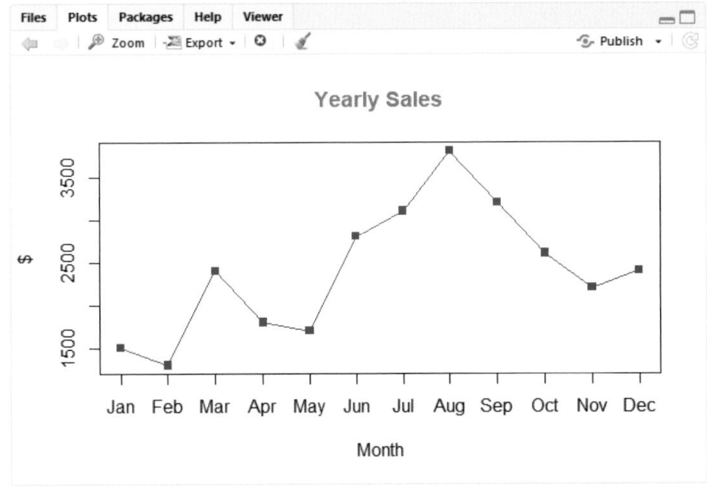

Color values can be specified by name **"Red"**, or hexadecimal **"#FF0000"**, or RGB components **rgb(1,0,0)**.

Controlling objects

When you execute R code to store data in any structure, such as a variable or list, a data structure object is created in the RStudio environment. These objects appear listed on the Environment tab in the Workspace pane in one of two possible views – List view or Grid view. Large data structures are collapsed to save space in List view but you can expand them to reveal their contents. In Grid view, large data structures can be examined by producing an expanded list in the Code Editor pane.

You can call the built-in **ls( )** function to list all objects within the current environment in the Console. Individual objects can be removed from the environment by specifying their name as a comma-separated argument to the built-in **rm( )** function, or all objects can be removed by specifying a **list=ls( )** argument:

Beware

If the **ls( )** function is called from within a user-defined function it will only list that function's local variables.

Environment.R

1. Open the RStudio Code Editor and create a list and two variables

```
iso.codes <- list( "United Kingdom"="UK",
                   "United States of America"="US",
                   France="FR", Germany="DE" )
iso.japan <- "JP"
iso.china <- "CN"
```

Hot tip

You must enclose list names within quotes to include space characters.

2. Next, press **Ctrl** + **A** to select all the code, then press **Ctrl** + **Enter** to run the code and create the objects

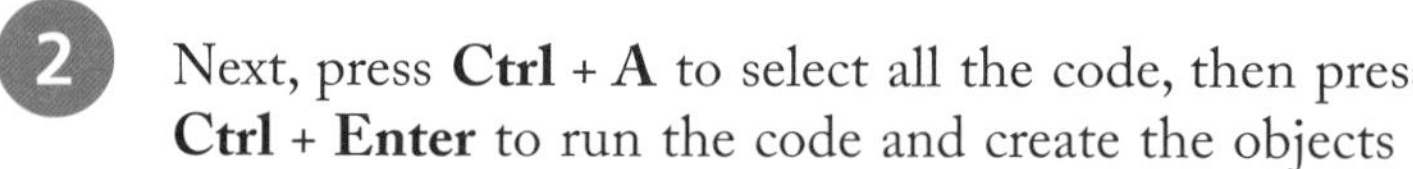

3. Open the Environment tab in List view, then click the button to expand the list object and see its key=value pairs

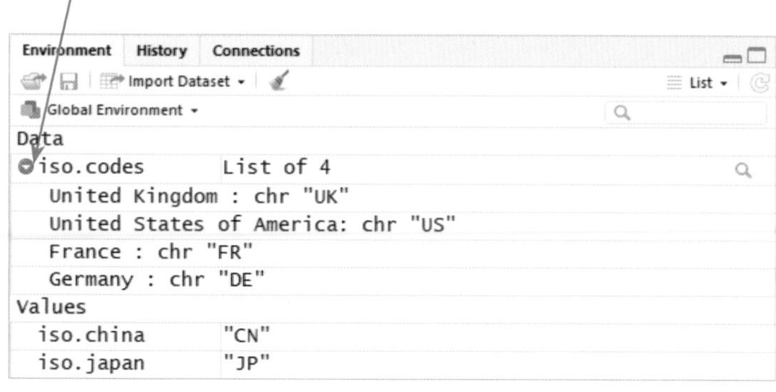

Don't forget

The R Script that created objects can be closed and another R Script started to work with those objects as they are retained in the current environment.

4. Now, click the arrow button on the tab's menu bar and switch to Grid view

Name	Type	Length	Size	Value
iso.china	charact...	1	96 B	"CN"
iso.codes	list	4	864 B	List of 4
iso.japan	charact...	1	96 B	"JP"

List of 4

5 Click the spyglass icon beside the list in Grid view to produce an expanded list in the Code Editor pane

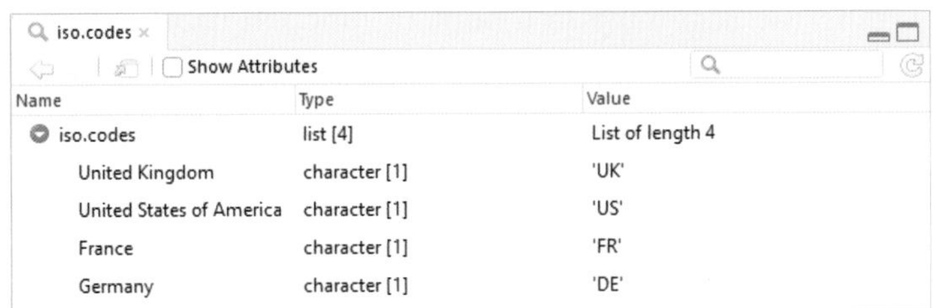

6 Return to the Code Editor and enter an instruction to list the current environment objects

```
ls( )
```

7 Add an instruction to remove both variable objects, then list the current environment objects to confirm removal

```
rm( iso.japan, iso.china )
ls( )
```

8 Select the three instructions, then click the Run button, or press **Ctrl** + **Enter**, to execute the code

You can use the **Save** button on the Environment tab's menu bar to save objects in an RData file, and the **Open** button to restore objects to the environment.

You can also click the brush icon on the tab's menu bar to remove all objects from the current environment.

Getting help

There are a number of ways to seek help in RStudio. The most obvious one is to enter the name of the topic you want help on into the Search box on the Help tab. This will search through the help files and present the results on the Help tab.

Alternatively, you can supply the topic name as a string argument to the built-in **help( )** function. This will search the help files for a word or phrase and present the results on the Help tab. Additionally, you can seek help about any built-in function by entering its name preceded by a **?** character or **??** characters.

Typing the beginning of a built-in function name into the Code Editor produces an auto-completion popup box, from which you can select an option to complete the name of the function. This is accompanied by a brief description of that function and an invitation to "Press F1 for additional help". Pressing the **F1** key will then present relevant documentation on the Help tab:

Help.R

1. Open the Help tab, then type "list" into the Search box and hit **Enter** to see information on the **list( )** function

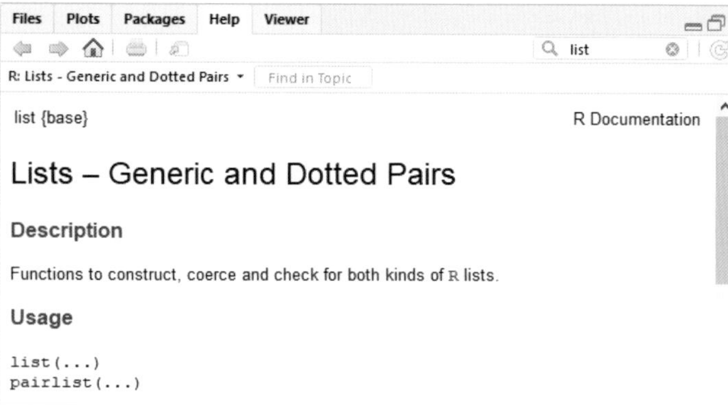

2. Open the Code Editor and run the command **help("color")** to seek help on how to specify colors

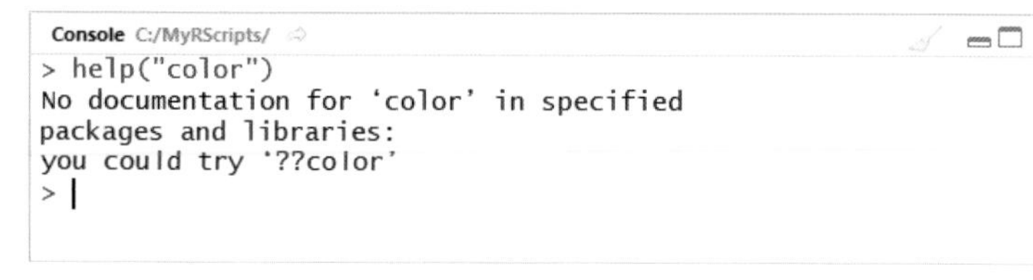

The **help("color")** and **?color** commands produce the same result, as **?** is a shorthand method for calling the **help( )** function.

3. The search fails to get help but suggests an alternative search – run the suggested command **??color** to see the results

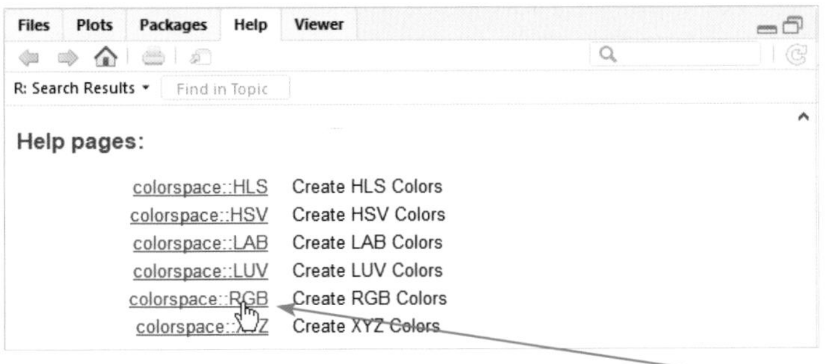

Choose a link from the search results to open relevant documentation on a particular topic, such as how to create RGB colors.

4. Type "plo" in the Code Editor, then choose the **plot** option on the auto-completion popup

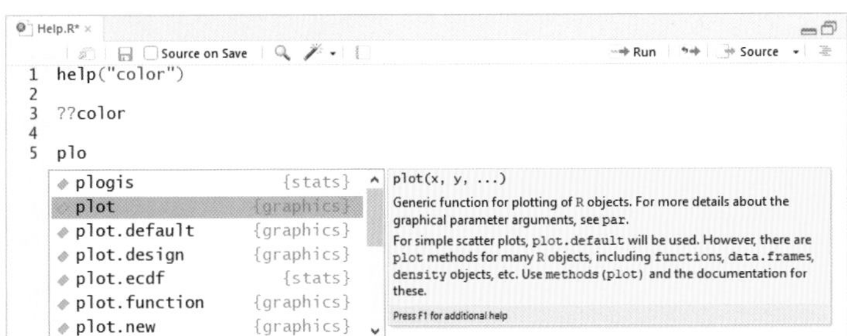

5. Press the **F1** key to see information on the **plot( )** function appear on the Help tab

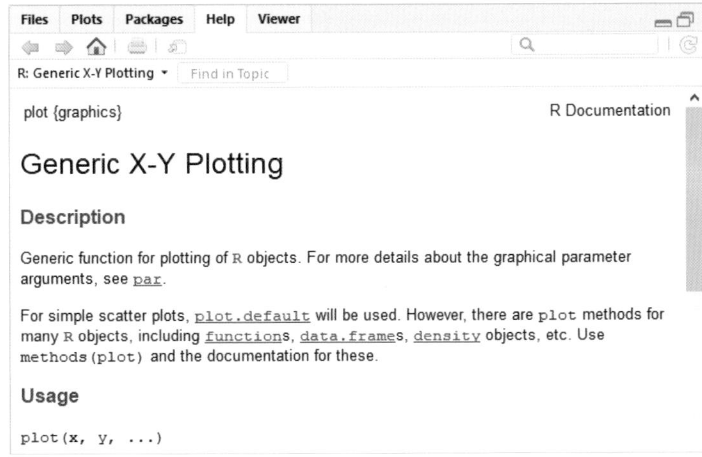

The help files contain links you can click to get help on specific items, and there are forward and back buttons on the Help tab, just like those on a web browser.

Summary

- A variable is a container in which a value may be stored for subsequent use in an R Script program.
- The name of a variable is a unique identifier that must avoid the R keywords.
- An identifier name in R must begin with a letter (or a period followed by a letter) and may subsequently contain only letters, digits, periods, or underscore characters.
- Identifier names are case-sensitive, and those with multiple words can separate each word with a period character.
- Values are assigned to variables in R programming using the **<-** assignment operator.
- The R interpreter ignores whitespace and ignores comments on lines that begin with a **#** hash character.
- The four main data types in R programming are character, double, integer, and Boolean.
- Each R variable is a vector that can contain multiple values.
- A vector may only contain values of the same data type, but a list structure may contain values of mixed data types.
- A list is created by specifying values as a comma-separated list of arguments to the built-in **list( )** function.
- Vectors and lists both store values within elements that are indexed starting at one.
- Single values in vectors and lists can be retrieved using the identifier name and an index number in **[ ]** square brackets.
- Single values in named elements can be retrieved using the identifier and element name separated by the **$** operator.
- The built-in **plot( )** function produces a scatter plot depicting data magnitude versus index.
- Data stored in any R structure creates an object in the RStudio environment.
- Help can be sought in RStudio on its Help tab, or using the **help( )** function, or via the auto-completion popup box.

3 Performing operations

This chapter demonstrates how to manipulate stored data in R Script programs.

Doing arithmetic

Arithmetical operators, listed in the table below, are used to create expressions in R Script programs that return a single resulting value. For example, the expression **4 * 2** returns the value **8**.

Integer division with the %/% operator will truncate any decimal part. For example, 11 %/% 4 = 2 but division with the / operator will retain the decimal part, so that 11 / 4 = 2.75.

Operator:	Operation:
+	Addition
-	Subtraction
*	Multiplication
/	Division
%/%	Integer division
^	Exponentiation
%%	Modulus

All arithmetic operators return the result of an operation performed on two given operands, and act as you would expect. For example, the expression **4 + 3** returns **7**.

The R documentation calls **%%** the "modulus" operator, whereas the operation it performs is typically called "modulo".

The **/** division operator divides the first operand by the second operand and returns the result as a decimal number. For example, the expression **4 / 3** returns **1.333333**. Conversely, the **%/%** integer division operator divides the first operand by the second operand and rounds down the result to a whole number. For example, the expression **4 %/% 3** returns **1** – not **1.333333**.

The **^** exponentiation operator returns the result of raising the first operand to the power of the second operand. For example, the expression **4 ^ 3** returns **64** – 4 cubed (4x4x4).

The **%%** modulus operator divides the first operand by the second operand and returns the remainder of the operation. For example, **4 % 3** returns **1** – 3 divides into 4 once, with 1 remainder.

Arithmetic.R

1. Open the RStudio Code Editor and create two variables containing integer values for arithmetic

```
large <- 5
small <- 2
```

2. Next, add statements to output the result of some basic arithmetical operations

```
print( paste( "Addition:", large + small ) )
print( paste( "Subtraction:", large - small ) )
print( paste( "Multiplication:", large * small ) )
```

3. Now, add statements to output the result of the two types of division operations

```
print( paste( "Division:", large / small ) )
print( paste( "Integer Division:", large %/% small ) )
```

4. Then, add a statement to output the result of an exponentiation operation

```
print( paste( "Exponentiation:", large ^ small ) )
```

5. Finally, add a statement to output the remainder after performing a division operation

```
print( paste( "Remainder:", large %% small ) )
```

6. Save the R Script file then click the Source button, or press **Ctrl** + **Shift** + **S**, to see the arithmetical output

Unlike other programming languages that support a ++ increment operator and -- decrement operator, there is no increment operator or decrement operator in R.

```
Console C:/MyRScripts/
> source('C:/MyRScripts/Arithmetic.R')
[1] "Addition: 7"
[1] "Subtraction: 3"
[1] "Multiplication: 10"
[1] "Division: 2.5"
[1] "Integer Division: 2"
[1] "Exponentiation: 25"
[1] "Remainder: 1"
> 
```

Making comparisons

Comparison operators, listed in the table below, are used to compare two values in an expression and return a single Boolean value of **TRUE** or **FALSE** – describing the result of that comparison.

The conditional operators are also known as the "relational" operators.

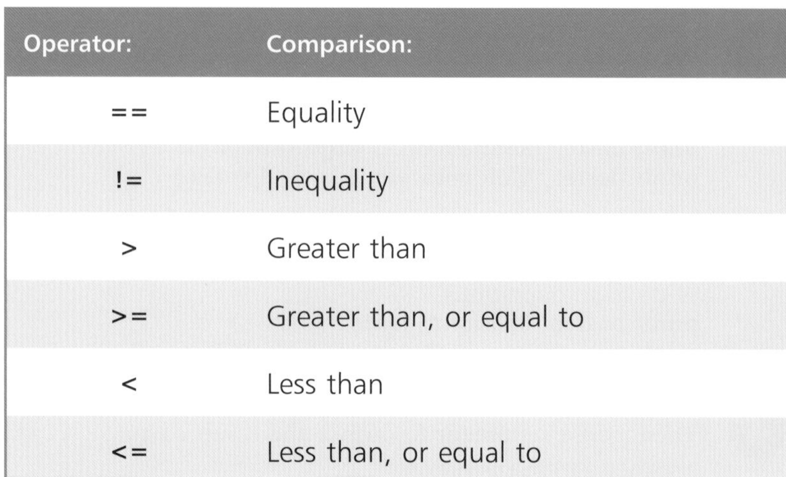

Operator:	Comparison:
==	Equality
!=	Inequality
>	Greater than
>=	Greater than, or equal to
<	Less than
<=	Less than, or equal to

The **==** equality operator compares two operands and will return **TRUE** if both are exactly equal in value. If both are the same number they are equal, or if both are text strings containing the same characters in the same order they are equal. Boolean operands that are both **TRUE**, or that are both **FALSE**, are equal.

The < less than operator is typically used to test a counter value in a loop – an example of this can be found on page 64.

Conversely, the **!=** inequality operator returns **TRUE** if two operands are not equal – applying the same rules as those followed by the equality operator.

Equality and inequality operators are useful in testing the state of two variables to perform "conditional branching" of a program – proceeding in different directions according to the condition.

The **>** "greater than" operator compares two operands and will return **TRUE** if the first is greater in value than the second.

The **<** "less than" operator makes the same comparison but returns **TRUE** if the first operand is less in value than the second.

Adding the **=** assignment operator after the **>** "greater than" operator, or after the **<** "less than" operator, makes it also return **TRUE** when the two operands are exactly equal in value.

Comparison.R

1. Open the RStudio Code Editor and create three variables containing integer values for comparison
```
nil <- 0
num <- 0
max <- 1
```

2. Next, create two variables containing character values for comparison
```
cap <- "A"
low <- "a"
```

The ASCII code value for uppercase "A" is 65 but for lowercase "a" it's 97 – so their comparison here returns **FALSE**.

3. Now, add statements to output the result of equality comparison of integer and character values
```
print( paste( "0 == 0 Equality:", nil == num ) )
print( paste( "A == a Equality:", cap == low ) )
```

4. Add a statement to output the result of inequality comparison of integer values
```
print( paste( "0 != 1 Inequality:", nil != max ) )
```

5. Then, add statements to output the results of greater than and less than comparisons of integer values
```
print( paste( "0 > 1 Greater:", nil > max ) )
print( paste( "0 < 1 Less:", nil < max ) )
```

When comparing numbers, remember to test for equality as well as testing for higher and lower values.

6. Finally, add statements to output the results of greater or equal and less or equal comparisons of integer values
```
print( paste( "0 >= 0 Greater or Equal:", nil >= num ) )
print( paste( "1 <= 0 Less or Equal:", max <= nil ) )
```

7. Save the R Script file then click the Source button, or press **Ctrl** + **Shift** + **S**, to see the comparison output

```
Console C:/MyRScripts/
> source('C:/MyRScripts/Comparison.R')
[1] "0 == 0 Equality: TRUE"
[1] "A == a Equality: FALSE"
[1] "0 != 1 Inequality: TRUE"
[1] "0 > 1 Greater: FALSE"
[1] "0 < 1 Less: TRUE"
[1] "0 >= 0 Greater or Equal: TRUE"
[1] "1 <= 0 Less or Equal: FALSE"
>
```

Assessing logic

Logical operators, listed in the table below, can be used to combine multiple expressions that each return a Boolean value into an expression that returns a single Boolean value.

Operator:	Operation:
!	Logical NOT
&&	Logical AND
&	Element-wise Logical AND
||	Logical OR
|	Element-wise Logical OR

The term "Boolean" refers to a system of logical thought developed by the English mathematician George Boole (1815-1864).

Logical operators are used with operands that have the Boolean values of **TRUE** or **FALSE**, or values that can convert to **TRUE** or **FALSE**. In R programming, zero is considered to be **FALSE** and all other numbers are considered to be **TRUE**.

The logical **!** NOT operator is a "unary" operator that is used before a single operand. It returns the inverse Boolean value of the given operand – reversing **TRUE** to **FALSE**, and **FALSE** to **TRUE**.

The logical **&&** AND operator will evaluate the first element of two operands and return **TRUE** only if both operands are themselves **TRUE**. Otherwise the logical **&&** operator will return **FALSE**. The element-wise logical **&** operator performs the same operation but on all elements of the operands.

Unlike the logical **&&** operator, which needs two operands to be **TRUE**, the logical **||** OR operator will evaluate the first element of its two operands and return **TRUE** if either one of the operands is **TRUE** – it will only return **FALSE** when neither operand is **TRUE**. The element-wise logical **|** operator performs the same operation but on all elements of the operands.

If the two operands have a different number of elements, the result will be of the same length as the operand with the most elements.

Logic.R

1. Open the RStudio Code Editor and create a variable containing a Boolean value
```
active <- TRUE
```

2. Next, add a statement to output the inverse of the stored Boolean value
```
print( paste( "NOT logic !active:", !active ) )
```

3. Now, create two more variables that each contain multiple Boolean values or values than can convert to Booleans
```
flags <- c( TRUE, TRUE, FALSE, ( 1 > 0 ), 0 )
marks <- c( FALSE, TRUE, TRUE, 16, FALSE )
```

4. Add a statement to output the result of logical AND and logical OR evaluation of first elements only
```
print( paste( "AND logic:", flags && marks ) )
print( paste( "OR logic:", flags || marks ) )
```

5. Finally, assign the result of logical AND and OR evaluation of all elements to two further variables
```
and.result <- flags & marks
or.result <- flags | marks
```

6. Save the R Script file then click the Source button, or press **Ctrl** + **Shift** + **S**, to see the output and results

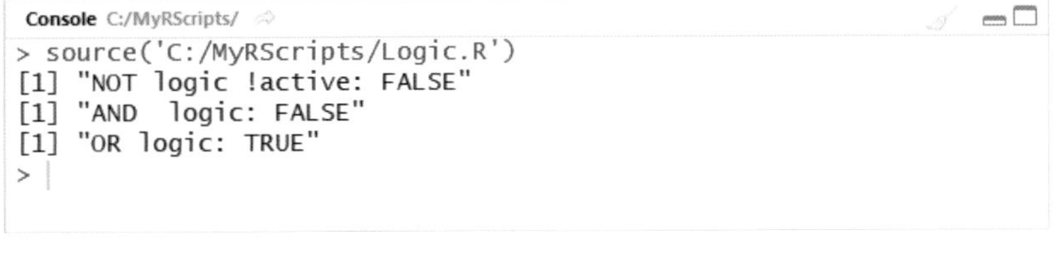
```
Console C:/MyRScripts/
> source('C:/MyRScripts/Logic.R')
[1] "NOT logic !active: FALSE"
[1] "AND  logic: FALSE"
[1] "OR logic: TRUE"
>
```

Global Environment

Values	
active	TRUE
and.result	logi [1:5] FALSE TRUE FALSE TRUE FALSE
flags	num [1:5] 1 1 0 1 0
marks	num [1:5] 0 1 1 16 0
or.result	logi [1:5] TRUE TRUE TRUE TRUE FALSE

The value returned by the ! NOT logical operator is the inverse of the stored value – the stored value itself remains unchanged.

Notice that the variables containing multiple values are stored numerically as they contain numbers and an expression that can convert to Boolean values.

Operating on elements

The elements of a vector can be easily filled with a numeric sequence using the : colon operator. A numeric "from" operand is required before the : operator, and a numeric "to" operand is required after the : operator to specify a range. The operation generates an inclusive sequence, in steps of one, between the specified range. The generated sequence will be either ascending or descending according to the specified "from" and "to" values.

A numeric sequence can be specified as the argument to the combining **c( )** function to fill the elements of a vector. Additionally, a numeric sequence can be specified within **[ ]** square brackets to specify an index range – to copy a "slice" of a vector.

When you want to output all elements of a vector to the Console, the combination of **print( )** and **paste( )** functions will be called for each element. For example, consider this statement and its output:

```
Console C:/MyRScripts/
> print( paste( "Series:", c(1:3) ) )
[1] "Series: 1" "Series: 2" "Series: 3"
>
```

Note that the **cat( )** function provides no quotes in the output and does not automatically add a newline after its output. You can include a final **"\n"** escape sequence argument to manually add a newline.

This may not be what you want, but R provides a useful built-in **cat( )** function that concatenates (joins) together its arguments then outputs them to the Console, like this:

```
Console C:/MyRScripts/
> cat( "Series:", c(1:3) )
Series: 1 2 3
>
```

One of the great advantages of R variables is the ability to perform vector arithmetic on all their numeric element values simply by placing any arithmetic operator between variable names. If the vectors have an equal number of elements, the operation will be performed between the corresponding element in each vector. If the vectors have an unequal number of elements, the shorter one will be "recycled" in order to match the longer vector length. Where the size of the longer vector is not an exact multiple of the shorter vector, the operations will be performed but the R interpreter will provide a warning.

VectorArithmetic.R

1. Open the RStudio Code Editor and create a variable containing a numeric sequence from one to nine
```
series <- c( 1:9 )
```

2. Next, add a statement to output a text string, the numeric sequence, and a newline
```
cat( "Series:", series, "\n" )
```

3. Now, create a second variable containing a slice of the first variable's element values, then output that sequence
```
slice <- series[ 1:3 ]
cat( "Slice:", slice, "\n" )
```

4. Create a third variable containing the total of element values in the other two variables, then output the totals
```
totals <- series + slice
cat( "Totals:", totals, "\n" )
```

5. Extend the slice, then output that sequence
```
slice <- series[ 1:4 ]
cat( "New Slice:", slice, "\n" )
```

6. Recalculate the total of element values that are now in the other two variables, then output those totals
```
totals <- series + slice
cat( "New Totals:", totals, "\n" )
```

7. Save the R Script file then click the Source button, or press **Ctrl** + **Shift** + **S**, to see the values and a warning

```
Console C:/MyRScripts/
> source('C:/MyRScripts/VectorArithmetic.R')
Series: 1 2 3 4 5 6 7 8 9
Slice: 1 2 3
Totals: 2 4 6 5 7 9 8 10 12
New Slice: 1 2 3 4
New Totals: 2 4 6 8 6 8 10 12 10
Warning message:
In series + slice :
  longer object length is not a multiple of shorter object length
>
```

The vector arithmetic in this example simply uses the + operator for addition, but you can use any arithmetical operator to perform an operation on the element values within two specified vector variables.

Notice that the length of the series in this example is an exact multiple of three times the length of the original slice, which gets recycled twice. The length of the series is not an exact multiple of the extended slice.

Comparing elements

Just as arithmetical operators can be used to perform arithmetic on elements within two vectors, so can comparison operators be used to perform comparison of elements within two vectors. Comparisons can be made of both numeric and text string values. The result is returned as a vector of Boolean **TRUE** and **FALSE** values indicating each corresponding element comparison.

In comparing short vectors of just a few elements, it's easy to determine the result by examining the returned vector of Booleans but this becomes more difficult when comparing larger vectors. Happily, R provides a built-in **which( )** function for this purpose. This function accepts a Boolean vector as its argument and returns a list of the index numbers containing a **TRUE** value.

Comparison of text strings to discover matching values within corresponding elements of two vectors can be made with the == equality operator, but the character case and order must be precisely identical for the comparison to return a **TRUE** value.

Comparison of text strings to discover matching values within any elements of two vectors can be made with the built-in **intersect( )** function. This accepts the names of two vector variables as a comma-separated list, and returns all values that precisely match:

VectorComparison.R

1. Open the RStudio Code Editor and create two variables that each contain a numeric sequence
```
ascend <- c( 1:5 )
descend <- c( 5:1 )
```

2. Next, add a statement to output a text string and the numeric sequences, formatted with newlines
```
cat( "Vectors:\n", ascend, "\n", descend )
```

3. Now, compare the numeric values within each corresponding element of the two vectors
```
result <- ascend > descend
```

4. Then, output the returned vector of Boolean values
```
cat( "\n1st Vector Greater?:", result )
```

5. Also, output the index numbers containing a **TRUE** value
```
cat( "\nAt Index No.:", which( result ) )
```

You can change the > comparison to the >= operator to also produce a **TRUE** result for the third elements here.

6. Next, create two variables that each contain string values within each element
```
pets <- c( "Dog", "Cat", "Gerbil", "Rabbit" )
animals <- c( "Lion", "Tiger", "Cat", "Rabbit" )
```

7. Now, add a statement to output a text string and the element values, formatted with newlines
```
cat( "\n\nVectors:\n", pets, "\n", animals )
```

You can also include the **\t** tab escape sequence to format output.

8. Compare the character string values within each corresponding element of the two vectors
```
result <- pets == animals
```

9. Then, output the returned vector of Boolean values
```
cat( "\nElement Match?:", result )
```

10. Also, output the index numbers containing a **TRUE** value
```
cat( "\nAt Index No.:", which( result ) )
```

11. Finally, output the matching values within any elements of the two vectors
```
cat( "\nCommon:", intersect( pets, animals ) )
```

12. Save the R Script file then click the Source button, or press **Ctrl** + **Shift** + **S**, to see the comparison results

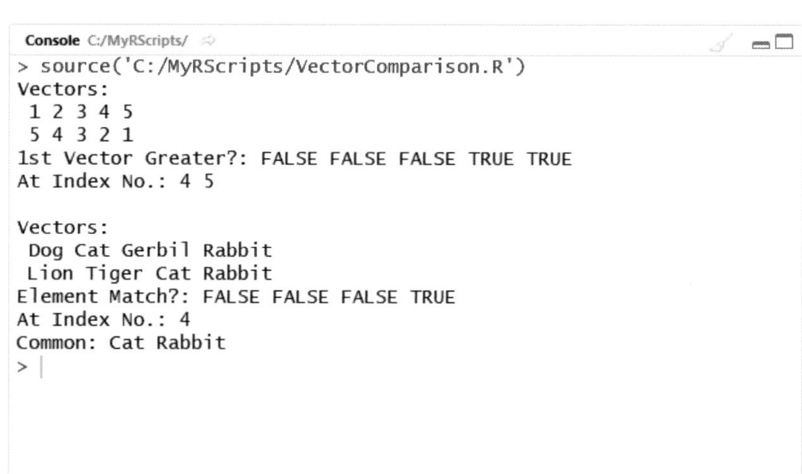

Console C:/MyRScripts/
> source('C:/MyRScripts/VectorComparison.R')
Vectors:
 1 2 3 4 5
 5 4 3 2 1
1st Vector Greater?: FALSE FALSE FALSE TRUE TRUE
At Index No.: 4 5

Vectors:
 Dog Cat Gerbil Rabbit
 Lion Tiger Cat Rabbit
Element Match?: FALSE FALSE FALSE TRUE
At Index No.: 4
Common: Cat Rabbit
>

Although "Cat" is contained in both vectors, it is not contained in corresponding elements.

Recognizing precedence

Operator precedence determines the order in which R evaluates expressions. For example, the expression **1 + 5 * 3** evaluates to **16**, not **18**, because the * multiplication operator has a higher precedence than the **+** addition operator. Parentheses can be used to specify precedence, so that **(1 + 5) * 3** evaluates to **18**.

When operators have equal precedence, their "associativity" determines how expressions are grouped. For example, the - subtraction operator is left-associative, grouping left-to-right (LTR), so **8 - 4 - 2** is grouped as **(8 - 4) - 2** and thus evaluates to **2**. Other operators are right-associative, grouping right-to-left (RTL).

The table below lists common operators in order of precedence, with the highest-precedence ones at the top. Operators on the same line have equal precedence, so operator associativity determines how expressions are grouped and evaluated.

The * multiply operator is on a higher row than the + addition operator – so in the expression **num <- 1 + 5 * 3** multiplication is completed first, before the addition.

Category:	Operator:	Associativity:
Subset	**$**	LTR ☞
Exponent	**^**	☜ RTL
Sign (unary)	**+ -**	LTR ☞
Sequence	**:**	LTR ☞
Modulus	**%% (and %/%)**	LTR ☞
Multiplicative	*** /**	LTR ☞
Additive	**+ -**	LTR ☞
Comparative	**< <= > >= == !=**	LTR ☞
Logical NOT	**!**	LTR ☞
Logical AND	**&& &**	LTR ☞
Logical OR	**|| |**	LTR ☞
Assignment	**=**	☜ RTL
Assignment	**<-**	☜ RTL
Help	**? ??**	LTR ☞

1. Open the RStudio Code Editor and create a variable containing the result of an arithmetical expression
sum <- 1 + 4 * 3

Precedence.R

2. Next, add a statement to output the result that relies upon the default order of operator precedence
print(paste("Default Order:", sum))

3. Now, assign to the variable the result of a clarified arithmetical expression, which forces the expression to be evaluated in a specific order
sum <- (1 + 4) * 3

The * multiplication operator takes precedence over the + addition operator – so multiplication is performed first.

4. Add a statement to output the clarified result
print(paste("Forced Order:", sum))

5. Assign to the variable the result of an expression whose arithmetical operators have the same level of precedence
sum <- 7 - 4 + 2

The - subtraction operator and the + addition operator have equal precedence but also have left-to-right associativity – so subtraction is performed first before addition.

6. Next, add a statement to output the result that relies upon the default associativity of operator precedence
print(paste("Default Direction:", sum))

7. Now, assign to the variable the result of a clarified arithmetical expression, then output the clarified result
sum <- 7 - (4 + 2)
print(paste("Forced Direction:", sum))

8. Save the R Script file, then click the Source button, or press **Ctrl** + **Shift** + **S**, to see the output and results

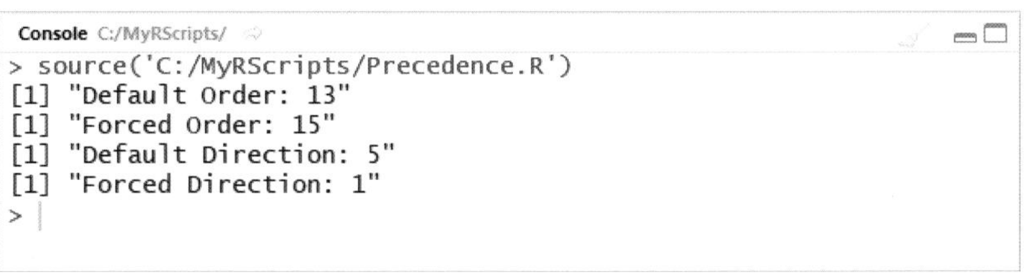
Console C:/MyRScripts/

```
> source('C:/MyRScripts/Precedence.R')
[1] "Default Order: 13"
[1] "Forced Order: 15"
[1] "Default Direction: 5"
[1] "Forced Direction: 1"
>
```

It is best to clarify all expressions by adding parentheses to group operations.

Manipulating elements

In addition to the various operators described in this chapter, R provides a number of built-in functions that can be used to manipulate the elements within vector variables. Each of the functions below accept a vector as their argument:

- The **sort( )** function sorts the element values into numerical or alphabetical order. By default, the element values will be sorted into ascending order, but can be sorted into descending order by including a **decreasing=TRUE** argument in the function call. Elements that have missing values, denoted in R by a **NA** constant value, will be automatically removed by default, but can be retained at the end of the order by including a **na.last=TRUE** argument in the function call.
- The **rev( )** function simply reverses the order of all elements within the vector variable.
- The **unique( )** function removes elements containing duplicated values from the vector variable.

The **sort( )** function can alternatively include a **na.last=FALSE** argument to retain elements that have missing values at the start of the order.

Manipulate.R

1. Open the RStudio Code Editor and create a vector variable containing three text string values
   fruit <- c("Banana", "Apple", "Cherry")

2. Next, add a statement to output the values contained in each element – in their current order
   cat("Fruit:", fruit, "\n")

3. Now, assign a sorted arrangement of the elements to the vector variable, using the default ascending order
   fruit <- sort(fruit)

4. Then, output the values contained in each element – in their new sorted order
   cat("Sorted:", fruit, "\n\n")

5. Create a second vector variable containing numerical values and some elements with missing values
   nums <- c(NA, 8:2, NA, 1:7, NA)

6. Next, output the values contained in each element of the second variable – in their current order
```
cat( "Numbers:", nums, "\n" )
```

7. Now, assign a sorted arrangement of the elements to the variable, using the default ascending order and placing elements with missing values at the end
```
nums <- sort( nums, na.last=TRUE )
```

8. Then, output the values contained in each element – in their new sorted order
```
cat( "Increasing:", nums, "\n" )
```

9. Assign a sorted arrangement of the elements to the vector variable in descending order, then output the values
```
nums <- sort( nums, decreasing=TRUE )
cat( "Decreasing:", nums, "\n" )
```

10. Assign a reversed arrangement of the elements to the vector variable, then output the values
```
nums <- rev( nums )
cat( "Reversed:", nums, "\n" )
```

11. Assign only elements with unique values to the vector variable, then output the values
```
nums <- unique( nums )
cat( "Unique:", nums, "\n" )
```

12. Save the R Script file then click the Source button, or press **Ctrl** + **Shift** + **S**, to see the output element values

If the call to the **sort( )** function does not specify a **na.last** argument, elements with missing values will be automatically removed.

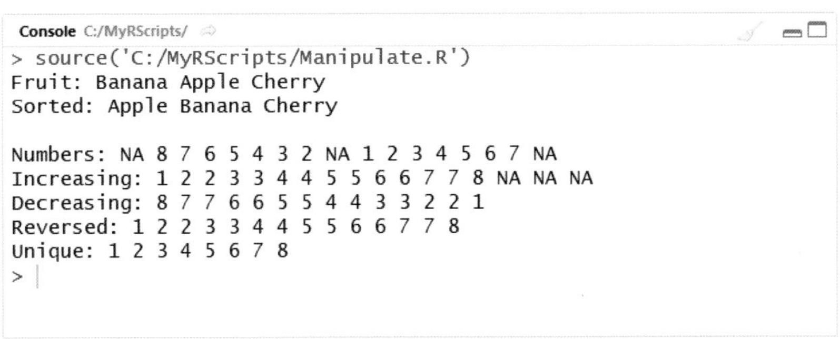
```
Console C:/MyRScripts/
> source('C:/MyRScripts/Manipulate.R')
Fruit: Banana Apple Cherry
Sorted: Apple Banana Cherry

Numbers: NA 8 7 6 5 4 3 2 NA 1 2 3 4 5 6 7 NA
Increasing: 1 2 2 3 3 4 4 5 5 6 6 7 7 8 NA NA NA
Decreasing: 8 7 7 6 6 5 5 4 4 3 3 2 2 1
Reversed: 1 2 2 3 3 4 4 5 5 6 6 7 7 8
Unique: 1 2 3 4 5 6 7 8
>
```

Summary

- The arithmetical operators in R programming are **+** addition, **-** subtraction, ***** multiplication, **/** division, **%/%** integer division, **^** exponentiation, and **%%** modulus.
- The comparison operators in R programming are **==** equality, **!=** inequality, **>** greater than, **<** less than, **>=** greater than or equal to, and **<=** less than or equal to.
- The logical operators in R programming are **!** logical NOT, **&&** logical AND, **&** element-wise logical AND, **||** logical OR, and **|** element-wise logical OR.
- Comparison and logical operators return a Boolean value of **TRUE** or **FALSE** as the result of their operation.
- The : colon operator generates an inclusive sequence in steps of one between the range specified by its numeric operands.
- The : colon operator can be used to specify a numeric sequence within **[ ]** square brackets to copy a slice of a vector.
- The **cat( )** function concatenates its arguments for output and is a useful alternative to the **print( )** and **paste( )** functions.
- Vector arithmetic on numeric element values is performed by placing an arithmetic operator between two variable names.
- When performing vector arithmetic, if vectors have an unequal number of elements, the shorter one will be recycled in order to match the longer vector length.
- The R comparison operators can be used to perform comparison of corresponding elements within two vectors.
- Operator precedence determines the order in which R evaluates expressions.
- Where operators have equal precedence, their associativity determines how expressions are grouped.
- Parentheses can be used to specify precedence, in which case expressions within innermost parentheses are performed first.
- Vector elements can be manipulated using the **sort( )**, **rev( )** and **unique( )** functions.

4 Testing conditions

This chapter demonstrates how to control the flow of R Script programs.

Seeking truth

The **if** keyword performs a conditional test to evaluate an expression for a Boolean value. A statement following the expression will only be executed when the evaluation is **TRUE**, otherwise the program proceeds on to subsequent code – pursuing the next "branch". The **if** statement syntax looks like this:

if (*test-expression* **) {** *code-to-be-executed-when-true* **}**

The code to be executed can contain multiple statements if they are enclosed within curly brackets to form a "statement block" :

If.R

1. Open the RStudio Code Editor and add a conditional test that evaluates an expression comparing two numbers

```
if ( 5 > 1 )
{
  print( "Five is greater than one." )
}
```

2. Add a second conditional test, which executes an entire statement block when one number is less than another

```
if ( 2 < 4 )
{
        print( "Two is less than four." ) ;
        print( "Test succeeded." ) ;
}
```

3. Select all lines of both statements, then click the Run button, or press **Ctrl** + **Enter**, to execute the code

```
Console C:/MyRScripts/
> if ( 5 > 1 )
+ {
+   print( "Five is greater than one.")
+ }
[1] "Five is greater than one."
>
> if ( 2 < 4)
+ {
+   print( "Two is less than four." )
+   print( "Test succeeded." )
+ }
[1] "Two is less than four."
[1] "Test succeeded."
>
```

Expressions can utilize the **TRUE** and **FALSE** keywords. The test expression **(2 < 4)** is shorthand for **(2 < 4 == TRUE)**.

A conditional test can also evaluate a complex expression to test multiple conditions for a Boolean value. Parentheses enclose each test condition to establish precedence – so they get evaluated first. The Boolean **&&** AND operator ensures the complex expression will only return **TRUE** when both tested conditions are true:

if ((*test-condition1* **) && (** *test-condition2* **)) {** *execute-this-code* **}**

The Boolean **||** OR operator ensures a complex expression will only return **TRUE** when either one of the tested conditions is true:

if ((*test-condition1* **) || (** *test-condition2* **)) {** *execute-this-code* **}**

A combination of these can form longer complex expressions:

4. Declare a variable containing a single integer value

```
num <- 8
```

5. Add a third conditional test that executes a statement when the value of the **num** variable is within a specified range, or when it's exactly equal to a specified value

```
if( ( num > 5 ) && ( num < 10 ) || ( num == 12 ) )
{
  print( "Number is 6-9 inclusive, or 12" )
}
```

6. Select the variable declaration and all lines of the third statement, then press **Ctrl** + **Enter** or click the Run button to execute the code

```
Console C:/MyRScripts/
> num = 8
>
> if( ( num > 5 ) && ( num < 10 ) || ( num == 12 ) )
+ {
+   print( "Number is 6-9 inclusive, or 12" )
+ }
[1] "Number is 6-9 inclusive, or 12"
>
```

7. Change the value assigned to the variable so it is neither within the specified range 6-9, or exactly 12, then run the third statement code again to now see the statement after the complex expression is not executed.

The range can be extended to include the upper and lower limits using the >= and <= operators.

The complex expression uses the == equality operator to specify an exact match, not the = assignment operator.

Branching alternatives

The **else** keyword is used in conjunction with the **if** keyword to create **if else** statements that provide alternative branches for a program to pursue – according to the evaluation of a tested expression. In its simplest form this merely nominates an alternative statement for execution when the test fails:

```
if ( test-expression )
{
        code-to-be-executed-when-true
} else
  {
        code-to-be-executed-when-false
  }
```

Each alternative branch may be a single statement or a statement block of multiple statements – enclosed within curly brackets.

More powerful **if else** statements can be constructed that evaluate a test expression for each alternative branch. These may have "nested" **if** statements within each **else** block to specify a further test. When the program discovers an expression that evaluates as **TRUE** it executes the statements associated with just that test then exits the **if else** statement without exploring any further branches:

Else.R

1. Open the RStudio Code Editor and create a variable containing an integer value

```
hour <- 11
```

2. Insert this simple conditional test, which executes a single statement when the value of the variable is below 13

```
if ( hour < 13 )
{
        print( paste( "Good Morning:", hour ) )
}
```

3. Click the Source button to run the code and see the statement get executed

```
Console C:/MyRScripts/
> source('C:/MyRScripts/Else.R')
[1] "Good Morning: 11"
>
```

4. Change the variable value to 15, then add this alternative branch immediately after the closing **}** curly bracket of the **if** statement

```
else
{
  if ( hour < 18 ) print( paste( "Good Afternoon:", hour ) )
}
```

5. Click the Source button to run the code and see just the alternative statement get executed

```
Console C:/MyRScripts/
> source('C:/MyRScripts/Else.R')
[1] "Good Afternoon: 15"
>
```

The **else** keyword must be added on the same line as the closing curly bracket of the preceding statement block.

It is sometimes desirable to provide a final **else** branch, without a chained **if** statement, to specify a "default" statement to be executed when no tested expression evaluates as **TRUE**:

6. Change the variable value to 21, then add this alternative branch immediately after the nested **if** statement

```
else
{
   print( paste( "Good Evening:", hour ) )
}
```

7. Select the entire code, then click the Run button to run the code and see the appropriate statement get executed

```
Console C:/MyRScripts/
> hour <- 21
>
> if( hour < 13 )
+ {
+   print( paste( "Good Morning:", hour ) )
+ } else
+   {
+     if( hour < 18 ) print( paste( "Good Afternoon:", hour ) )
+     else
+     {
+       print( paste( "Good Evening:", hour ) )
+     }
+   }
[1] "Good Evening: 21"
>
```

Conditional branching is the fundamental process by which computer programs proceed.

Chaining branches

When you want to provide several alternative branches, the technique of nesting **if else** statements can produce code that is difficult to read. A better solution is possible by "chaining" alternative branches using **else if** statements. These too provide alternative branches for a program to pursue according to the evaluation of a tested expression, but in a more succinct format:

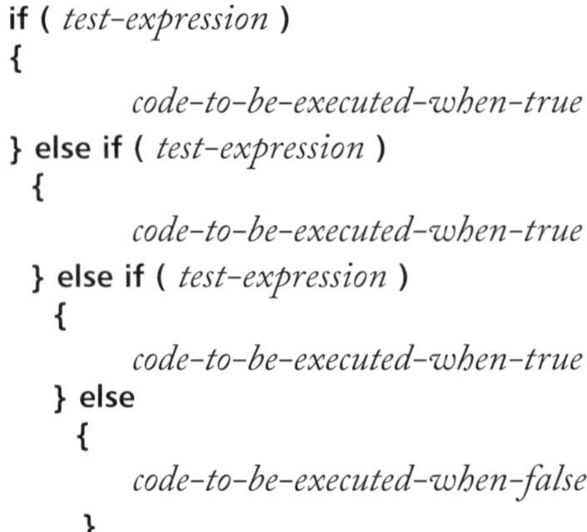

```
if ( test-expression )
{
        code-to-be-executed-when-true
} else if ( test-expression )
  {
        code-to-be-executed-when-true
  } else if ( test-expression )
    {
        code-to-be-executed-when-true
    } else
      {
        code-to-be-executed-when-false
      }
```

The **else** keyword must be added on the same line as the closing curly bracket of the preceding statement block.

When the program discovers an expression that evaluates as **TRUE**, it executes the statements associated with just that test then exits the **if** or **else if** statement without exploring any further branches. The previous example that used nested conditional tests can therefore be better written to use chained conditional tests:

ElseIf.R

1. Open the RStudio Code Editor and create a variable containing an integer value

```
hour <- 11
```

2. Insert this simple conditional test, which executes a single statement when the value of the variable is below 13

```
if ( hour < 13 )
{
        print( paste( "Good Morning:", hour ) )
}
```

3. Click the Source button to run the code

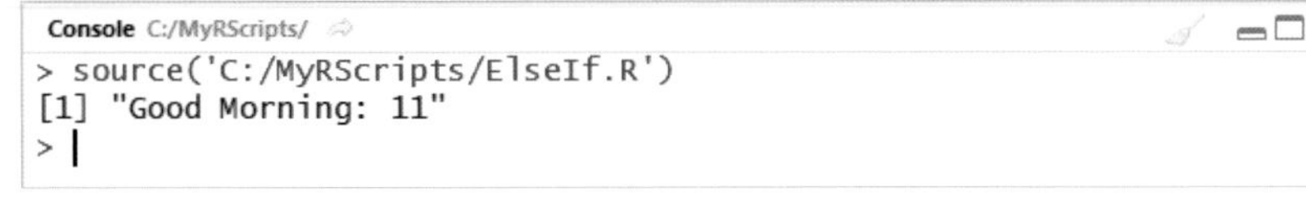

```
Console C:/MyRScripts/
> source('C:/MyRScripts/ElseIf.R')
[1] "Good Morning: 11"
>
```

4. Change the value assigned to the variable to 15, then add this alternative branch immediately after the closing **}** curly bracket of the **if** statement

```
else if ( hour < 18 )
{
        print( paste( "Good Afternoon:", hour ) )
}
```

5. Click the Source button to run the code and see just the alternative statement get executed

```
Console C:/MyRScripts/
> source('C:/MyRScripts/ElseIf.R')
[1] "Good Afternoon: 15"
> |
```

6. Change the value assigned to the variable to 21, then add this default branch immediately after the closing **}** curly bracket of the **else** statement

```
else
{
  print( paste( "Good Evening:", hour ) )
}
```

7. Select the entire code, then click the Run button to run the code and see just the default statement get executed

```
Console C:/MyRScripts/
> hour <- 21
>
> if( hour < 13 )
+ {
+   print( paste( "Good Morning:", hour ) )
+ } else if( hour < 18 )
+   {
+     print( paste( "Good Afternoon:", hour ) )
+   } else
+     {
+       print( paste( "Good Evening:", hour ) )
+     }
[1] "Good Evening: 21"
>
```

The final **else** statement provides a default statement to execute when all conditional tests fail.

Switching branches

Lengthy **if else** statements, which offer many conditional branches for a program to pursue, can become unwieldy. Where the test expression returns an integer or character string value, a more elegant solution can be provided by the built-in **switch( )** function.

The basic syntax of the **switch( )** function looks like this:

switch (*expression* **,** *list* **)**

The list contains comma-separated items that can themselves be returned by the **switch( )** function, or be expressions to be executed by the function, or be named items with associated values or expressions to be returned or executed by the function.

The **switch( )** function examines the value returned by the specified expression. If the value is an integer, or can convert to an integer, the **switch( )** function returns the value at that index position. For example, **switch(2, "A", "B", "C")** returns "B".

Alternatively, list items may be complex expressions that contain code to be executed within **{ }** curly brackets. In this case, the **switch( )** function will execute the code at that index position. For example, **switch(2, { print("A") }, { print("B") })** prints "B".

When the integer returned by the specified expression is beyond the final index position of the list, the **switch( )** function returns a **NULL** value. For example, **switch(4, "A", "B", "C")** returns **NULL**.

If the value returned by the specified expression is a character string, the **switch( )** function seeks to match that string in the list. When it finds a match in the list, the **switch( )** function returns the value associated with that character string. For example, **switch("bar", foo="A", bar="B")** returns "B".

Where the list items are complex expressions that contain code to be executed within **{ }** curly brackets, the **switch( )** function will execute the code associated with the character string. For example, **switch("bar", foo={ print("A") }, { bar=print("B") })** prints "B".

When no match is found to the character string returned by the specified expression, the **switch( )** function returns a **NULL** value. For example, **switch("num", foo="A", bar="B")** returns **NULL**.

Notice that the list names do not need to be enclosed within quote marks.

Switch.R

1. Open the RStudio Code Editor and create three variables

```
month <- "Jan"
year <- 2020
num <- 0
```

2. Next, add a statement to examine the first variable and assign a new value to the last variable

```
switch( month,
        "Jan"  =    { num <- 31 },
        "Feb"  =    { if( year %% 4 == 0 )
                    num <- 29 else num <- 28 },
        "Mar"  =    { num <- 31 },
        "Apr"  =    { num <- 30 },
        "May"  =    { num <- 31 },
        "Jun"  =    { num <- 30 },
        "Jul"  =    { num <- 31 },
        "Aug"  =    { num <- 31 },
        "Sep"  =    { num <- 30 },
        "Oct"  =    { num <- 31 },
        "Nov"  =    { num <- 30 },
        "Dec"  =    { num <- 31 }
)
```

The **num** variable must be created outside the **switch( )** statement block to be visible to code elsewhere – otherwise it will only be available locally, to code inside the **switch** block. This is variable "scope" – see page 84 for details.

3. Now, add a statement to output the number of days in the specified month

```
print( paste( month, year, "has", num, "days" ) )
```

4. Click the Source button to run the code and see the output

```
Console C:/MyRScripts/
> source('C:/MyRScripts/Switch.R')
[1] "Jan 2020 has 31 days"
>
```

Notice that complex expressions containing code to be executed enclose the code within curly brackets.

5. Change the value of the first variable to match any list name, then run the code again to see its associated output

```
Console C:/MyRScripts/
> source('C:/MyRScripts/Switch.R')
[1] "Feb 2020 has 29 days"
> source('C:/MyRScripts/Switch.R')
[1] "Mar 2020 has 31 days"
> source('C:/MyRScripts/Switch.R')
[1] "Apr 2020 has 30 days"
>
```

Looping while true

A loop is a block of code that repeatedly executes the statements it contains until a tested condition is met – then the loop ends and the program proceeds on to its next task.

The basic loop structure in R programming employs the **while** keyword and has this syntax:

```
while ( test-expression )
{
        statements-to-be-executed-on-each-iteration
        updater
}
```

The test expression must evaluate some value that gets updated in the loop's statement block as the loop proceeds – otherwise an infinite loop is created that will relentlessly execute its statements.

The test expression is evaluated at the start of each iteration of the loop for a Boolean **TRUE** value. When the evaluation returns **TRUE**, the iteration proceeds but when it returns **FALSE**, the loop is immediately terminated, without completing that iteration.

Note that if the test expression returns **FALSE** when it is first evaluated, the loop statements are never executed.

A **while** loop can be made to evaluate a counter variable in its test expression, by creating a counter variable outside the loop and updating its value within the loop's statement block that it executes on each iteration. For example, a **while** loop can output the value of its counter variable on each iteration, like this:

```
count <- 1

while ( count < 4 )
{
        print( paste( "Loop Counter =", count ) )
        count <- ( count + 1 )
}
```

This positions the counter externally, before the **while** loop structure, and its updater within the statement block.

Loop structures may also be nested – so that an inner loop executes all its iterations on each iteration of the outer loop.

The updater is often referred to as the "incrementer" as it more often increments, rather than decrements, the counter variable.

While.R

1. Open the RStudio Code Editor and create a variable to count the total number of loop iterations

```
sum <- 0
```

2. Next, create a counter variable and a loop to increment the total counter, output this loop counter and total counter, then increment this loop's counter value

```
i <- 1
while( i < 4 )
{
  sum <- ( sum + 1 )
  cat( "Outer Loop i =", i, "\t\tTotal =", sum, "\n" )
  i <- ( i + 1 )

  # Nested loop to be inserted here.

}
```

The "trivial" variables that are used as loop counters are traditionally named **i** , **j**, and **k**.

3. Now, create a second counter variable and a similar loop to increment the total counter, output this loop counter and total counter, then increment this loop's counter value

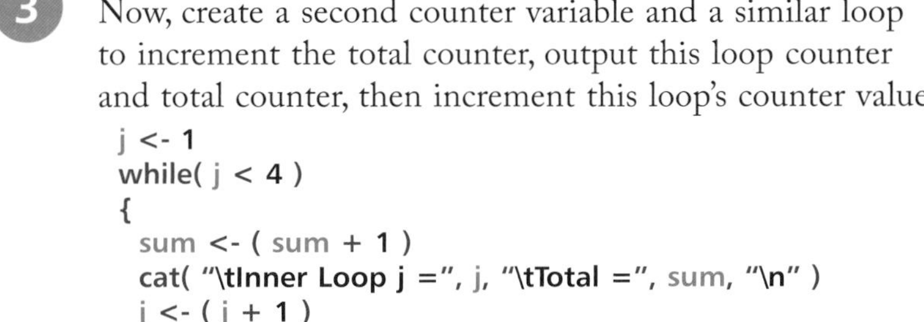

```
  j <- 1
  while( j < 4 )
  {
    sum <- ( sum + 1 )
    cat( "\tInner Loop j =", j, "\tTotal =", sum, "\n" )
    j <- ( j + 1 )
  }
```

You can halt execution of an infinite loop by pressing the **Esc** key, or by clicking the Stop button that appears on the Console menu bar as the loop is running.

4. Click the Source button to run the code and see the output display the counter values on each iteration of the loops

```
Console C:/MyRScripts/
> source('C:/MyRScripts/While.R')
Outer Loop i = 1                Total = 1
        Inner Loop j = 1        Total = 2
        Inner Loop j = 2        Total = 3
        Inner Loop j = 3        Total = 4
Outer Loop i = 2                Total = 5
        Inner Loop j = 1        Total = 6
        Inner Loop j = 2        Total = 7
        Inner Loop j = 3        Total = 8
Outer Loop i = 3                Total = 9
        Inner Loop j = 1        Total = 10
        Inner Loop j = 2        Total = 11
        Inner Loop j = 3        Total = 12
>
```

Performing for loops

Unlike the **while** loop structure, which evaluates a test expression to determine whether it should continue its iterations, R provides an alternative that is especially useful with sequences. This loop uses the **for** and **in** keywords and has this syntax:

for (*variable* **in** *sequence* **)**
{
statements-to-be-executed-on-each-iteration
}

The **for** loop iterates over each element **in** a sequence and executes the statements contained within its statement block on each iteration of the loop. When the end of the sequence is reached, the loop ends and the program proceeds to its next task.

The variable named in the parentheses of a **for** loop is assigned the value of the current element **in** the sequence on each iteration of the loop. For example, a **for** loop can output the value of its variable on each iteration over a vector, like this:

```
seq <- c( 100, 200, 300 )

for( var in seq )
{
        print( paste( "Loop Variable =", var ) )
}
```

The : colon operator can be used to easily specify a numeric range. For example, to perform one hundred iterations, like this:

```
for( var in 1:100 )
{
        print( paste( "Loop Variable =", var ) )
}
```

It is sometimes more efficient to iterate by index number.

Where the **for** loop is to iterate over a specified sequence whose length may vary, the **length( )** function can be used, like this:

```
seq <- c( 100, 200, 300, 400, 500 )

for( var in 1:length( seq ) )
{
        print( paste( "Loop Variable =", seq[ var ] ) )
}
```

In this case the variable is assigned the index number of the element, which is used to retrieve its value in the statement.

...cont'd

ForIn.R

1. Open the RStudio Code Editor and create a variable to contain a list sequence of character strings

```
seq <- list( A="Alpha", B="Bravo", C="Charlie" )
```

2. Next, add a loop to iterate over the sequence and output the current element value on each iteration

```
for( var in seq )
{
  print( var )
}
```

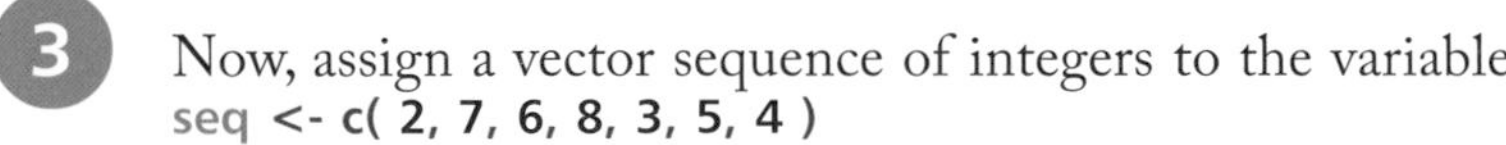

3. Now, assign a vector sequence of integers to the variable

```
seq <- c( 2, 7, 6, 8, 3, 5, 4 )
```

In R, the execution of loops is relatively slow so it is better to use vector arithmetic wherever possible – see page 46.

4. Then, add a loop to iterate over the sequence and output the current element value and its parity on each iteration

```
for( var in seq )
{
  if( var %% 2 == 1 )
  {
    cat( var, "Is Odd\n" )
  } else
  {
    cat( var, "Is Even\n" )
  }
}
```

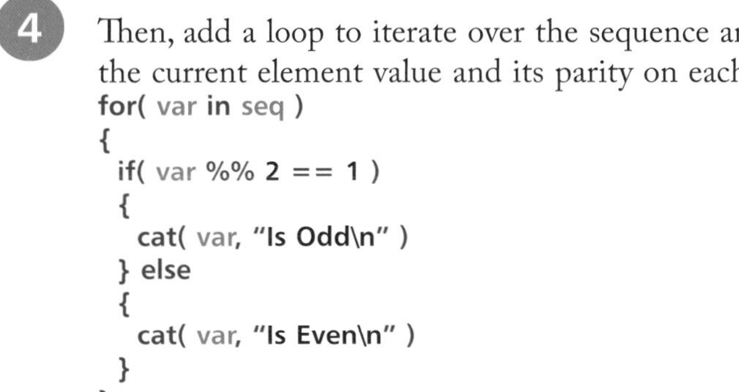

5. Click the Source button to run the code and see the output display the values on each iteration of the loops

```
Console C:/MyRScripts/
> source('C:/MyRScripts/ForIn.R')
[1] "Alpha"
[1] "Bravo"
[1] "Charlie"
2 Is Even
7 Is Odd
6 Is Even
8 Is Even
3 Is Odd
5 Is Odd
4 Is Even
>
```

Breaking from loops

The **break** keyword can be used to prematurely terminate a loop when a specified condition is met. The **break** statement is situated inside the loop statement block and is preceded by a test expression. When the test returns **TRUE**, the loop ends immediately and the program proceeds to its next task. For example, in a nested **for** loop it proceeds to the next iteration of its outer loop.

BreakNext.R

1. Open the RStudio Code Editor and create an outer loop that will perform three iterations

```
for( i in 1:3 )
{

  # Inner loop to be inserted here.

}
```

2. Insert an inner loop that will also perform three iterations, and output the variable values on each iteration

```
  for( j in 1:3 )
  {
          # Statement for next to be inserted here.

          # Statement for break to be inserted here.

          cat( "Running i=", i, " j=", j, "\n" )
  }
```

3. Click the Source button to run the code and see the output display the values on each iteration of the loops

```
Console C:/MyRScripts/
> source('C:/MyRScripts/BreakNext.R')
Running i= 1  j= 1
Running i= 1  j= 2
Running i= 1  j= 3
Running i= 2  j= 1
Running i= 2  j= 2
Running i= 2  j= 3
Running i= 3  j= 1
Running i= 3  j= 2
Running i= 3  j= 3
> |
```

4. Add this **break** statement to the beginning of the inner loop statement block, to break out of the inner loop – then click the Source button to re-run the program

```
if ( i == 2 && j == 1 )
{
        cat( "Breaks Inner Loop at i=", i, " j=", j, "\n" )
        break
}
```

```
Console C:/MyRScripts/
> source('C:/MyRScripts/BreakNext.R')
Running i= 1  j= 1
Running i= 1  j= 2
Running i= 1  j= 3
Breaks Inner Loop at i= 2  and j= 1
Running i= 3  j= 1
Running i= 3  j= 2
Running i= 3  j= 3
>
```

Here, the **break** statement halts all three iterations of the inner loop when the outer loop tries to run it for the second time.

The **next** keyword can be used to skip a single iteration of a loop when a specified condition is met. The **next** statement is situated inside the loop statement block and is preceded by a test expression. When the test returns **TRUE**, that iteration ends.

5. Add this **next** statement to the beginning of the inner loop statement block, to skip the first iteration of the inner loop – then click Source to re-run the program

```
if ( i == 1 && j == 1 )
{
        cat( "Skips Iteration at i=", i, " j=", j, "\n" )
        next
}
```

```
Console C:/MyRScripts/
> source('C:/MyRScripts/BreakNext.R')
Skips Iteration at i= 1  and j= 1
Running i= 1  j= 2
Running i= 1  j= 3
Breaks Inner Loop at i= 2  and j= 1
Running i= 3  j= 1
Running i= 3  j= 2
Running i= 3  j= 3
>
```

Here, the **next** statement skips just the first iteration of the inner loop when the outer loop tries to run it for the first time.

Summary

- The **if** keyword performs a conditional test to evaluate an expression for a Boolean value of **TRUE** or **FALSE**.
- An **if** statement block can contain one or more statements that are only executed when the test expression returns **TRUE**.
- The Boolean **&&** AND operator and **||** OR operator can be used to perform multiple conditional tests.
- The **else** keyword specifies alternative statements to execute when the test performed by the **if** keyword returns **FALSE**.
- Multiple **if else** statements can be nested to test several conditions in the process of conditional branching.
- A final **else** statement can be used to specify default statements to be executed when all conditional tests fail.
- Combined **else if** statements can be chained to test several conditions more succinctly than nested statements.
- The **switch( )** function can sometimes provide an elegant solution to unwieldy **if else** statements.
- When the value returned by the expression specified to **switch( )** is an integer, the function returns the value at that index position in its list, but when it's a character string, the function seeks to match that string in its list.
- A loop repeatedly executes the statements it contains until a tested expression returns **FALSE**.
- Statements in a **while** loop must change a value used in their test expression to avoid an infinite loop.
- The parentheses that follow the **for** keyword specify a variable, the **in** keyword, and a sequence to iterate over.
- A loop iteration can be skipped using the **next** keyword.
- A loop can be terminated using the **break** keyword.

5 Employing functions

This chapter demonstrates how to use built-in R functions and how to create your own functions in R Script programs.

Doing mathematics

The R programming language provides many built-in functions that are useful to perform mathematical calculations. For example, the **sqrt( )** function returns the square root of the number specified as its sole argument. A variety of functions are provided to round decimal numbers up or down according to your requirements.

All trigonometric operations are supported in R to return sine, cosine, tangent, and their inverse equivalents. Conveniently, R also has a built-in constant named **pi**, representing Π (3.14159265...).

The natural logarithm of a number is returned by the **log( )** function and the inverse of this operation can be performed using the **exp( )** function. Frequently-used mathematical R functions are listed in the table below:

To discover more on trigonometric functions, enter **?Trig** to see their Help page.

Function:	Returns:
abs(*x*)	Absolute value of ***x***
sqrt(*x*)	Square root of ***x***
ceiling(*x*)	Integer of ***x*** rounded up
floor(*x*)	Integer of ***x*** rounded down
trunc(*x*)	Integer of ***x*** truncated
round(*x* , digits=*n*)	Nearest number to ***x*** , to ***n*** decimal places
signif(*x* , digits=*n*)	Nearest number to ***x*** , to ***n*** significant digits
cos(*x*), sin(*x*), tan(*x*) **acos(*x*), asin(*x*), atan(*x*)**	Cosine, sine, tangent, arc-cosine, arc-sine, and arc-tangent of ***x***
log(*x*)	Natural logarithm of ***x***
log10(*x*)	Common (base 10) logarithm of ***x***
exp(*x*)	Exponential value of ***x***

Angles in R must be expressed in radians, not degrees, so degrees must be converted to radians when specifying arguments to the trigonometric functions.

Math.R

1. Begin an R Script by displaying the value of the mathematical constant of Π

```
cat( "Pi Constant =", pi, "\n" )
```

2. Next, add statements to display the value of the mathematical constant Π rounded down, rounded up, and rounded to two decimal places

```
cat( "Pi Floor\t", floor( pi ), "\n" )
cat( "Pi Ceiling\t", ceiling( pi ), "\n" )
cat( "Pi Rounded\t", round( pi, digits=2 ), "\n\n" )
```

3. Now, create a variable containing an integer value, then display the square root of that value

```
num <- 64
cat( "Square Root of", num, "=", sqrt( num ), "\n\n" )
```

4. Then, assign an angle represented in radians to the variable and display that angle's cosine

```
num <- ( 120 * ( pi / 180 ) )
cat( "Cosine of 120° = ", cos( num ), "\n\n" )
```

5. Finally, assign the natural logarithm of an integer to the variable, then display its inverse value and the logarithm

```
num <- log( 100 )
cat( "Log of", exp( num ), "=", num, "\n" )
```

6. Run the code to see the output results from the mathematical functions

R also supports scientific notation to represent very large numbers as a decimal and exponent separated by the letter **e**. For example, 12,500 can be written as **1.25e4** – meaning 1.25 x 10^4.

Console C:/MyRScripts/

```
> source('C:/MyRScripts/Math.R')
Pi Constant = 3.141593
Pi Floor        3
Pi Ceiling      4
Pi Rounded      3.14

Square Root of 64 = 8

Cosine of 120° =  -0.5

Log of 100 = 4.60517
> |
```

Manipulating strings

The R programming language provides built-in functions to manipulate character strings. The familiar **paste( )** function joins strings together. Conversely, there are several functions provided to extract substrings from a given string to suit your requirements. The character case of a given string can be easily transformed by **toupper( )** and **tolower( )** functions. Frequently-used R functions for string manipulation are listed in the table below:

Function:	Returns:
substr(***x*** **,** ***start, stop*** **)**	Substring of ***x*** from ***start*** to ***stop***
sub(***pattern, new, x*** **)**	String substituted first match of ***pattern*** with ***new*** in ***x***
strsplit(***x, separator*** **)**	Substrings of ***x*** split around the specified ***separator***
toupper(***x*** **)**	String ***x*** transformed to all uppercase characters
tolower(***x*** **)**	String ***x*** transformed to all lowercase characters

The **Sys.time( )** function returns the current system date and time, which can be manipulated to suit your requirements using the built-in **format( )** function. This requires two arguments to specify the date and time, plus a string incorporating format specifiers:

There are many other format specifiers available. Enter **?strptime** to discover more.

Specifier:	Format:	Example:
%e	Day number (1-31)	7
%a	Short day name	Mon
%A	Full day name	Monday
%b	Short month name	Aug
%B	Full month name	August
%H	Hour number (00-23)	12
%M	Minute number (00-59)	30
%Y	Year number 4-digit	2018

String.R

1. Begin an R Script by assigning a character string to a variable for manipulation
string <- "R for Data Analysis"

2. Next, add a statement to display an extracted substring of the variable string
cat("Substring:\t", substr(string, 7, 10), "\n")

3. Now, add a statement to display a substring in which a matched pattern has been replaced
cat("Replaced:\t", sub("sis", "tics", string), "\n\n")

4. Then, print substrings extracted from the variable string around each space character
print(paste("Split: ", strsplit(string, " ")))

5. Add a statement to display an uppercase version of the variable string
cat("\nUppercase:\t", toupper(string), "\n\n")

6. Finally, assign the current date and time to a variable, then print its components in formatted strings
now <- Sys.time( )
print(format(now, format="Date: %A, %B %e"))
print(format(now, format="Time: %H:%M"))

7. Run the code to see the output results from the string manipulations

```
Console C:/MyRScripts/
> source('C:/MyRScripts/String.R')
Substring:       Data
Replaced:        R for Data Analytics

[1] "Split:  c(\"R\", \"for\", \"Data\", \"Analysis\")"

Uppercase:       R FOR DATA ANALYSIS

[1] "Date: Friday, November 3"
[1] "Time: 15:12"
> 
```

Notice that the **strsplit( )** function returns a list that has \" escaped quote marks around each item to avoid conflict with the quote marks enclosing the entire string.

Producing sequences

The : colon operator is useful for quickly producing a sequence of numbers in steps of one, but the built-in **seq( )** function offers greater possibilities. This function accepts two arguments to specify the start and end value of the sequence, but can also accept a third integer argument to specify the step value. Alternatively, the third argument can be **length.out=** to specify the length of the sequence. In this case, R will calculate the step value to evenly distribute the sequence between the specified start and end values. The length may also be specified using **along.with=** as the third argument to nominate a vector whose length will be matched.

Where you want to replicate items repeatedly in a sequence, you can specify the item and sequence length as arguments to the built-in **rep( )** function. The item may be a single value, a vector, or a list – each element will be repeated in turn within the sequence. Additionally, a fourth **each=** argument can be included to specify how many times each element should be repeated in the sequence.

R also provides these useful sequences as built-in constants:

The built-in "constant" values in R can actually be assigned new values so be careful to avoid using their names for your variable names.

Constant:	Sequence:
LETTERS	"A", "B", "C", "D", "E", "F", "G", "H", "I", "J", "K", "L", "M", "N", "O", "P", "Q", "R", "S", "T", "U", "V", "W", "X", "Y", "Z"
letters	"a", "b", "c", "d", "e", "f", "g", "h", "i", "j", "k", "l", "m", "n", "o", "p", "q", "r", "s", "t", "u", "v", "w", "x", "y", "z"
month.name	"January", "February", "March", "April", "May", "June", "July", "August", "September", "October", "November", "December"
month.abb	"Jan", "Feb", "Mar", "Apr", "May", "Jun", "Jul", "Aug", "Sep", "Oct", "Nov", "Dec"

The built-in constants are vectors, so individual elements can be addressed using their index number as usual. For example, writing **month.name[4]** to retrieve "April". A slice can also be addressed using the : colon operator to specify the start and end index numbers, such as **LETTERS[1:3]** to retrieve "A", "B", "C".

...cont'd

Sequence.R

1. Begin an R Script by assigning a slice of a constant to a variable, then output the assigned values
```
half.year <- month.abb[ 1:6 ]
cat( "Constant:", half.year, "\n" )
```

2. Next, add statements to display sequences stepped by increments of one and two respectively
```
cat( "Sequence:", seq( 1, 8 ), "\n" )
cat( "Two Step:", seq( 1, 8, 2 ), "\n\n" )
```

3. Now, add statements to display sequences whose element values are distributed evenly between specified lengths
```
cat( "Distributed:", seq( 1, 8, length.out=4 ), "\n" )
cat( "Distributed:", seq( 1, 8, along.with=half.year ), "\n\n" )
```

4. Then, output a replicated sequence of a specified integer nine times
```
cat( "Replicated:", rep( 5, 9 ), "\n" )
```

5. Output a replicated sequence of a specified sequence that will be repeated three times
```
cat( "Replicated:", rep( 1:4, 3 ), "\n" )
```

6. Finally, output a replicated sequence of a specified sequence that will be repeated three times, in which each element will be repeated twice
```
cat( "Replicated:", rep( 1:4, 3, each=2 ), "\n" )
```

7. Run the code to see the output sequences

```
Console C:/MyRScripts/
> source('C:/MyRScripts/Sequence.R')
Constant: Jan Feb Mar Apr May Jun
Sequence: 1 2 3 4 5 6 7 8
Two Step: 1 3 5 7

Distributed: 1 3.333333 5.666667 8
Distributed: 1 2.4 3.8 5.2 6.6 8

Replicated: 5 5 5 5 5 5 5 5 5
Replicated: 1 2 3 4 1 2 3 4 1 2 3 4
Replicated: 1 1 2 2 3 3 4 4 1 1 2 2 3 3 4 4 1 1 2 2 3 3 4 4
>
```

The next step in the two step increment sequence (9) is not output, as it is beyond the specified end value (8).

Generating random numbers

The R programming language provides the ability to generate random uniformly distributed numbers with its built-in **runif( )** function, which by default returns random numbers between zero and one. This function requires a single argument to specify how many random numbers to generate.

Multiplying a random number will specify a wider range. For example, multiplying by 10 will create a random number in the range of 0 to 10. Now, rounding the random number up with the **ceiling()** function will make it within the range 1-10 inclusive:

Random.R

1. Begin an R Script by assigning a single generated random number to a variable, then output its value

```
rand <- runif( 1 )
cat( "Random Number:\t\t", rand, "\n" )
```

2. Next, multiply the variable value to increase its range, then output its new value

```
rand <- ( rand * 10 )
cat( "Multiplied Number:\t", rand, "\n" )
```


3. Now, round the variable value, then output its new value

```
rand <- ceiling( rand )
cat( "Random Integer:\t\t", rand, "\n\n" )
```

4. Run the code several times to see the random numbers

In statistics, a "uniform" distribution describes a probability in which all outcomes are equally likely. For example, a coin toss has uniform distribution, as the probability of getting heads or tails is equally likely.

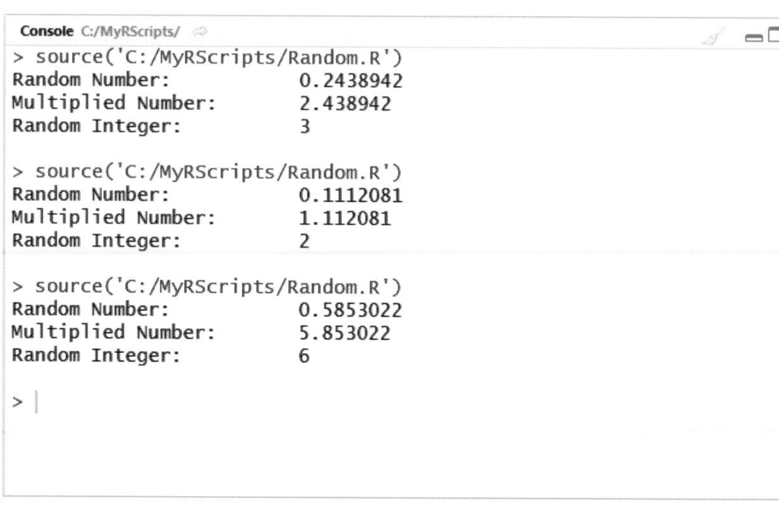

Console C:/MyRScripts/
> source('C:/MyRScripts/Random.R')
Random Number: 0.2438942
Multiplied Number: 2.438942
Random Integer: 3

> source('C:/MyRScripts/Random.R')
Random Number: 0.1112081
Multiplied Number: 1.112081
Random Integer: 2

> source('C:/MyRScripts/Random.R')
Random Number: 0.5853022
Multiplied Number: 5.853022
Random Integer: 6

>

A random sample of element values can be produced by specifying a range and the required number of element values as arguments to the built-in **sample( )** function. This might be used to produce a sequence of six non-repeating random numbers within the range 1-59 inclusive for a random lottery selection:

1. Create an R Script that assigns integers 1-59 to a vector variable and displays six random element values
```
nums <- c( 1:59 )
cat( "My Lucky Numbers:", sample( nums, 6 ), "\n\n" )
```

Lottery.R

2. Run the code several times to see the random sequences of six non-repeating numbers within the range 1-59

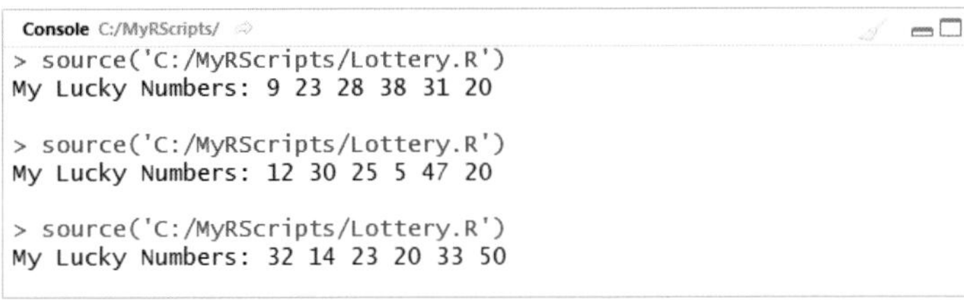

```
Console C:/MyRScripts/
> source('C:/MyRScripts/Lottery.R')
My Lucky Numbers: 9 23 28 38 31 20

> source('C:/MyRScripts/Lottery.R')
My Lucky Numbers: 12 30 25 5 47 20

> source('C:/MyRScripts/Lottery.R')
My Lucky Numbers: 32 14 23 20 33 50
```

In statistics, "mean" is the expected value and "standard deviation" is the amount of variation. A low standard deviation indicates data points close to the mean value.

Random normally distributed numbers can be generated with the built-in **rnorm( )** function. This function requires a single argument to specify how many random numbers to generate. Optionally, it can accept two further arguments to specify a mean value and standard deviation value. By default, the **mean=** value is zero and the **sd=** standard deviation argument is one:

1. Create an R Script that assigns three random numbers to a variable and displays the generated values
```
nums <- rnorm( 3 )
cat( "Random Normal Distribution:", nums, "\n\n" )
```

RandomNormal.R

2. Run the code several times to see the random numbers

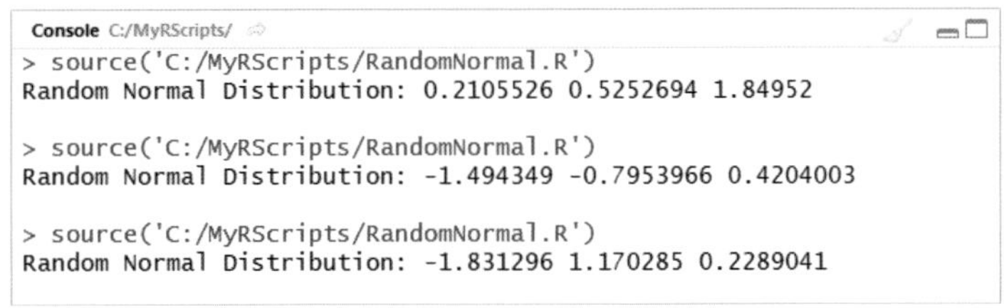

```
Console C:/MyRScripts/
> source('C:/MyRScripts/RandomNormal.R')
Random Normal Distribution: 0.2105526 0.5252694 1.84952

> source('C:/MyRScripts/RandomNormal.R')
Random Normal Distribution: -1.494349 -0.7953966 0.4204003

> source('C:/MyRScripts/RandomNormal.R')
Random Normal Distribution: -1.831296 1.170285 0.2289041
```

Distributing patterns

The **rnorm( )** function, introduced on the previous page, generates a vector of random numbers that is sampled from a "normal distribution" of values. The normal distribution plots all its values in a symmetrical fashion around the specified mean value. The values are tightly grouped close to the mean, then tail off symmetrically away from the mean, across the standard deviation. This is represented graphically as a bell curve. The graph illustrated below depicts the normal distribution pattern for a mean value of zero and standard distribution of one (the defaults).

The **σ** sigma character is used in math notation to denote the standard deviation values.

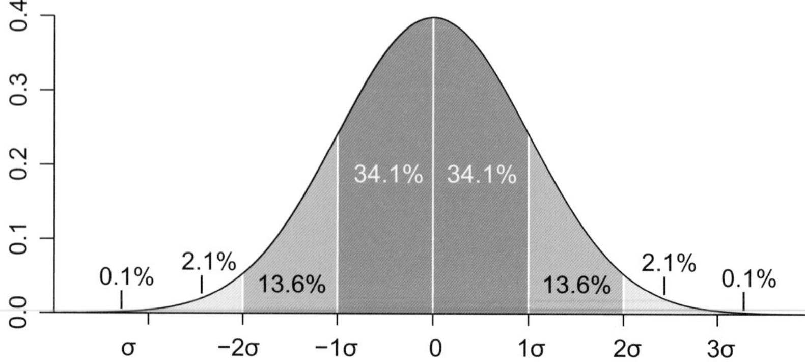

To understand the Law of Large Numbers, imagine tossing a coin – where there is a 50% chance for heads and tails. 10 coin tosses might produce 7 heads and 3 tails (70%/30%), 100 coin tosses might produce 55 heads and 45 tails (55%/45%), and 1000 coin tosses might produce 510 heads and 490 tails (51%/49%) – getting increasingly closer to average 50% as the number of coin tosses increase.

The pattern demonstrates that there is a greater probability of the randomly generated number being closer to the mean value. The probability that the average value will be closer to the mean value increases as the number of generated random numbers increases. This pattern is recognized by the "Law of Large Numbers" (LLN), which is written in math notation like this:

$$\bar{X}_n \rightarrow E(X) \; when \; n \rightarrow \infty$$

The law states that the average of the actual measured values $\bar{X}_n$ converges towards the expected value $E(X)$ when the number of values n grows towards infinity ∞ . The graph above shows a 34.1% probability on either side of the mean value zero. This means that there is a total expectation of 68.2% that the generated random number will fall within the range -1 to +1.

The Law of Large Numbers can be tested by calculating the percentage of generated random numbers that fall within the expected range as the quantity of generated numbers increases.

1. Begin an R Script by creating a variable to specify the quantity of random numbers to generate
   ```
   qty <- 10
   ```

LLN.R

2. Next, add a loop structure that will iterate to 1 million
   ```
   while( qty <= 1000000 )
   {
     # Statements to be inserted here – Steps 3-6.
   }
   ```

3. Now, insert a variable to count the number that fall within the expected range
   ```
   num <- 0
   ```

You could, optionally, omit the **mean** and **sd** arguments as the values specified here are the **rnorm( )** default values.

4. Then, insert a nested loop to generate random numbers, and to increment the counter for each generated random number that falls within the expected range
   ```
   for( i in rnorm( qty, mean=0, sd=1 ) )
   {
     if( ( i >= -1 ) && ( i <= 1 ) ) num <- ( num + 1 )
   }
   ```

5. Insert statements to calculate and output the percentage of values that fall within the expected range
   ```
   num <- ( num / ( qty / 100 ) )
   cat( "For", qty, "Generated Random Numbers:", num, "%\n" )
   ```

6. Finally, insert a statement to multiply by 10 the quantity of random numbers to be generated on each iteration
   ```
   qty <- ( qty * 10 )
   ```

7. Run the code to test the Law of Large Numbers

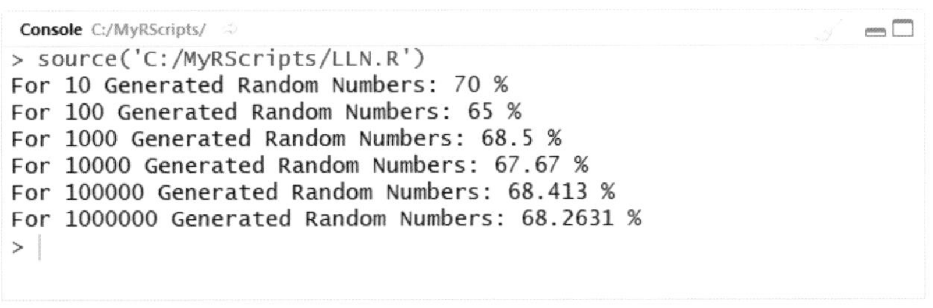

```
Console C:/MyRScripts/
> source('C:/MyRScripts/LLN.R')
For 10 Generated Random Numbers: 70 %
For 100 Generated Random Numbers: 65 %
For 1000 Generated Random Numbers: 68.5 %
For 10000 Generated Random Numbers: 67.67 %
For 100000 Generated Random Numbers: 68.413 %
For 1000000 Generated Random Numbers: 68.2631 %
>
```

See that the percentage on the final iteration is closest to the expectation of 68.2% – thereby demonstrating the Law of Large Numbers.

Extracting statistics

The R programming language provides a number of built-in utility functions that allow you to easily extract statistics from a range of values stored within a vector variable:

Function:	Returns:
mean(*x*)	Average of the values in ***x*** – computed by adding up all values and dividing the total by the number of values
median(*x*)	Number at the mid-point of the values in ***x*** – computed by listing all values in ascending order then locating the central number
sd(*x*)	Standard deviation of the values in ***x***
quantile(*x*)	Cut points that divide the values in ***x*** into four equal parts
sum(*x*)	Sum total of all the values in ***x***
range(*x*)	Maximum and minimum values in ***x***
max(*x*)	Maximum value in ***x***
min(*x*)	Minimum value in ***x***

Hot tip

The mean is used for normal distributions, whereas the median is generally used for skewed distributions.

Stats.R

1. Begin an R Script by creating a variable containing 20 generated random numbers, targeting a mean of five and a standard deviation of two

```
nums <- rnorm( 20, mean=5, sd=2 )
```

2. Next, add statements to output the mean value and median value of the generated random numbers

```
cat( "Mean:\t", mean( nums ), "\n" )
cat( "Median:\t", median( nums ), "\n\n" )
```

3. Now, add a statement to output the actual standard deviation of the generated random numbers

```
cat( "Actual SD:\t", sd( nums ), "\n\n" )
```

4. Add a statement to output the cut points that divide the generated numbers into four equal parts
cat("Cut Points:\t", quantile(nums **), "\n")**

5. Next, add a statement to output the sum total of all the generated random numbers
cat("Total:\t", sum(nums **), "\n\n")**

6. Now, add statements to output the minimum and maximum values of the generated random numbers
cat("Range:\t\t", range(nums **), "\n")**
cat("Minimum:\t", min(nums **), "\n")**
cat("Maximum:\t", max(nums **), "\n")**

7. Finally, add a statement to visualize the generated random numbers
plot(1:20, nums**, type="o")**

8. Run the code to see the extracted statistics

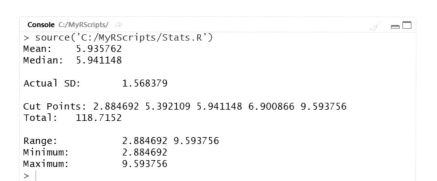

```
Console C:/MyRScripts/
> source('C:/MyRScripts/Stats.R')
Mean:    5.935762
Median:  5.941148

Actual SD:       1.568379

Cut Points: 2.884692 5.392109 5.941148 6.900866 9.593756
Total:   118.7152

Range:           2.884692 9.593756
Minimum:         2.884692
Maximum:         9.593756
> |
```

Notice that the median value is also the central cut point number.

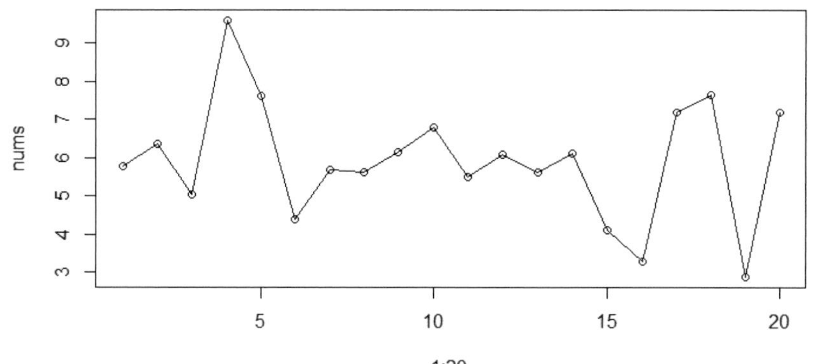

Creating functions

Previous examples in this book have featured built-in R functions, but you can easily create your own custom functions that can be called as required during execution of the program.

Custom functions have a "function block" that contains one or more statements that are executed each time the function gets called. Once the function statements have been executed, program flow resumes at the point directly following the function call.

Custom functions are created using the **function** and **return** keywords, and their declaration has this syntax:

```
function-name <- function( arg1, arg2, arg3 )
{
  statements-to-be-executed
  return( object )
}
```

The naming conventions for identifier names are described on page 22.

The function name can be any name that adheres to the usual R identifier naming conventions, and the object returned by the function can be of any data type, or **NULL** if none is required.

A custom function is called simply by stating its name followed by parentheses, just as built-in functions are called.

If your code contains repeated statements it would be better to enclose the statement within a function.

Values can be passed to custom functions by specifying valid names for each argument in the comma-separated parameter list within the **( )** parentheses that follow the **function** keyword. The passed values can then be addressed within the function block using their specified names, just as variable values can be addressed by their specified variable names. The parameter list is optional so can be omitted from the parentheses if the function does not require argument values to be passed when called.

Where a custom function declaration includes a parameter list, the function call must generally include a value for each argument, and in the same order in which they appear in the declaration.

It is important to recognize that variables created within a function block have "local scope", which means they are only visible within that function block – they cannot be addressed from code outside the function block.

...cont'd

FirstFunction.R

1. Begin an R Script by declaring a custom function to print out a message whenever this function is called

```
greet <- function( )
{
  print( "Hello from R!" )
}
```

2. Next, add a statement to call the custom function

```
greet( )
```

3. Now, declare a second custom function that will require one argument value whenever it gets called

```
f2c <- function( degrees )
{
  # Statements to be inserted here – Step 4.
}
```

4. Then, insert statements to assign a value to a variable using the passed in value, then return the variable value

```
result <- ( ( degrees - 32 ) * ( 5 / 9 ) )
return( result )
```

Variables that are created outside of function blocks are visible throughout the R Script code and are said to have "global scope".

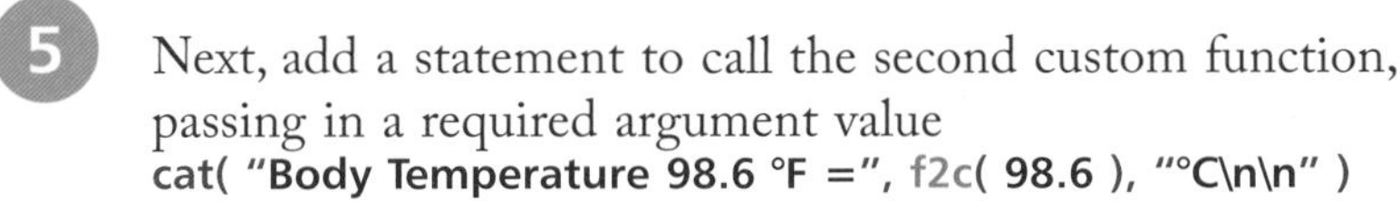

5. Next, add a statement to call the second custom function, passing in a required argument value

```
cat( "Body Temperature 98.6 °F =", f2c( 98.6 ), "°C\n\n" )
```

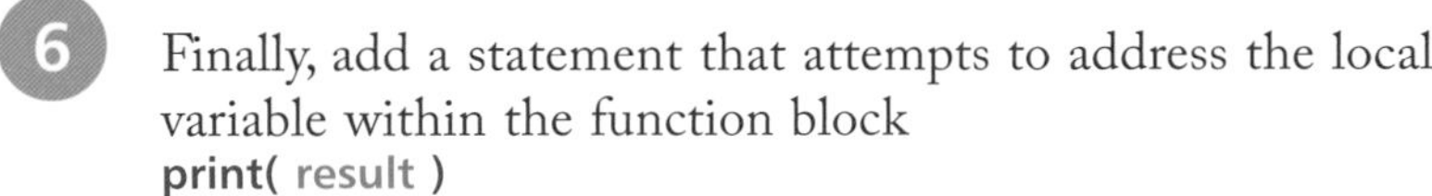

6. Finally, add a statement that attempts to address the local variable within the function block

```
print( result )
```

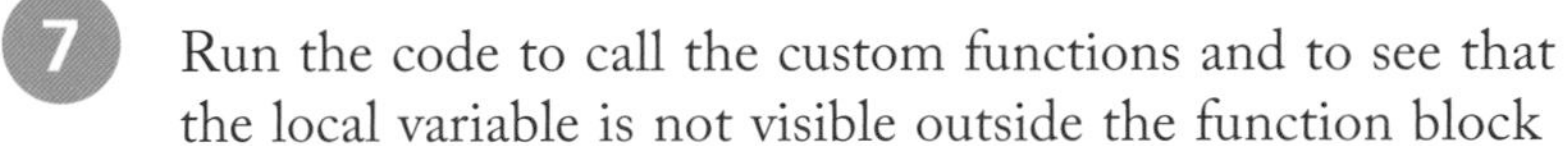

7. Run the code to call the custom functions and to see that the local variable is not visible outside the function block

```
Console C:/MyRScripts/
> source('C:/MyRScripts/FirstFunction.R')
[1] "Hello from R!"
Body Temperature 98.6 °F = 37 °C

Error in print(result) : object 'result' not found
> |
```

Calling the **f2c()** function without an argument will also produce an error.

Providing defaults

Custom functions can allow arguments to be optional by specifying a default value to the parameters in the declaration. Where the function call supplies an argument value, that value will be used by the function – otherwise the default value will be used by the function. Each default value must be assigned to the parameter in the declaration using the = operator, like this:

```
function-name <- function( arg1=value, arg2=value )
{
  statements-to-be-executed
  return( object )
}
```

The three dots operator

The ... three dots operator is more correctly known as the "ellipsis operator".

Custom functions can allow an arbitrary number of arguments to be passed from the caller by specifying a ... three dots operator parameter at the end of the arguments list in the declaration. Typically, this is used to accept arguments that will be passed to another function call within the function block. The three dots operator must also be added at the end of the function call in the function block in order to pass further arguments, like this:

```
function-name <- function( arg1, arg2, ... )
{
  statements-to-be-executed
  function-call( arg1, arg2, ... )
  return( object )
}
```

Recursive functions

You can halt continuous execution of a recursive function by pressing the **Esc** key, or by clicking the Stop button that appears on the Console menu during execution.

A custom function block can include a function call to itself recursively, to repeatedly execute statements within its own function block. As with loops, it is important that the function block includes a statement to modify a test expression to avoid continuous execution – so the function will end at some point:

```
function-name <- function( arg1, arg2 )
{
  statements-to-be-executed

  if( test-expression )
  { return( object ) }
  else
  { function-name( arg1, arg2 ) }
}
```

Default.R

1. Begin an R Script by declaring a custom function to print out and decrement an argument value when called

```
launch <- function( num=5 )
{
  cat( num, "- " )
  num <- ( num - 1 )

  # Statement to be inserted here – Step 2.
}
```

2. Next, add a conditional test to exit the function or call the function recursively, according to the tested value

```
if( num < 0 ) { return NULL } else { launch( num ) }
```

3. Now, declare a function that will accept an arbitrary number of arguments to be passed to another function

```
graph <- function( x, y, ... )
{
  plot( x, y, col="Red", type="o", ... )
}
```

4. Then, insert statements to call each function

```
launch( )
graph( 1:20, rnorm( 20 ), xlab="X Axis", ylab="Y Axis" )
```

5. Run the code to call the custom functions and see the default and arbitrary argument values applied

Here, the **...** three dots operator allows the label text to be passed to the **plot( )** function.

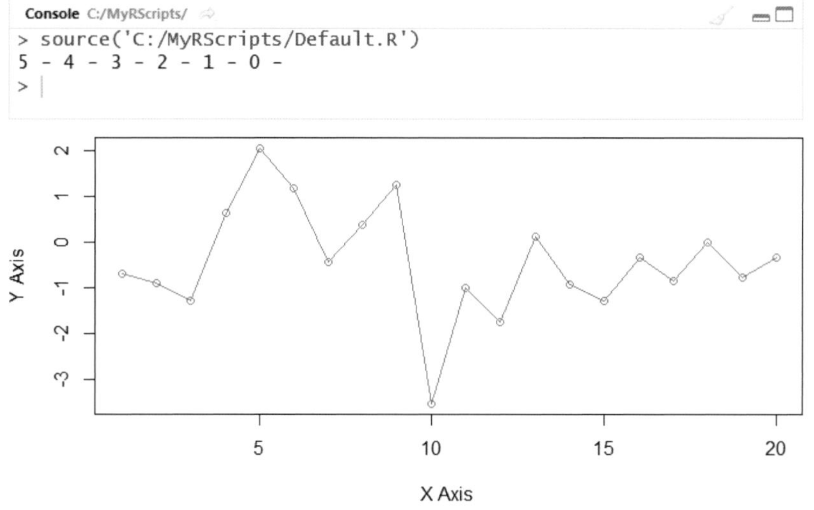

Summary

- The R programming language provides built-in math functions, such as **sqrt( )**, for mathematical calculation.
- The built-in **pi** constant value represents 3.141593.
- The R programming language provides built-in character string functions, such as **substr( )**, for string manipulation.
- The built-in **format( )** function accepts format specifiers, such as **%A**, to format date and time strings.
- The built-in **seq( )** function offers greater possibilities than the : colon operator for producing sequences.
- The R programming language provides built-in **LETTER**, **letter**, **month.name**, and **month.abb** character constants.
- Random uniformly distributed numbers between zero and one are generated by the built-in **runif( )** function.
- Random normally distributed numbers can be generated by the built-in **rnorm( )** function.
- The Law of Large Numbers recognizes that the probability that the average value will be closer to the mean value increases as the number of observations increase.
- The R programming language provides built-in utility functions, such as **range( )**, for the extraction of statistics.
- Custom functions are created using the **function** and **return** keywords, and are given a user-defined identifier name.
- A comma-separated parameter list can be added in a function declaration to accept argument values from the caller.
- Variables created within a function block have local scope, so they are only visible within that function block.
- Default argument values can be specified in a parameter list using the **=** operator, to allow arguments to be optional.
- The ... three dots operator can be used to allow an arbitrary number of arguments to be passed from the caller.
- A recursive function includes a function call to itself, to repeatedly execute statements within its own function block.

6 Building matrices

This chapter demonstrates how to store data in matrix structures and how to output stored data values in a plotted chart.

Building a matrix

Column →

Row ↓	[0]	[1]
[0]	1	4
[1]	2	5
[2]	3	6

In R programming, a "matrix" is a two-dimensional structure that stores data in a tabular format of cell rows and cell columns. As with vector structures, the values stored within a matrix must all be of the same data type.

A matrix can be created in R Script by writing a unique identifier name of your choice in the Code Editor, then assigning values using the built-in **matrix( )** function. This function requires a vector containing the values as its first argument, followed by **nrow=** and **ncol=** arguments to specify the desired number of rows and columns you wish to create. The number of rows and columns must match the length of the assigned vector or be an exact multiple of its length, or a warning message will appear. In this case, the matrix will still be created but the vector values will be recycled into additional cells. A matrix might be used to record a value for each day of a year in a table of 52 rows (one per week) and 7 columns (one per day), like this:

daily.record <- matrix(***vector*** **, nrow=52, ncol=7)**

A matrix in R resembles a multi-dimensional array structure found in other programming languages.

Individual values are addressed in a matrix using the appropriate index numbers of the row and column. For example, in this case you can retrieve the value for the second day in the third week using **daily.record [3, 2]**. New values can also be assigned to individual cells using their index number of row and column. For example, for the first day of the sixth week, like this:

daily.record[6, 1] <- ***value***

In order to confirm that a structure is indeed a matrix, R provides a built-in **is.matrix( )** function that will only return **TRUE** when its specified argument is a matrix object.

Usefully, you can seek a value within a matrix using the built-in **which( )** function. This requires a test expression as its argument, stating the matrix name and the value to seek. The **which( )** function examines the cells as if they were a vector and, if the sought value exists, returns the index numbers at which the value is found within that vector. If the sought value is not found, the function returns zero. Optionally, you can include an **arr.ind=TRUE** argument to the **which( )** function, so it will return the row and column index number of each cell containing the sought value.

FirstMatrix.R

1. Begin an R Script by creating a vector containing a sequence of 32 integer values

```
data <- seq( 1:32 )
```

2. Next, create a matrix that stores the vector values in tabular format, then output the matrix to see the cells

```
table <- matrix( data, nrow=4, ncol=8 )
print( table )
```

3. Now, confirm the type of structure storing the values

```
cat( "\nVector?:", is.vector( table ) ,
          "\tMatrix?:", is.matrix( table ) )
```

4. Retrieve a cell value, then assign a new value to that cell

```
cat( "\n\nCell 4,5 Contains:", table[ 4, 5 ] )
table[ 4, 5 ] <- 10
```

5. Finally, search all cells for a specific value, and identify the location of cells that do contain that value

```
cell <- which( table == 10, arr.ind=TRUE )
cat( "\n\nValue 10 Search:\n" )
print( cell )
```

6. Run the code to see the cell values and search result

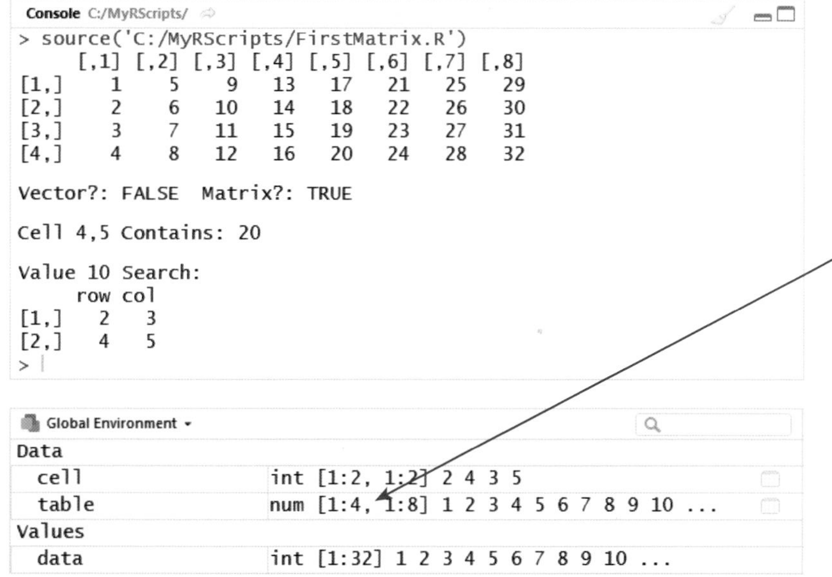

Console C:/MyRScripts/
> source('C:/MyRScripts/FirstMatrix.R')
     [,1] [,2] [,3] [,4] [,5] [,6] [,7] [,8]
[1,]   1   5   9   13   17   21   25   29
[2,]   2   6   10   14   18   22   26   30
[3,]   3   7   11   15   19   23   27   31
[4,]   4   8   12   16   20   24   28   32
Vector?: FALSE Matrix?: TRUE
Cell 4,5 Contains: 20
Value 10 Search:
     row col
[1,]   2   3
[2,]   4   5
>
Global Environment
Data
cell int [1:2, 1:2] 2 4 3 5
table num [1:4, 1:8] 1 2 3 4 5 6 7 8 9 10 ...
Values
data int [1:32] 1 2 3 4 5 6 7 8 9 10 ...

Note that the matrix is created with two indices – denoting rows first then columns second.

Transposing data

When creating a matrix, the **matrix( )** function will, by default, insert the data you supply into cells arranged by column order. This means that cells in the first column will be filled with data from the elements at the beginning of the specified vector before filling the second column, then the third column, and so on.

If you prefer to control how the cells are filled with data, you can include a **byrow=** argument in the call to the **matrix( )** function. When this is assigned a **TRUE** value, the function will then insert the data you supply into cells arranged by row order. Cells in the first row will now be filled with data from the elements at the beginning of the specified vector, before filling the second row, then the third row, and so on. Assigning a **FALSE** value to the **byrow=** argument will insert the data you supply into cells arranged by column order – the default order.

The arrangement of cells in a matrix can also be transposed, so that the rows become columns and the columns become rows, simply by specifying the matrix name to the built-in **t( )** function.

Transpose.R

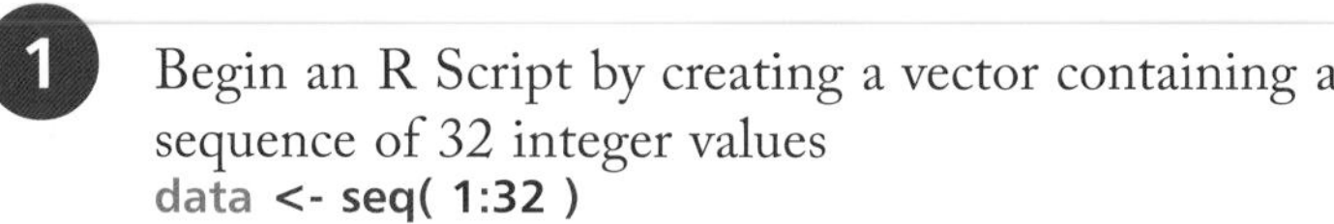

1. Begin an R Script by creating a vector containing a sequence of 32 integer values

```
data <- seq( 1:32 )
```

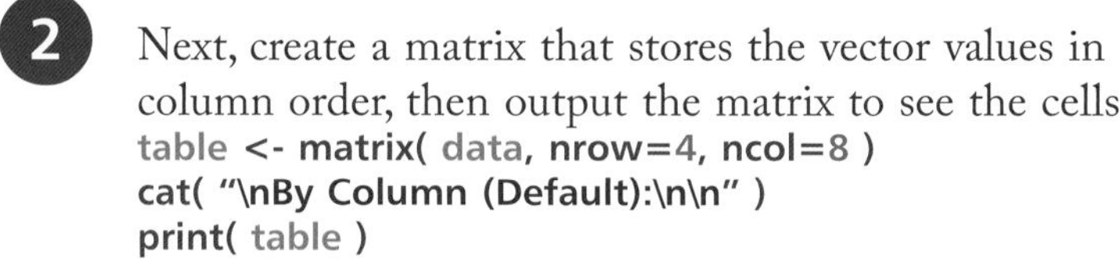

2. Next, create a matrix that stores the vector values in column order, then output the matrix to see the cells

```
table <- matrix( data, nrow=4, ncol=8 )
cat( "\nBy Column (Default):\n\n" )
print( table )
```

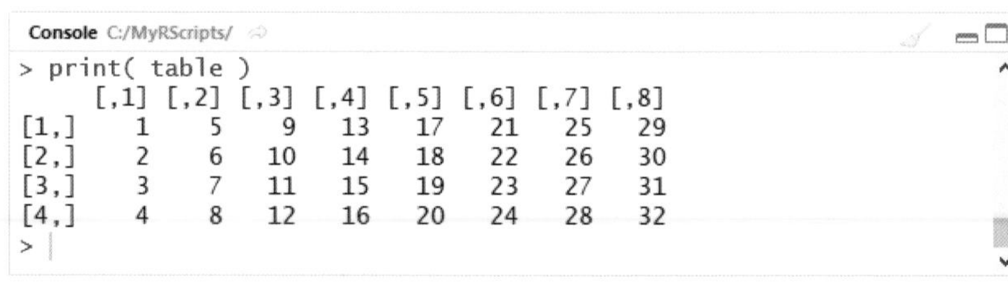

Select the code, then click the Run button, or press **Ctrl** + **Enter**, to execute the code.

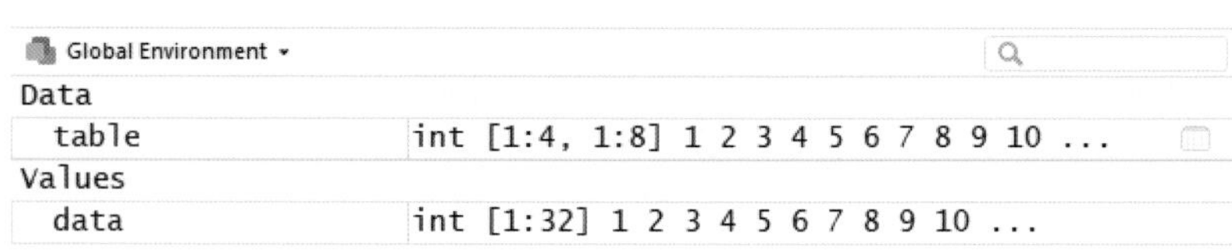

3. Now, recreate the matrix to store the vector values in row order, then output the matrix to see the cells

```
table <- matrix( data, nrow=4, ncol=8, byrow=TRUE )
cat( "\nBy Row:\n\n" )
print( table )
```

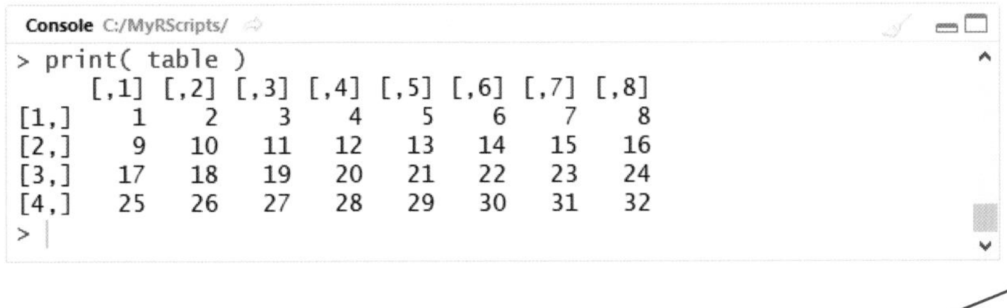

```
Console C:/MyRScripts/
> print( table )
     [,1] [,2] [,3] [,4] [,5] [,6] [,7] [,8]
[1,]    1    2    3    4    5    6    7    8
[2,]    9   10   11   12   13   14   15   16
[3,]   17   18   19   20   21   22   23   24
[4,]   25   26   27   28   29   30   31   32
>
```

See that the cell data is rearranged when stored by row.

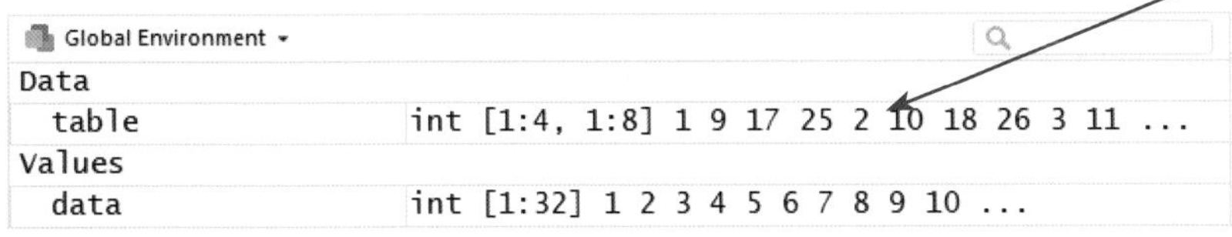

```
Global Environment
Data
  table     int [1:4, 1:8] 1 9 17 25 2 10 18 26 3 11 ...
Values
  data      int [1:32] 1 2 3 4 5 6 7 8 9 10 ...
```

4. Finally, transpose the matrix to exchange rows and columns, then output the matrix to see the cells

```
table <- t( table )
cat( "\nTransposed (Rows to Columns):\n\n" )
print( table )
```

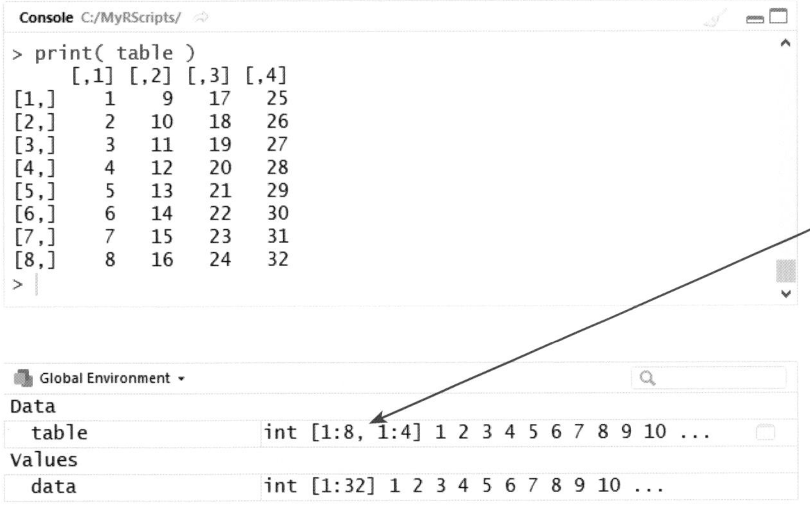

```
Console C:/MyRScripts/
> print( table )
     [,1] [,2] [,3] [,4]
[1,]    1    9   17   25
[2,]    2   10   18   26
[3,]    3   11   19   27
[4,]    4   12   20   28
[5,]    5   13   21   29
[6,]    6   14   22   30
[7,]    7   15   23   31
[8,]    8   16   24   32
>

Global Environment
Data
  table     int [1:8, 1:4] 1 2 3 4 5 6 7 8 9 10 ...
Values
  data      int [1:32] 1 2 3 4 5 6 7 8 9 10 ...
```

See that the matrix elements are rearranged when it gets transposed.

Binding vectors

When you need to combine data from multiple vectors into a single matrix the R programming language offers two possibilities:

- A sequence of vector names can be specified as arguments to the built-in **rbind( )** function to create a matrix that will contain the data from each vector on individual rows.
- A sequence of vector names can be specified as arguments to the built-in **cbind( )** function to create a matrix that will contain the data from each vector in individual columns.

The length of all specified vectors should be identical or a warning message will appear. In this case, the matrix will still be created but the vector values will be recycled into additional cells.

The data contained within the vectors to be combined must be of the same data type, otherwise it may be converted so the matrix will contain cell data of only one data type:

Bind.R

1. Begin an R Script by creating three vectors of identical length, containing different data types

```
start <- LETTERS[ 1:10 ]
finish <- LETTERS[ 17:26 ]
numeric <- seq( 1:10 )
```

2. Next create a matrix that stores the vector values on individual rows, then output the matrix to see the cells

```
table <- rbind( start, finish, numeric )
cat( "\nBind Rows:\n\n" )
print( table )
```

```
Console C:/MyRScripts/
> source('C:/MyRScripts/Bind.R')

Bind Rows:

        [,1] [,2] [,3] [,4] [,5] [,6] [,7] [,8] [,9] [,10]
start   "A"  "B"  "C"  "D"  "E"  "F"  "G"  "H"  "I"  "J"
finish  "Q"  "R"  "S"  "T"  "U"  "V"  "W"  "X"  "Y"  "Z"
numeric "1"  "2"  "3"  "4"  "5"  "6"  "7"  "8"  "9"  "10"
>
```

3. Open the Environment tab in the Workspace pane to see the vector data types differ, but see that the matrix contains only values of the character data type

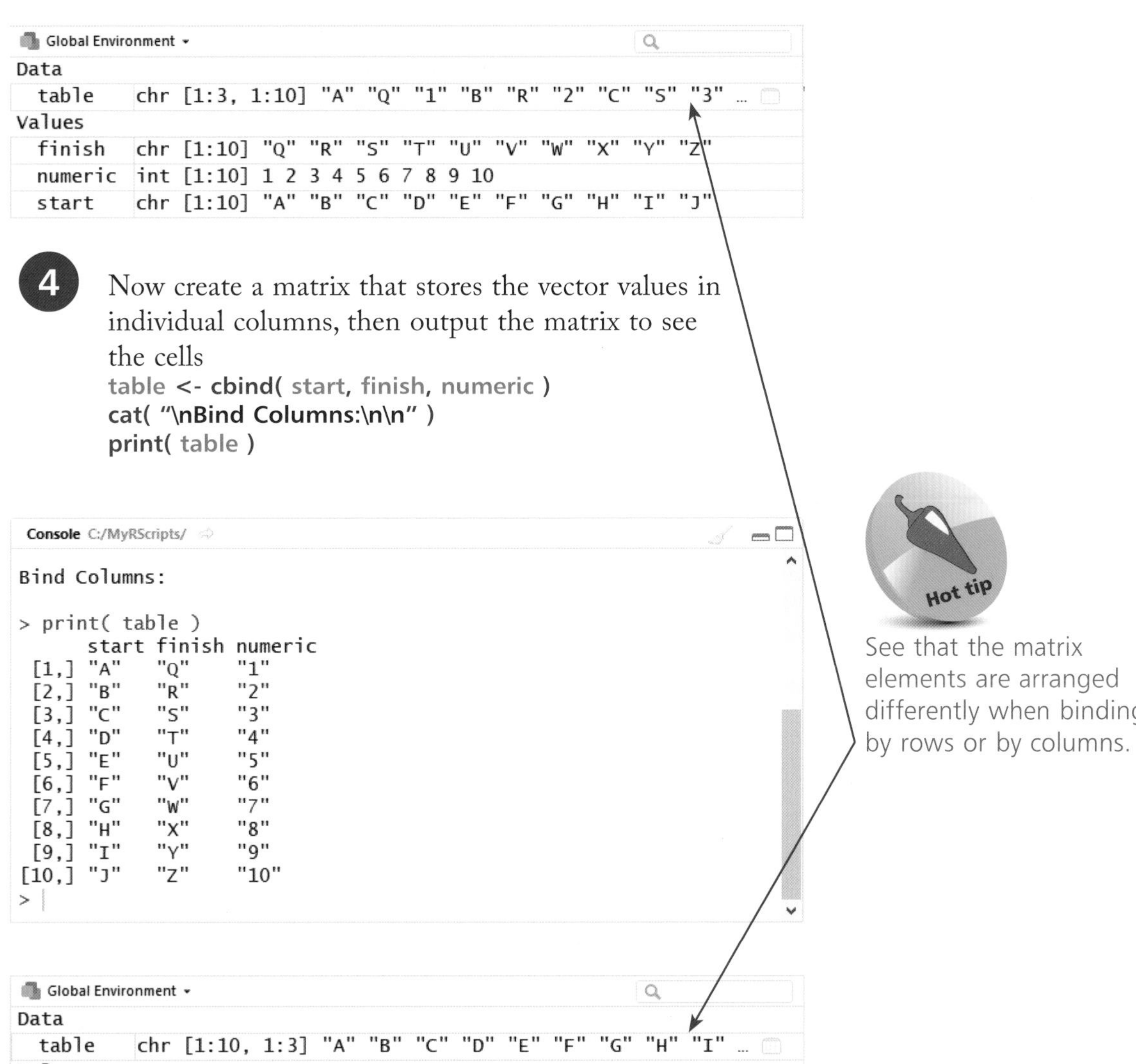

4. Now create a matrix that stores the vector values in individual columns, then output the matrix to see the cells

```
table <- cbind( start, finish, numeric )
cat( "\nBind Columns:\n\n" )
print( table )
```

Hot tip

See that the matrix elements are arranged differently when binding by rows or by columns.

The data type of any object can be examined by specifying that object as the argument to the built-in **typeof( )** function. For example, with the matrix above **typeof(table[1, 3])** confirms that the cell contains the value "1" of the character data type.

Character data can be converted to numeric data for use in an R Script by the built-in **as.numeric( )** function. For example, **as.numeric(table[1, 3])** converts to the double data type.

Naming rows and columns

The R interpreter automatically displays row labels and column headings when a matrix is output in the Console pane. These may simply denote the index number of each row ([1,], [2,],[3,], etc.) and each column ([,1], [,2], [,3], etc.) if the **matrix( )** function was used to create the matrix.

Matrices created with the **rbind( )** function will automatically display the vector variable name in place of the index number for each row label when output. Similarly, matrices created with the **cbind( )** function will automatically display the vector variable name in place of the index number for each column heading when output.

Meaningful names can be given by specifying the matrix name as the argument to the **rownames( )** and **colnames( )** functions. These can then each be assigned a comma-separated list of names by the **c( )** function, for row labels and column headings respectively. Naturally, the length of each list must match the number of rows and columns within the matrix.

Individual rows or columns can be addressed using their index number or specified name. Copying data from a matrix with named rows and columns into a vector will also copy the names to create a named vector with key=value elements:

Name.R

1. Begin an R Script by creating three vectors of identical length, each containing data of the double data type

```
ny <- c( 3.8, 5.5, 9.9, 15.7, 21.5, 26.3 )
la <- c( 19.5, 19.4, 19.7, 20.8, 21.3, 22.7 )
fw <- c( 13.7, 15.4, 20.0, 24.6, 28.5, 32.7 )
```

2. Next, create a matrix that stores the vector values on individual rows, then output the matrix to see the cells

```
table <- rbind( ny, la, fw )
print( table )
```

3. Now, assign meaningful names for the row labels and column headings

```
rownames( table ) <- c( "New York",
                        "Los Angeles",
                        "Fort Worth" )

colnames( table ) <- month.abb[ 1:6 ]
```

Notice how the R constant **month.abb** is used here to specify column heading names.

4. Then, output a text string and the revised matrix
cat("\nAverage High Temperature (°C):\n\n")
print(table **)**

5. Create a new vector to store the data from a single row of the matrix, using either the row name or index number
nyc **<-** table**["New York" ,]** **# Or table[1,]**

6. Next, display the data stored in the new vector variable
cat("\nNew York:", nyc**, "\n\n")**

7. Now, display the entire contents of the new vector variable
print(nyc **)**

8. Run the code to see the row labels, column headings, and the named vector

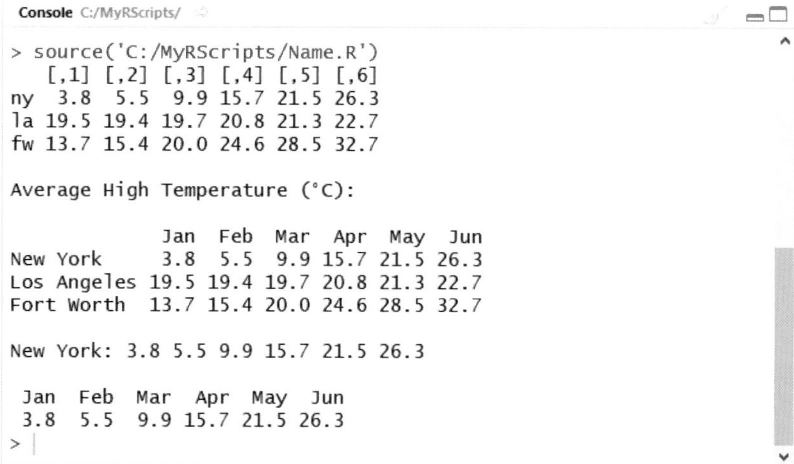

```
> source('C:/MyRScripts/Name.R')
   [,1] [,2] [,3] [,4] [,5] [,6]
ny  3.8  5.5  9.9 15.7 21.5 26.3
la 19.5 19.4 19.7 20.8 21.3 22.7
fw 13.7 15.4 20.0 24.6 28.5 32.7

Average High Temperature (°C):

             Jan  Feb  Mar  Apr  May  Jun
New York     3.8  5.5  9.9 15.7 21.5 26.3
Los Angeles 19.5 19.4 19.7 20.8 21.3 22.7
Fort Worth  13.7 15.4 20.0 24.6 28.5 32.7

New York: 3.8 5.5 9.9 15.7 21.5 26.3

 Jan  Feb  Mar  Apr  May  Jun
 3.8  5.5  9.9 15.7 21.5 26.3
>
```

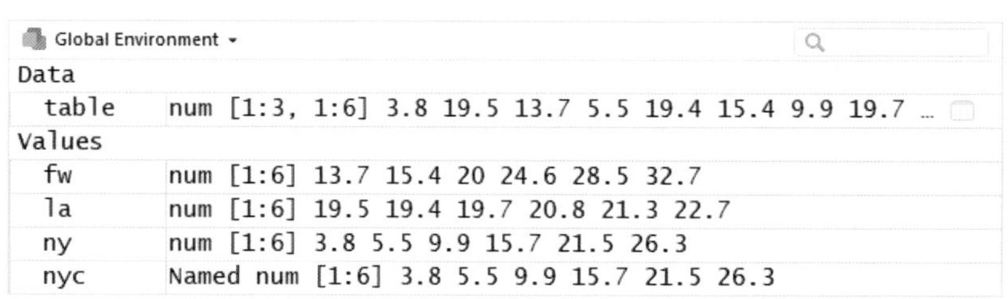

Global Environment	
Data	
table	num [1:3, 1:6] 3.8 19.5 13.7 5.5 19.4 15.4 9.9 19.7 ...
Values	
fw	num [1:6] 13.7 15.4 20 24.6 28.5 32.7
la	num [1:6] 19.5 19.4 19.7 20.8 21.3 22.7
ny	num [1:6] 3.8 5.5 9.9 15.7 21.5 26.3
nyc	Named num [1:6] 3.8 5.5 9.9 15.7 21.5 26.3

The **cat( )** function retrieves only the stored data here, whereas the **print( )** function also retrieves the column headings.

The **names( )** function can be used to retrieve the names within a named vector. For example, **names(nyc[1])** in this example retrieves "Jan", whereas **nyc[1]** retrieves the value 3.8.

Plotting matrices

The R programming language provides a **matplot( )** function that allows you to easily produce graphic visualizations of data contained within a matrix structure. This function requires the matrix name as an argument, plus several other arguments to specify how you would like the visualization to appear:

- **type=** – the type of plot to be drawn. Options include “p” for points only, “l” for lines only, and “b” for both plots and lines.
- **pch=** – the plotting character to use. Options are specified numerically for one or more of the symbols below:

- **col=** – the plotting color to use. Options are specified by name or numerically for one or more colors, and include the basic palette below:

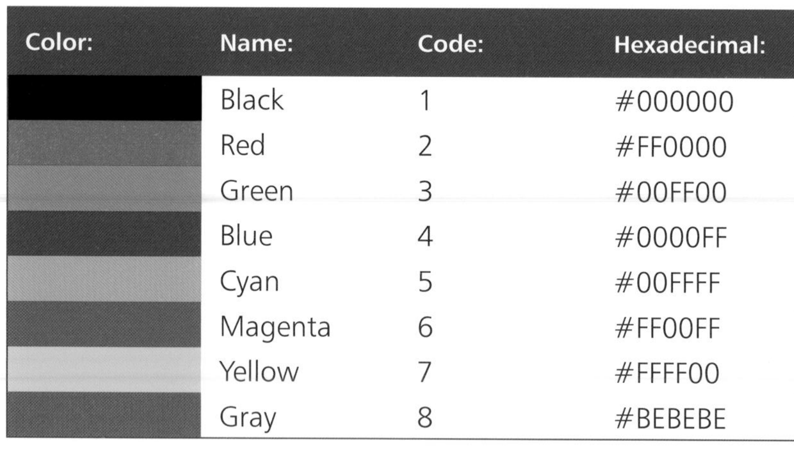

Color:	Name:	Code:	Hexadecimal:
	Black	1	#000000
	Red	2	#FF0000
	Green	3	#00FF00
	Blue	4	#0000FF
	Cyan	5	#00FFFF
	Magenta	6	#FF00FF
	Yellow	7	#FFFF00
	Gray	8	#BEBEBE

Multiple options may be specified as a comma-separated list of arguments to the **c( )** function, or as a sequence using the : colon operator.

Hexadecimal color values must be specified as character strings within quote marks.

1. Begin an R Script by creating three vectors of identical length, each containing data of the double data type

```
ny <- c( 3.8, 5.5, 9.9, 15.7, 21.5, 26.3 )
la <- c( 19.5, 19.4, 19.7, 20.8, 21.3, 22.7 )
fw <- c( 13.7, 15.4, 20.0, 24.6, 28.5, 32.7 )
```

MatrixPlot.R

2. Next, create a matrix that stores the vector values in individual columns, then output the matrix to see the cells

```
table <- cbind( ny, la, fw )
print( table )
```

3. Now, add a statement to create a graphic visualization of the data – showing points and lines, using three different plot characters, and drawn in three different colors

```
matplot( table, type="b", pch=15:17, col=2:4 )
```

Don't forget

Here, the multiple options could alternatively be specified as **pch=c(15, 16, 17)** and **col=c(2, 3, 4)**.

4. Run the code to see the matrix in the Console and to see its graphic visualization on the Plots tab

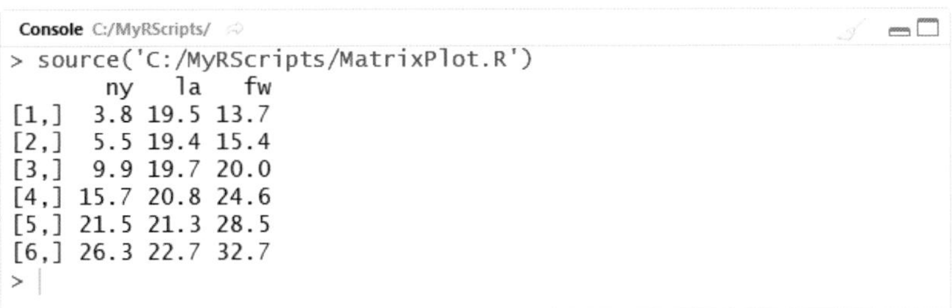

```
Console C:/MyRScripts/
> source('C:/MyRScripts/MatrixPlot.R')
       ny   la   fw
[1,]  3.8 19.5 13.7
[2,]  5.5 19.4 15.4
[3,]  9.9 19.7 20.0
[4,] 15.7 20.8 24.6
[5,] 21.5 21.3 28.5
[6,] 26.3 22.7 32.7
> 
```

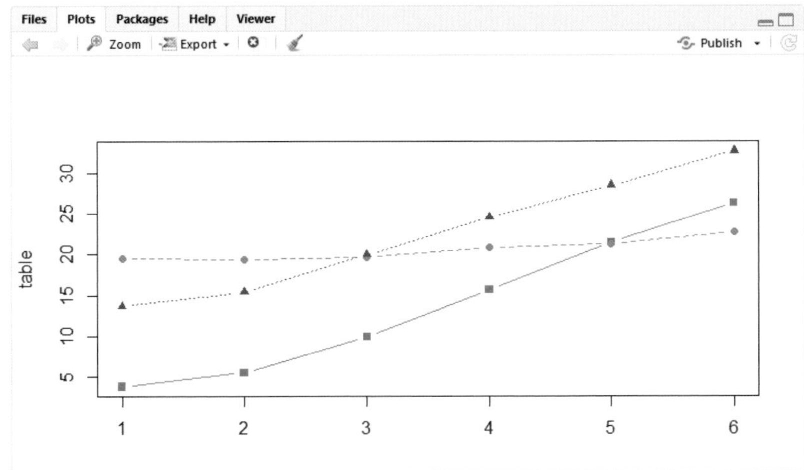

Adding labels

The R programming language **matplot( )** function, introduced in the previous example, can accept further arguments to specify labels for the plot and to control the range along each axis:

- **xlab=** , **ylab=** – title for the x axis and y axis, respectively.
- **xlim=** , **ylim=** – range for the x axis and y axis, respectively.
- **main=** – headline title for the plot.

The R interpreter will automatically supply plot axes with labeled tick marks, but you can suppress these to specify your own axes. This first requires you to include an **axes=FALSE** argument in the **matplot( )** function call to suppress the automatic axes, then you can use the built-in **axis( )** function to specify each required axis. This function requires a first integer argument to specify at which side of the plot to draw the axis – below (**1**), left (**2**), above (**3**), or right (**4**). If no further arguments are included, the range and labels will be automatically added. To supply your own range and labels, an **at=** argument is required, to specify the points at which to draw tick marks, and a **labels=** argument to specify label names. Label names are assigned as a vector of comma-separated character strings whose length must match the specified tick range. Typically, this might use the **rownames( )** or **colnames( )** functions to assign the matrix row or column names as axis labels.

Legends

The R programming language **legend( )** function allows you to easily add a descriptive legend to a plot. This function requires a first argument to specify a position at which to draw the legend. Special keywords, such as "topleft", can be used for this purpose. The position can be further adjusted by including an **inset=** argument to distance the legend away from the plot margins. Most importantly, the **legend( )** function should include **pch=** and **col=** arguments whose assigned values must precisely match those specified to the **matplot( )** function for correct identification of the plot's point characters and colors. Finally, the **legend( )** function should include a **legend=** argument to describe the plot components by assignment of a vector of comma-separated character strings. Typically, this might use the **rownames( )** or **colnames( )** functions to assign the matrix row or column names.

Available keywords for positioning legends are **bottomright**, **bottom**, **bottomleft**, **left**, **topleft**, **top**, **topright**, **right**, and **center**.

Label.R

1. Copy the previous **MatrixPlot.R** script file and assign row and column names before calling the **print( )** function

```
colnames( table ) <-
        c( "New York", "Los Angeles", "Fort Worth" )
rownames( table ) <- month:abb[ 1:6 ]
```

2. Modify the **matplot( )** function call to add arguments

```
matplot( table, type="b", pch=15:17, col=2:4,
          xlab="Months" ylab="Average High (°C)",
          xlim=c( 1, 6 ), ylim=c( 0, 35 ), axes=FALSE,
          main="City Temperature Comparison" )
```

The value assigned to the **inset=** argument is a fraction of the plot region, not an absolute measure of length.

3. Create axis labels and add a descriptive legend

```
axis( 1, at=1:6, labels=rownames( table ) )
axis( 2 )
legend( "topleft", inset=0.02, pch=15:17, col=2:4,
          legend=colnames( table ) )
```

4. Run the code to see the matrix in the Console and to see its labeled graphic visualization on the Plots tab

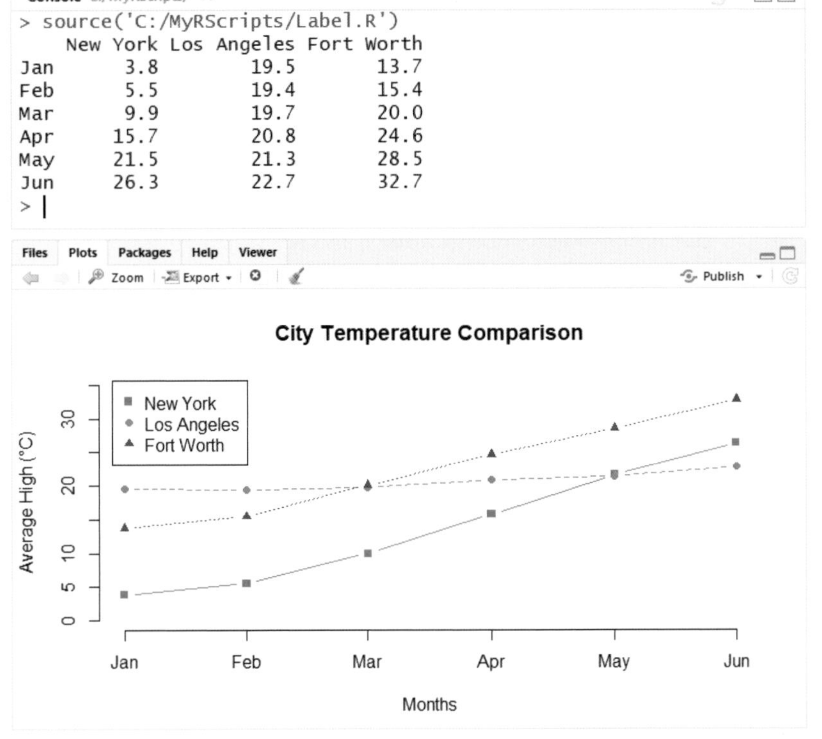

Insights from this plot: Los Angeles has the most consistent high temperature, Fort Worth reaches the Los Angeles temperature in March, but New York does not reach the Los Angeles temperature until May.

Extracting matrix subsets

A "subset" is simply a group of data values that are part of another larger set of data values. In R programming, it is often useful to extract subsets for comparison of specific areas of interest. With vector variables, a subset can be extracted by specifying the index numbers of specific elements, like this:

```
alphabet <- LETTERS[ ]
vowel.subset <- alphabet[ 1, 5, 9, 15, 21 ]
```

Notice that the **c( )** function must be included in the square brackets to specify the index names of elements to be extracted.

Alternatively, with named vector variables, a subset can be extracted by specifying the index names of specific elements:

```
nato <- c( A="Alpha", B="Bravo", C="Charlie", D="Delta" )
abc.subset <- nato[ c( A, B, C ) ]
```

Subsets that are extracted from a vector have one dimension and are returned as a vector data structure.

With matrices, a subset can be extracted by specifying the index numbers of specific cells, like this:

```
table <- matrix( 1:60, nrow=12, ncol=5 )
table.subset <- table[ 1:3, 1:5 ]
```

The rows and columns of a matrix can be named using the **rownames( )** and **colnames( )** functions, or by including a **dimnames=** argument in the call to the **matrix( )** function. This argument requires a list of length one to name the rows only, or a list of length two to name both the rows and columns, like this:

```
table <- matrix( 1:60, nrow=12, ncol=5,
         dimnames=list( month.abb[ ], LETTERS[ 1:5 ] ) )
```

A subset can then be extracted by specifying the row or column names of specific cells, like this:

```
table.subset <- table[ month.abb[ 1:3 ], LETTERS[ 1:5 ] ]
```

A comma is still required when omitting an index name or number from the square brackets.

When an entire row or column is to be extracted, its index number or name can be entirely omitted from the square brackets. For example, the assignments above can be made, like this

```
table.subset <- table[ 1:3 , ]

table.subset <- table[ c( "Jan", "Feb", "Mar ) , ]
```

Extracted subsets that contain more than one dimension (i.e. more than one row or column) are returned as a matrix data structure.

Subset.R

1. Begin an R Script by creating three vectors of identical length, each containing data of the double data type

```
ny <- c( 3.8, 5.5, 9.9, 15.7, 21.5, 26.3 )
la <- c( 19.5, 19.4, 19.7, 20.8, 21.3, 22.7 )
fw <- c( 13.7, 15.4, 20.0, 24.6, 28.5, 32.7 )
```

2. Next, create a matrix that stores the vector values in individual columns, then name the rows and columns

```
table <- cbind( ny, la, fw )
rownames( table ) <- month.name[ 1:6 ]
colnames( table ) <- c( "New York",
                        "Los Angeles", "Fort Worth" )
```

3. Add statements to output the entire matrix

```
cat( "\nMatrix...\n" )
print( table )
```

Here the : colon operator is used to select rows 1-TO-3 and the , comma operator is used in the **c( )** function to select columns 1-AND-3.

4. Now, create a subset that only stores values from the first three rows of just two columns of the matrix

```
table.q1 <- table[ 1:3 , c( 1, 3 ) ]
```

5. Add statements to output the entire subset

```
cat( "\nSubset...\n" )
print( table.q1 )
```

6. Run the code to see the matrix and subset in the Console

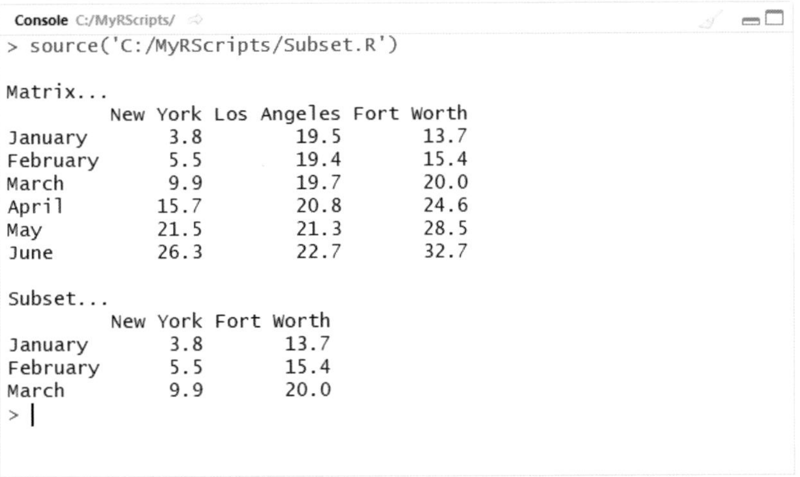

```
Console C:/MyRScripts/
> source('C:/MyRScripts/Subset.R')

Matrix...
         New York Los Angeles Fort Worth
January       3.8        19.5       13.7
February      5.5        19.4       15.4
March         9.9        19.7       20.0
April        15.7        20.8       24.6
May          21.5        21.3       28.5
June         26.3        22.7       32.7

Subset...
         New York Fort Worth
January       3.8       13.7
February      5.5       15.4
March         9.9       20.0
> |
```

Maintaining dimensions

When extracting subsets from a matrix it is important to recognize the type of data structure in which the data is returned – the default behavior may not be what you require!

The default behavior is sensible as you will generally want data from single rows or columns of a matrix to be returned as a vector.

If the subset has more than one dimension, the subset will be returned in a matrix data structure, but if the subset has only one dimension, the subset will, by default, always be returned in a vector data structure. This is because R is trying to anticipate your requirements by automatically dropping (deleting) dimensions that it considers to contain redundant information.

Where the subset extracts data from a single row, the row name dimension will be deleted, and the column names will be used as element names in the returned vector. Conversely, where the subset extracts data from a single column, the column name dimension will be deleted and the row names will be used as element names in the returned vector.

The default behavior can be overridden by including a final **drop=FALSE** argument within the **[ ]** square brackets that specify the rows or columns to be extracted. This means that subsets that extract data from a single row, or from a single column, will now be returned in a matrix data structure.

Dimension.R

1. Begin an R Script by creating a vector containing a numerical sequence

```
data <- 1:28
```

2. Next, create a matrix that stores the vector values in rows, and name the rows and columns alphabetically

```
table <- matrix( data, nrow=4, ncol=7, byrow=TRUE,
         dimnames=list( letters[ 1:4 ], LETTERS[ 1:7 ] ) )
```

3. Add statements to output the entire matrix

```
cat( "\nMatrix...\n" )
print( table )
```

4. Now, create a subset that extracts data from a single row of the matrix – using the default behavior

```
tier <- table[ 2,  ]
```

5. Add statements to output the subset
```
cat( "\nSubset...\n\nRow #2 (Default)...\n" )
print( tier )
```

6. Add statements to identify the subset's data structure
```
cat( "\nMatrix?:", is.matrix( tier ) )
cat( "\tVector?:", is.vector( tier ), "\n\n" )
```

7. Then, recreate the subset that extracts data from a single row of the matrix – overriding the default behavior
```
tier <- table[ 2, , drop=FALSE ]
```

8. Add statements to output the revised subset
```
cat( "\nRow #2 (Drop=FALSE)...\n" )
print( tier )
```

9. Add statements to identify the subset's data structure now
```
cat( "\nMatrix?:", is.matrix( tier ) )
cat( "\tVector?:", is.vector( tier ), "\n" )
```

10. Run the code to see the matrix and subsets in the Console – notice that the row name dimension is retained when the default behavior has been overridden

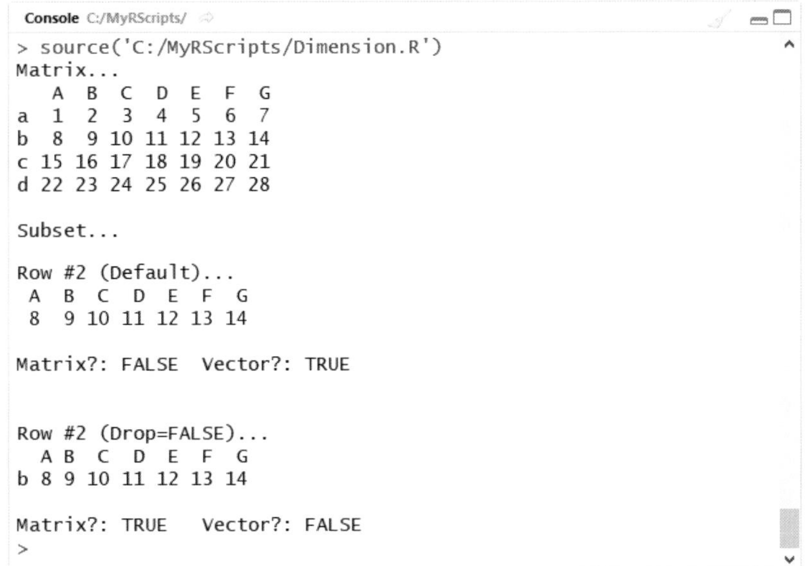

Console C:/MyRScripts/
> source('C:/MyRScripts/Dimension.R')
Matrix...
   A B C D E F G
a 1 2 3 4 5 6 7
b 8 9 10 11 12 13 14
c 15 16 17 18 19 20 21
d 22 23 24 25 26 27 28
Subset...
Row #2 (Default)...
 A B C D E F G
 8 9 10 11 12 13 14
Matrix?: FALSE Vector?: TRUE
Row #2 (Drop=FALSE)...
  A B C D E F G
b 8 9 10 11 12 13 14
Matrix?: TRUE   Vector?: FALSE
>

Don't forget the extra space and comma within the square brackets to denote an entire row or a entire column.

Adding a **drop=FALSE** argument ensures that data will always be returned in the same class of object as the one from which it has been retrieved.

Summary

- A matrix is a two-dimensional structure that stores data in a tabular format of cell rows and cell columns.
- The **matrix( )** function requires a vector argument and arguments to specify the desired number of rows and columns.
- Unless the number of matrix rows and columns match the length of the vector, values will be recycled in additional cells.
- Individual matrix values are addressed by stating the index number of their row and column within square brackets.
- The **is.matrix( )** function can be used to identify a matrix object, and the **which( )** function can seek a stored value.
- The **matrix( )** function can optionally include a **byrow=TRUE** argument to insert data by row order, and a **dimnames=** argument to name the rows and columns.
- Matrix rows and columns arrangement can be transposed using the **t( )** function – so that rows become columns.
- The **rbind( )** function creates a matrix of each vector on rows, and the **cbind( )** function places each vector in columns.
- The **rownames( )** and **colnames( )** functions can be used to name the rows and columns of a specified matrix argument.
- The **matplot( )** function can produce graphic visualizations of data contained within a matrix structure.
- The **axis( )** function can be used to specify axis appearance, and the **legend( )** function can add a descriptive legend.
- A subset is a group of data values that are part of another larger set of data values.
- A subset can be extracted from a matrix by specifying the index numbers of specific elements, or by stating their names.
- A subset that has one dimension will, by default, be returned as a vector – otherwise it will be returned as a matrix.
- A **drop=FALSE** argument can be included within the **[ ]** square brackets that specify rows or columns to be extracted from a matrix to ensure that the subset will be returned as a matrix.

7 Constructing data frames

This chapter demonstrates how to store and manipulate data in data frame structures.

Constructing a data frame

In R programming, a "data frame" is a two-dimensional structure that stores data in a tabular format of cell rows and cell columns. Unlike matrix structures, the values stored within a data frame do not need to all be of the same data type – they may contain values of any data type. This means that data frames are especially versatile and are the most useful data structure in R programming.

Remember to include the period character in the **data.frame( )** and **is.data.frame( )** function names.

A data frame can be created in R Script by writing a unique identifier name of your choice in the Code Editor, then assigning values using the built-in **data.frame( )** function. This function requires vectors containing values as its arguments. Each vector should be of the same length, or values will be recycled in additional cells to match the length of the longest vector.

The values in each vector will appear in separate columns of the data frame, and each column will, by default, be given the name of the corresponding vector as its column name. Row names will, by default, be numbered in ascending order from one. As with matrices, the arrangement of data frame rows and columns can be transposed using the **t( )** function – to switch rows to columns.

If you prefer to supply your own names for data frame rows and columns, these can be assigned using the **rownames( )** and **colnames( )** functions – as with matrices. Alternatively, you can include a **row.names=** argument in the call to the **data.frame( )** function to specify a list of names for the data frame rows.

Individual values are addressed in a data frame using the appropriate index numbers of the row and column. New values can also be assigned to individual cells using their index number of row and column, but care must be taken to observe the data type of that cell.

In order to confirm that a structure is indeed a data frame, R provides a built-in **is.data.frame( )** function that will only return **TRUE** when its specified argument is a data frame object.

Usefully, you can seek a value within a data frame using the built-in **which( )** function to specify a logical argument and, optionally, you can include an **arr.ind=TRUE** argument to return the row and column index number of each cell containing the sought value.

1. Begin an R Script by creating three vectors of differing data type values

```
bools <- c( TRUE, FALSE, TRUE )
chars <- LETTERS[ 1:3 ]
nums <- 1:3
```

FirstDataframe.R

2. Next, create a data frame that stores the vector values, then output the data frame and confirm its structure

```
frame <- data.frame( bools, chars, nums )
print( frame )
cat( "\nData Frame?:", is.data.frame( frame ), "\n\n" )
```

3. Now, name the data frame's rows and columns

```
rownames( frame ) <- c( "Tier 1:", "Tier 2:", "Tier 3:" )
colnames( frame ) <- c( "Logical", "Alphabetical", "Numerical" )
```

Alternatively, the row names could be assigned to a **row.names=** argument in the call to the **data.frames( )** function.

4. Then, assign a new value to one cell and output the data frame once more to see the named rows and columns

```
frame[ 2, 2 ] <- "A"
print( frame )
```

5. Finally, search all cells for a specific value, and identify the location of cells that do contain that value

```
cat( "Search for 'A'...\n" )
print( which( frame == "A", arr.ind=TRUE ) )
```

6. Run the code to see the cell values and search result

```
Console C:/MyRScripts/
> source('C:/MyRScripts/FirstDataframe.R')
  bools chars nums
1  TRUE     A    1
2 FALSE     B    2
3  TRUE     C    3

Data Frame?: TRUE

        Logical Alphabetical Numerical
Tier 1:    TRUE            A         1
Tier 2:   FALSE            A         2
Tier 3:    TRUE            C         3

Search for 'A'...
        row col
Tier 1:   1   2
Tier 2:   2   2
> |
```

Importing data sets

Collections of tabular data are often stored as a “data set” in a comma-separated values (CSV) file. These data sets can be easily imported into RStudio and their data copied into a data frame using the built-in **read.csv( )** function. This function simply requires the CSV file path as its argument.

You can find many free CSV data sets using a web search engine, and spreadsheet data can be exported from Microsoft Excel in CSV file format.

The path to a CSV file can be supplied to the **read.csv( )** function by specifying the **file.choose( )** function as its argument. This launches a “Select file” dialog that allows you to browse to the location of the CSV file. Once selected, the path is supplied to the **read.csv( )** function so the data can be copied into a data frame. For example, the statement **frame <- read.csv(file.choose( ))** provides a dialog to select a CSV file whose data will subsequently be copied into a data frame named “frame”.

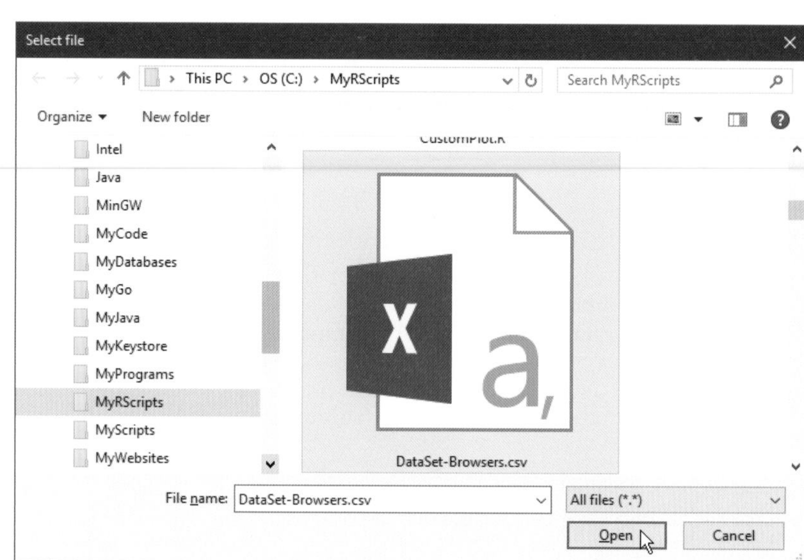

You can set the default working directory in RStudio by clicking **Tools**, **Global Options**, and the **General** option.

Alternatively, the full path to a CSV file can be specified to the **read.csv( )** function as its argument. For example, this statement provides the full path to the selected CSV file illustrated above: **frame <- read.csv("C:/MyRScripts/DataSet-Browsers.csv")**. Full path names can be lengthy, so it is convenient to set the CSV file location as RStudio’s working directory by specifying its directory as the argument to the **setwd( )** function. The **read.csv( )** function then only requires the CSV file name as its argument. You can discover the current working directory at any time by calling the built-in **getwd( )** function.

Paths can use the forward slash / character or escaped backslash, such as **C:\\MyRScripts\\DataSet-Browsers.csv**.

1. Begin an R Script by setting the working directory, then confirm its path address
   setwd("C:/MyRScripts")
   cat("Working Directory:", getwd( ), "\n\n")

ImportData.R

2. Next, create a data frame that imports data from a CSV file located in the working directory
   frame **<- read.csv("DataSet-Browsers.csv")**

3. Now, output the data frame's rows and columns
   print(frame **)**

4. Run the code to see the imported data

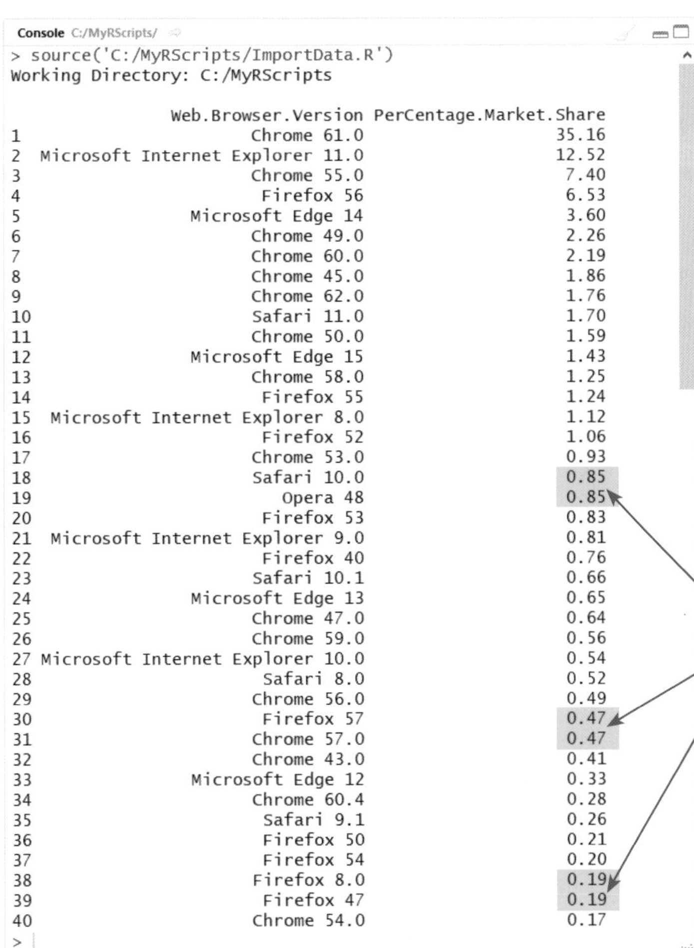

```
Console C:/MyRScripts/
> source('C:/MyRScripts/ImportData.R')
Working Directory: C:/MyRScripts

               Web.Browser.Version PerCentage.Market.Share
1                      Chrome 61.0                   35.16
2  Microsoft Internet Explorer 11.0                  12.52
3                      Chrome 55.0                    7.40
4                       Firefox 56                    6.53
5                Microsoft Edge 14                    3.60
6                      Chrome 49.0                    2.26
7                      Chrome 60.0                    2.19
8                      Chrome 45.0                    1.86
9                      Chrome 62.0                    1.76
10                     Safari 11.0                    1.70
11                     Chrome 50.0                    1.59
12               Microsoft Edge 15                    1.43
13                     Chrome 58.0                    1.25
14                      Firefox 55                    1.24
15  Microsoft Internet Explorer 8.0                   1.12
16                      Firefox 52                    1.06
17                     Chrome 53.0                    0.93
18                     Safari 10.0                    0.85
19                        Opera 48                    0.85
20                      Firefox 53                    0.83
21  Microsoft Internet Explorer 9.0                   0.81
22                      Firefox 40                    0.76
23                     Safari 10.1                    0.66
24               Microsoft Edge 13                    0.65
25                     Chrome 47.0                    0.64
26                     Chrome 59.0                    0.56
27 Microsoft Internet Explorer 10.0                   0.54
28                      Safari 8.0                    0.52
29                     Chrome 56.0                    0.49
30                      Firefox 57                    0.47
31                     Chrome 57.0                    0.47
32                     Chrome 43.0                    0.41
33               Microsoft Edge 12                    0.33
34                     Chrome 60.4                    0.28
35                      Safari 9.1                    0.26
36                      Firefox 50                    0.21
37                      Firefox 54                    0.20
38                     Firefox 8.0                    0.19
39                      Firefox 47                    0.19
40                     Chrome 54.0                    0.17
> 
```

Here, the column names are supplied by the first line of the CSV file but the rows are automatically numbered by the R interpreter. Notice that there are three instances of identical market share.

Examining data frames

The R programming language provides a number of functions for the examination of data frame structures:

It is useful to check that the total number of imported rows and columns match what is expected from the source data set.

- **nrow( )** – returns an integer that is the total number of rows within the data frame specified as its argument.
- **ncol( )** – returns an integer that is the total number of columns within the data frame specified as its argument.
- **head( )** – by default returns the top six rows of the data frame specified as its argument, plus its column and row names. Optionally, a **n=** argument can be added to specify how many rows to return. For example, **n=3** returns the top three rows.
- **tail( )** – by default returns the bottom six rows of the data frame specified as its argument plus column and row names. An **n=** argument can be added to specify how many rows to return. For example, **n=3** returns the bottom three rows.
- **str( )** – outputs an overview of the structure of the data frame specified as its argument – listing the total number of objects and variables it contains, together with the number of unique factors in each column. Internally, the factors are ranked numerically in descending order where the top rank is level 1.
- **summary( )** – outputs a summary of the contents of the data frame specified as its argument – by default, six levels of factors are displayed but an optional **maxsum=** argument can be added to specify how many levels to display. For columns that contain numerical data, the summary provides statistics:

  Minimum – the lowest number in the column.

  1st Quartile – the mid-point value between the minimum number and the median value.

  Median – the mid-point value of the column.

  Mean – the average value of the numbers in the column.

  3rd Quartile – the mid-point value between the median value and the maximum number.

  Maximum – the highest number in the column.

In R programming, the **str( )** function refers to "structure", unlike in other programming languages in which it refers to "string".

ExamineData.R

1. Begin an R Script by creating a data frame that imports data from a CSV file located in the working directory
```
frame <- read.csv( "DataSet-Browsers.csv" )
```

2. Next, display the total number of rows and columns
```
cat( "Rows:", nrow( frame ), "\tColumns:", ncol( frame ) )
```

3. Now, output the first and last three rows and columns
```
cat( "\nHead...\n" )
print( head( frame, n=3 ) )
cat( "\nTail...\n" )
print( tail( frame, n=3 ) )
```

4. Finally, display the structure and a summary
```
cat( "\nStructure...\n" )
print( str( frame ) )
cat( "\nSummary...\n" )
print( summary( frame ) )
```

5. Run the code to examine the data frame

```
Console C:/MyRScripts/
> source('C:/MyRScripts/ExamineData.R')
Rows: 40        Columns: 2
Head...
               Web.Browser.Version PerCentage.Market.Share
1                      Chrome 61.0                   35.16
2 Microsoft Internet Explorer 11.0                   12.52
3                      Chrome 55.0                    7.40

Tail...
   Web.Browser.Version PerCentage.Market.Share
38         Firefox 8.0                    0.19
39          Firefox 47                    0.19
40         Chrome 54.0                    0.17

Structure...
'data.frame':   40 obs. of  2 variables:
 $ Web.Browser.Version    : Factor w/ 40 levels "Chrome 43.0",..:
 15 32 8 24 29 4 13 2 16 38 ...
 $ PerCentage.Market.Share: num  35.16 12.52 7.4 6.53 3.6 ...
NULL

Summary...
  Web.Browser.Version PerCentage.Market.Share
 Chrome 43.0: 1       Min.   : 0.170
 Chrome 45.0: 1       1st Qu.: 0.470
 Chrome 47.0: 1       Median : 0.820
 Chrome 49.0: 1       Mean   : 2.373
 Chrome 50.0: 1       3rd Qu.: 1.617
 Chrome 53.0: 1       Max.   :35.160
 (Other)    :34
> |
```

Here, the first column contains data of the character data type, whereas the second column contains data of the numerical double data type – so statistics are provided for that column in the summary.

Addressing frame data

There are a number of ways to address data contained in a data frame. As with matrices, cells can be addressed by stating their row and column index number within **[ ]** square brackets. Alternatively, cells can be addressed by stating their row and column name within **[ ]** square brackets. Additionally, data frames can employ the **$** dollar operator, so that a column can be addressed with this convenient syntax:

data.frame.name$column.name

Similarly, cells can be addressed by appending **[ ]** square brackets to the above syntax in which to specify row index numbers. The factor levels of a column can be addressed by specifying the column as an argument to the built-in **levels( )** function using the same syntax:

AddressData.R

1. Begin an R Script by creating a data frame that imports data from a CSV file located in the working directory
```
frame <- read.csv( "DataSet-Browsers.csv" )
```

2. Next, output the first three rows and columns
```
cat( "\nHead...\n" )
print( head( frame, n=3 ) )
```

3. Address a single cell by row and column index number
```
data <- frame[ 1, 2 ]
cat( "\nRow #1, Column #2:", data, "\n" )
```

4. Now, address a single cell by row index number and column name
```
data <- frame[ 2, "PerCentage.Market.Share" ]
cat( "\nRow #2, Column #2:", data, "\n" )
```

5. Then, address a single cell by column name and row index number
```
data <- frame$PerCentage.Market.Share[ 3 ]
cat( "\nRow #3, Column #2:", data, "\n" )
```

6. Address an entire column by name to output all its levels
```
print( levels( frame$Web.Browser.Version ) )
```

7. Run the code to see the data content from the data frame

...cont'd

```
Console C:/MyRScripts/
> source('C:/MyRScripts/AddressData.R')
Head...
                Web.Browser.Version PerCentage.Market.Share
1                       Chrome 61.0                   35.16
2 Microsoft Internet Explorer 11.0                   12.52
3                       Chrome 55.0                    7.40

Row #1, Column #2: 35.16

Row #2, Column #2: 12.52

Row #3, Column #2: 7.4

 [1] "Chrome 43.0"
 [2] "Chrome 45.0"
 [3] "Chrome 47.0"
 [4] "Chrome 49.0"
 [5] "Chrome 50.0"
 [6] "Chrome 53.0"
 [7] "Chrome 54.0"
 [8] "Chrome 55.0"
 [9] "Chrome 56.0"
[10] "Chrome 57.0"
[11] "Chrome 58.0"
[12] "Chrome 59.0"
[13] "Chrome 60.0"
[14] "Chrome 60.4"
[15] "Chrome 61.0"
[16] "Chrome 62.0"
[17] "Firefox 40"
[18] "Firefox 47"
[19] "Firefox 50"
[20] "Firefox 52"
[21] "Firefox 53"
[22] "Firefox 54"
[23] "Firefox 55"
[24] "Firefox 56"
[25] "Firefox 57"
[26] "Firefox 8.0"
[27] "Microsoft Edge 12"
[28] "Microsoft Edge 13"
[29] "Microsoft Edge 14"
[30] "Microsoft Edge 15"
[31] "Microsoft Internet Explorer 10.0"
[32] "Microsoft Internet Explorer 11.0"
[33] "Microsoft Internet Explorer 8.0"
[34] "Microsoft Internet Explorer 9.0"
[35] "Opera 48"
[36] "Safari 10.0"
[37] "Safari 10.1"
[38] "Safari 11.0"
[39] "Safari 8.0"
[40] "Safari 9.1"
> |
```

Notice how the levels are automatically created in descending alphabetical and numerical order.

Extracting frame subsets

Subsets can be extracted from data frames by stating their row and column index numbers within **[ ]** square brackets – in the same way that subsets are extracted from matrices. For example, using **frame[1:3, 2]** to extract a subset containing only the second column of the first three rows of a data frame, or **frame[1:3,]** to extract a subset containing all columns of the first three rows.

Alternatively, a subset of specific cells can be extracted using the familiar **c( )** function. For example, using **frame[c(1, 3, 5), 2]** to extract a subset containing only the second column of the first, third, and fifth, rows of a data frame, or **frame[c(1, 3, 5),]** to extract a subset containing all columns of those specific rows.

When a subset extracts one or more rows or more than one column from a data frame, the data is returned in a data frame object. Conversely, when a subset extracts only one column, the data is, by default, returned in a vector object. The default behavior can be overridden by including a final **drop=FALSE** argument within the **[ ]** square brackets that specify the column to be extracted – so the data will now be returned in a vector structure:

SubsetData.R

1. Begin an R Script by creating a data frame that imports data from a CSV file located in the working directory
```
frame <- read.csv( "DataSet-Browsers.csv" )
```

2. Next, extract a subset containing data in all columns of four specific rows, then output the subset data
```
edge <- frame[ c( 33, 24, 5, 12 ), ]
print( edge )
```

3. From the original subset, extract a second subset containing data in all columns of one single row
```
edge.row <- edge[ 1 , ]
```

4. Output the second subset data to see the column headings and row numbering preserved
```
cat( "\nRow...\n" )
print( edge.row )
```

5. Confirm the data structure of the second subset
```
cat( "Data Frame?:", is.data.frame( edge.row ) )
```

6 From the original subset, extract a third subset containing all data in one single column, then output its data to see that column headings and row numbers are not preserved

```
edge.col <- edge[  , 2 ]
cat( "\n\nColumn...\n" )
print( edge.col )
```

7 Confirm the data structure of the third subset

```
cat( "Data Frame?:", is.data.frame( edge.col ) )
cat( "\tVector?:", is.vector( edge.col ) )
```

Don't forget the extra space and comma within the square brackets to denote an entire row or a entire column.

8 Now, recreate the third subset to override default behavior, then output its data to see that column headings and row numbers are now preserved

```
edge.col <- edge[  , 2, drop=FALSE ]
cat( "\n\nColumn...\n" )
print( edge.col )
```

9 Confirm the data structure of the recreated third subset

```
cat( "Data Frame?:", is.data.frame( edge.col ) )
cat( "\tVector?:", is.vector( edge.col ) )
```

10 Run the code to see the data in the subset objects

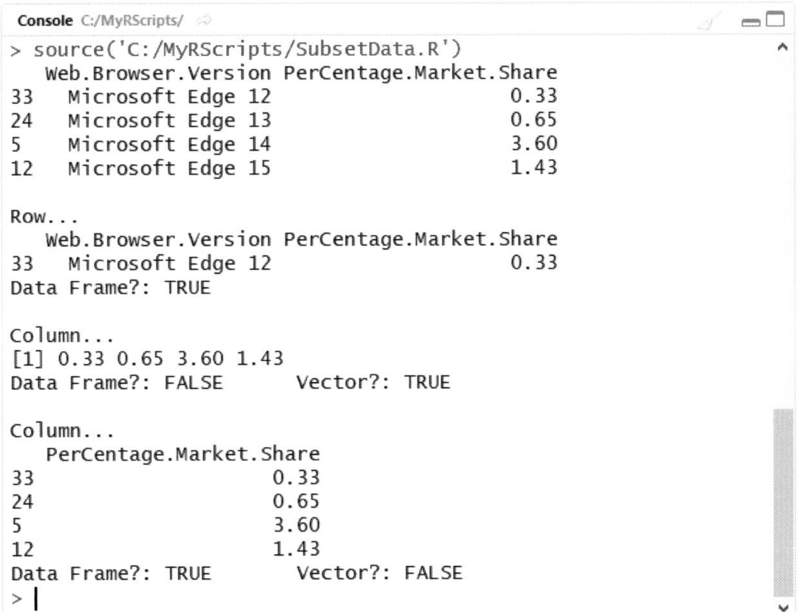

Changing frame columns

The column names of data frames created from data imported from a CSV file will typically be adopted from the header names specified on the first line of the CSV file. If you prefer to ignore the header names, you can add a **header=FALSE** argument in the call to the **read.csv( )** function.

Column names can be added to unnamed columns, or existing column names changed, by assigning column names to the **colnames( )** function, as with matrices.

A new column can be added to a data frame by assigning cell values to a new column name, like this:

```
frame[ "New Column" ] <- 1:10
```

Alternatively, the **$** dollar operator can be used to add a new column, but a column name that includes spaces must be enclosed within ` backtick characters, like this:

```
frame$`New Column` <- 1:10
```

The ` Backtick key is typically found at the top-left of the keyboard, beside the number 1 key.

An existing column can be removed from a data frame simply by assigning it a **NULL** value:

```
frame$Existing.Column <- NULL
```

Values assigned to a new column may be copied from an existing column and manipulated to provide new data values. For example, to total two columns in a third column:

```
frame$Total <- frame$Price + frame$Tax
```

Arithmetical and mathematical operations can only be performed on numerical data values, such as double or integer data type values.

Numeric data can be converted to the character data type for string manipulation by specifying the numeric data value as an argument to the built-in **as.character( )** function. It can then be concatenated to other character data using the **paste( )** function. By default, the **paste( )** function will automatically add space characters as separators between concatenated strings. This behavior can, however, be overridden by specifying an alternative separator to an optional **sep=** argument to the **paste( )** function. If you prefer to have no separator between concatenated strings, this argument can be assigned no characters whatsoever.

ColumnData.R

1. Begin an R Script by creating a data frame that imports data from a CSV file located in the working directory
```
frame <- read.csv( "DataSet-Browsers.csv" )
```

2. Next, create a function to output a title and the first two lines of a data frame – including row and column names
```
display <- function( title ) {
  cat( "\n", title, "...\n" )
  print( head( frame, n=2 ) )
}
```

3. Output two data frame rows and columns, then rename the existing columns and output the changes
```
display( "Original Columns" )
colnames( frame ) <- c( "Web.Browser", "PerCentage" )
display( "Renamed Columns" )
```

4. Copy existing numerical column data into a new column – converted to character data and concatenated
```
frame$Market.Share <-
  paste( as.character( frame$PerCentage ), "%", sep="" )
```

5. Delete the column containing numerical data, then output the changes once more
```
frame$PerCentage <- NULL
display( "Switched Columns" )
```

6. Run the code to see changes to the data frame columns

Removing columns will affect their index number. For example, removing the first column means that the second column assumes index number one.

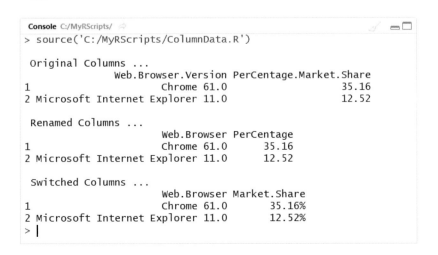

```
Console C:/MyRScripts/
> source('C:/MyRScripts/ColumnData.R')

 Original Columns ...
              Web.Browser.Version PerCentage.Market.Share
1                     Chrome 61.0                   35.16
2 Microsoft Internet Explorer 11.0                   12.52

 Renamed Columns ...
                      Web.Browser PerCentage
1                     Chrome 61.0      35.16
2 Microsoft Internet Explorer 11.0      12.52

 Switched Columns ...
                      Web.Browser Market.Share
1                     Chrome 61.0       35.16%
2 Microsoft Internet Explorer 11.0       12.52%
> |
```

Filtering data frames

The data contained in the cells of a data frame can be filtered by performing a conditional test upon the value in each cell, to select only data from cells where the conditional test returns **TRUE**.

Numerical data can be filtered by comparing the value in each cell with a value specified in a conditional test. For example, a filter might be created for a column containing numerical data, to examine the parity of data in each cell to select only even values with this statement **filter <- frame[, 1] %% 2 == 0**. The filter is created as a vector of Boolean values in which even values are represented by **TRUE** and odd values by **FALSE**. Including the filter within the **[ ]** square brackets that specify an area of the data frame will select only cells whose data passes the conditional test:

Here, the **t( )** function is used to transpose the data frame, so its columns appear as rows.

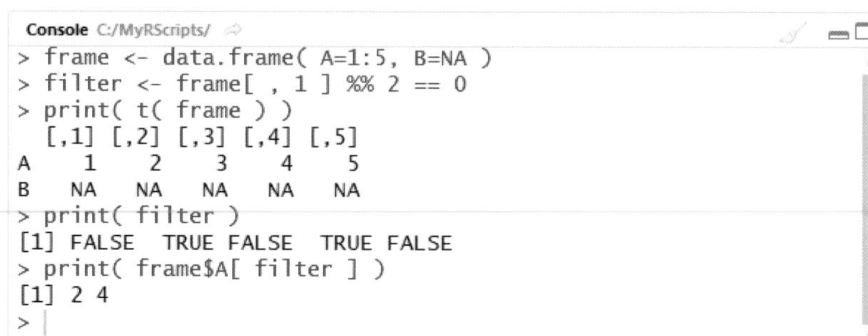

```
Console C:/MyRScripts/
> frame <- data.frame( A=1:5, B=NA )
> filter <- frame[ , 1 ] %% 2 == 0
> print( t( frame ) )
  [,1] [,2] [,3] [,4] [,5]
A    1    2    3    4    5
B   NA   NA   NA   NA   NA
> print( filter )
[1] FALSE  TRUE FALSE  TRUE FALSE
> print( frame$A[ filter ] )
[1] 2 4
>
```


Character data can be filtered by comparing the value in each cell with a value specified as the first argument to the built-in **grep( )** function. This function also requires a second argument to specify the area of the data frame whose cell values are to be compared.

A filter's conditional test result can be assigned to a variable, as in the screenshot above, or the conditional test can be made within the **[ ]** square brackets that specify an area of the data frame:

FilterData.R

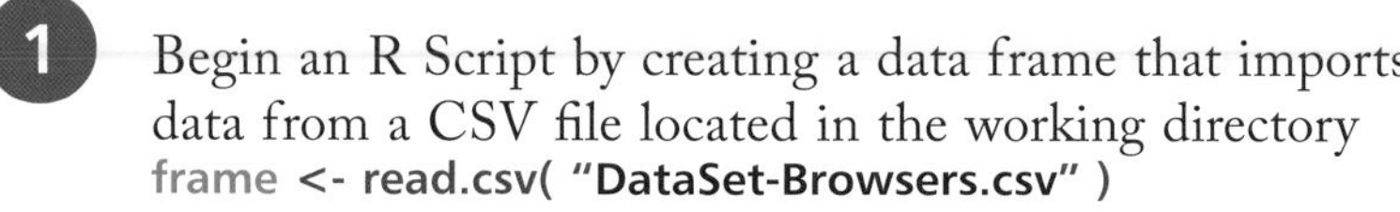

1. Begin an R Script by creating a data frame that imports data from a CSV file located in the working directory

```
frame <- read.csv( "DataSet-Browsers.csv" )
```

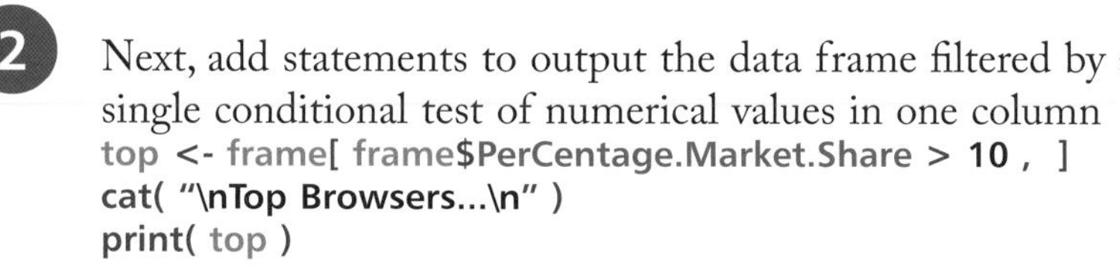

2. Next, add statements to output the data frame filtered by a single conditional test of numerical values in one column

```
top <- frame[ frame$PerCentage.Market.Share > 10 , ]
cat( "\nTop Browsers...\n" )
print( top )
```

3. Now, add statements to output the data frame filtered by two conditional tests of numerical values in one column

```
mid <- frame[ frame$PerCentage.Market.Share > 3 &
                 frame$PerCentage.Market.Share < 10 ,  ]
cat( "\nPopular Browsers...\n" )
print( mid )
```

4. Then, add statements to output the data frame filtered by a conditional test of character values in one column

```
google <-
  frame[ grep( "Chrome", frame$Web.Browser.Version ) ,  ]
cat( "\nGoogle Browsers...\n" )
print( google )
```

5. Run the code to see the filtered output

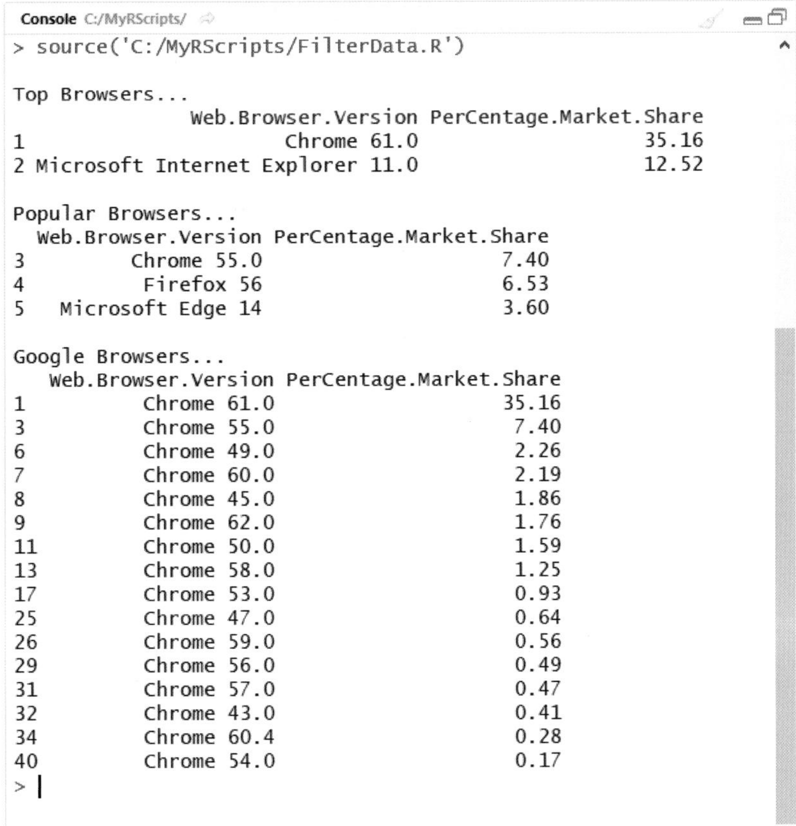

Console C:/MyRScripts/
> source('C:/MyRScripts/FilterData.R')
Top Browsers...
Web.Browser.Version PerCentage.Market.Share
1 Chrome 61.0 35.16
2 Microsoft Internet Explorer 11.0 12.52
Popular Browsers...
Web.Browser.Version PerCentage.Market.Share
3 Chrome 55.0 7.40
4 Firefox 56 6.53
5 Microsoft Edge 14 3.60
Google Browsers...
Web.Browser.Version PerCentage.Market.Share
1 Chrome 61.0 35.16
3 Chrome 55.0 7.40
6 Chrome 49.0 2.26
7 Chrome 60.0 2.19
8 Chrome 45.0 1.86
9 Chrome 62.0 1.76
11 Chrome 50.0 1.59
13 Chrome 58.0 1.25
17 Chrome 53.0 0.93
25 Chrome 47.0 0.64
26 Chrome 59.0 0.56
29 Chrome 56.0 0.49
31 Chrome 57.0 0.47
32 Chrome 43.0 0.41
34 Chrome 60.4 0.28
40 Chrome 54.0 0.17
>

The **grep( )** function can optionally include an **ignore.case=TRUE** argument if case sensitivity is not required.

The **grep( )** function is used here to select all rows whose first column cell contains the "Chrome" string.

Merging data frames

Data from two data frames can be combined into a single data frame by a common column name or a common row name using the built-in **merge( )** function. This function requires the names of the two source data frames as its first two arguments. It also requires the names of the column or row field containing common values to be specified to **by.x=** and **by.y=** arguments.

The common field in each data frame to be merged need not have the same name or position, and the common values need not be in the same order, but the case of character values needs to match in order for the fields to be merged. Only corresponding values will be merged – other values will be ignored by default.

If you prefer to retain all fields, regardless of whether they precisely match, you can include an **all=TRUE** argument in the call to the **merge( )** function. In this case, cells that do not directly correspond in each source data frame will be filled with the special **NA** (Not Available) constant in the merged data frame.

If merging two data frames by common fields that have identical names, the **by.x=** and **by.y=** arguments can be replaced by a single **by=** argument stating the common field name. For example, **by="State"**.

The two common fields of the source data frames will appear as a single field in the merged data frame, but other fields that contain data common to both source data frames will appear in separate fields. This means that the merged data frame can contain rows or columns of duplicated data. Assignment of a **NULL** value to unnecessary fields will remove them, so that only unique data remains in the merged data frame.

Additional columns can be added to a merged data frame as usual, and may contain data calculated from the data supplied from each source data frame:

MergeData.R

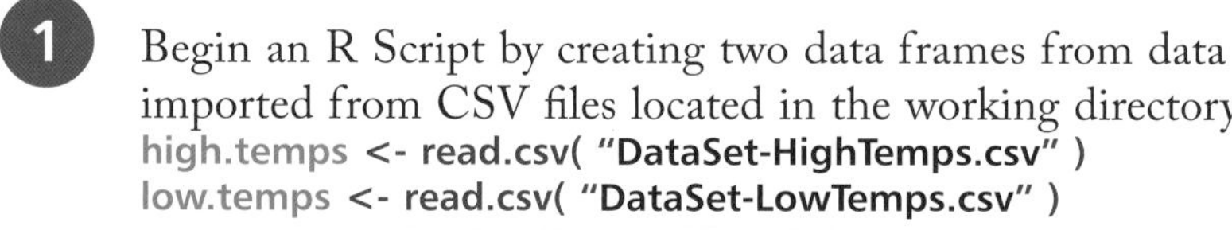

1. Begin an R Script by creating two data frames from data imported from CSV files located in the working directory

```
high.temps <- read.csv( "DataSet-HighTemps.csv" )
low.temps <- read.csv( "DataSet-LowTemps.csv" )
```

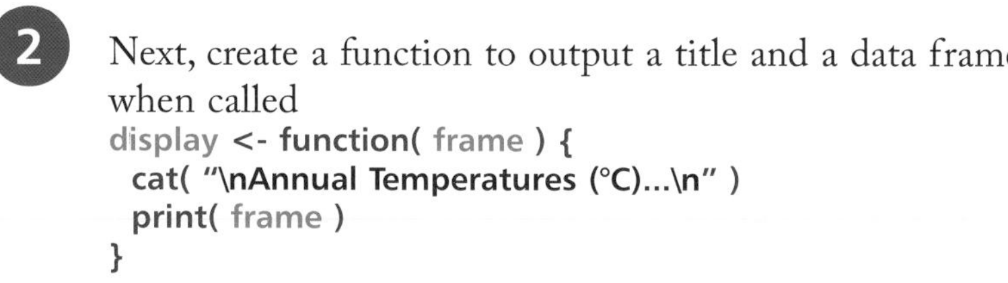

2. Next, create a function to output a title and a data frame when called

```
display <- function( frame ) {
  cat( "\nAnnual Temperatures (°C)...\n" )
  print( frame )
}
```

3. Now, add statements to output each source data frame

```
display( high.temp )
display( low.temp )
```

4. Then, add statements to merge the two data frames by common column values

```
avg.temp <- merge( high.temp, low.temp,
                        by.x="State", by.y="State.Code" )
display( avg.temp )
```

5. Add a statement to remove a column that contains duplicated data

```
avg.temp$Capital <- NULL
```

6. Add a new column containing data calculated from the data supplied by the two source data frames, then output the combined data once more

```
avg.temp$Average <- ( avg.temp$High + avg.temp$Low ) / 2
display( avg.temp )
```

7. Run the code to see the merged output

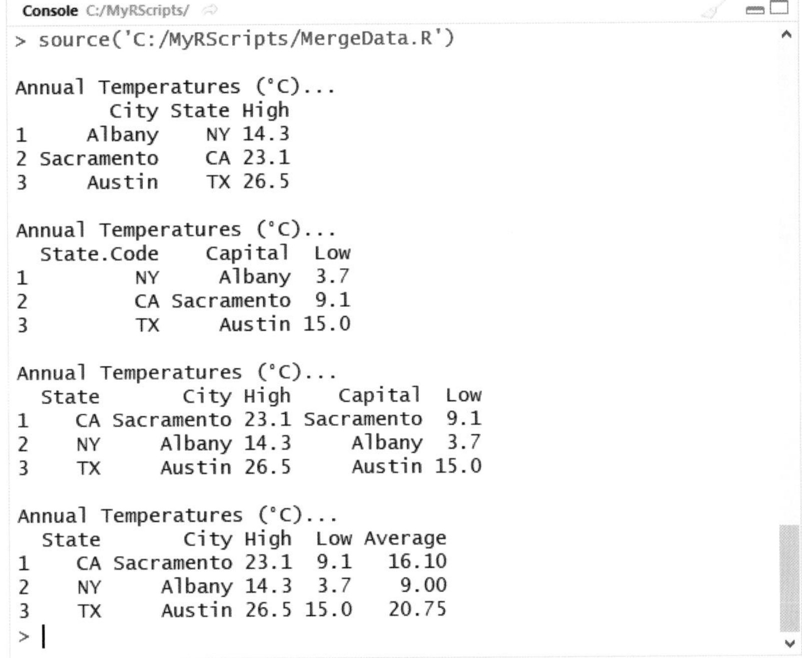

Console C:/MyRScripts/
> source('C:/MyRScripts/MergeData.R')
Annual Temperatures (°C)...
City State High
1 Albany NY 14.3
2 Sacramento CA 23.1
3 Austin TX 26.5
Annual Temperatures (°C)...
State.Code Capital Low
1 NY Albany 3.7
2 CA Sacramento 9.1
3 TX Austin 15.0
Annual Temperatures (°C)...
State City High Capital Low
1 CA Sacramento 23.1 Sacramento 9.1
2 NY Albany 14.3 Albany 3.7
3 TX Austin 26.5 Austin 15.0
Annual Temperatures (°C)...
State City High Low Average
1 CA Sacramento 23.1 9.1 16.10
2 NY Albany 14.3 3.7 9.00
3 TX Austin 26.5 15.0 20.75
>

The column fields containing state abbreviations have different names and appear in different positions within the source data frames.

The city names are duplicated in the merged data frame so one column is unnecessary and can be removed.

Adjusting factors

The structure of data copied into a vector variable from a data frame is maintained, so that the factors and levels are preserved. Vectors do not automatically provide factor categories and ranked levels, but a vector variable name can be specified as an argument to the built-in **factor( )** function to create factors and levels.

The **factor( )** function will, by default, rank the factor levels in alphabetical and numerical order. For example, given data values of "B", "C2", "A", and "C1", the factor levels will be ranked as "A" (1), "B" (2), "C1" (3), and "C2" (4).

You can optionally specify a ranking preference by including a **levels=** argument in the call to the **factor( )** function. This argument must be assigned a vector of the data values in the descending order of your preferred ranking level. For example, **levels=c("C1", "C2", "A", "B")** ensures that the factor levels will be ranked as "C1" (1), "C2" (2), "A" (3), and "B" (4).

Should you wish to reverse the ranking order of factor levels, the vector of data values can be specified as an argument to the built-in **rev( )** function in the assignment to the **levels=** argument:

Hot tip

The **factor( )** function produces a factor structure. You can confirm this using the **is.factor( )** function.

FactorData.R

1. Begin an R Script by creating a data frame

```
frame <- data.frame( 1:5, sizes=c( "S","L","XL", "S","M" ) )
```

2. Next, output the structure of one column of the data frame to see its factors and their ranking levels

```
cat( "\nColumn Data...\n" )
str( frame$sizes )
```

3. Now, create a vector containing the same data values as the column data, and in the same order

```
var.sizes <- c( "S", "L", "XL", "S", "M" )
```

4. Then, output the structure of the vector to see it merely contains character data with no factors or levels

```
cat( "\nVector Data...\n" )
str( var.sizes )
```

5. Reproduce the vector to create factors and ranking levels

```
var.sizes <- factor( var.sizes )
```

6. Output the structure of the vector once more to see it now has factors and levels
cat("\nFactored Vector Data...\n")
str(var.sizes **)**
print(levels(var.sizes **))**

The **levels( )** function provides access to the levels attribute of the variable specified as its argument.

7. Next, reproduce the vector to create factors and levels in a preferred ranking order
var.sizes **<- factor(** var.sizes**, levels=c("S","M", "L", "XL"))**

8. Output the revised structure of the vector factor levels
cat("\nRe-ordered Factored Vector Data...\n")
str(var.sizes **)**
print(levels(var.sizes **))**

9. Finally, reproduce the vector to create factors and levels in a reversed ranking order, then output the reversed structure
var.sizes **<- factor(** var.sizes**, levels=rev(levels(** var.sizes **)))**
cat("\nReversed Factored Vector Data...\n")
str(var.sizes **)**
print(levels(var.sizes **))**

10. Run the code to see the adjusted factor levels

```
Console C:/MyRScripts/
> source('C:/MyRScripts/FactorData.R')

Column Data...
 Factor w/ 4 levels "L","M","S","XL": 3 1 4 3 2

Vector Data...
 chr [1:5] "S" "L" "XL" "S" "M"

Factored Vector Data...
 Factor w/ 4 levels "L","M","S","XL": 3 1 4 3 2
[1] "L"  "M"  "S"  "XL"

Re-ordered Factored Vector Data...
 Factor w/ 4 levels "S","M","L","XL": 1 3 4 1 2
[1] "S"  "M"  "L"  "XL"

Reversed Factored Vector Data...
 Factor w/ 4 levels "XL","L","M","S": 4 2 1 4 3
[1] "XL" "L"  "M"  "S"
> |
```

Factors are unique values. This example has five data values but only four unique values – so there are only four factors.

Summary

- The **data.frame( )** function creates a tabular data frame structure that stores data of any type in rows and columns.
- Vectors assigned to a data frame should be the same length, or values will be recycled to match the longest vector length.
- Data frame columns are, by default, named with their vector name, and rows are, by default, numbered in ascending order.
- Data frame row and column names can be assigned using the **rownames( )** and **colnames( )** functions.
- The **which( )** function can be used to seek a value within a data frame and can identify the value's cell location.
- Data sets stored in comma-separated value (CSV) files can be imported using the **read.csv( )** function.
- The RStudio working directory can be specified using the **setwd( )** function, and discovered using the **getwd( )** function.
- The **str( )** function outputs the structure of a data frame, listing its unique factors and their ranking levels.
- Data frame cells can be addressed using their row and column index numbers or names within **[ ]** square brackets, and columns can be addressed using the **$** dollar operator.
- The factor levels of a column can be addressed by specifying the column as an argument to the built-in **levels( )** function.
- A data frame subset of only one field is returned as a vector object, otherwise the data is returned as a data frame object.
- A new column can be added to a data frame by assigning cell values to a new column name.
- Data frames can be filtered by performing a conditional test upon the value in each cell.
- Data from two data frames can be combined into a single data frame using the **merge( )** function.
- Vectors do not automatically provide factors and levels, but the **factor( )** function can be used to create factors and levels.

8 Producing quick plots

This chapter demonstrates how to create scatter plots, bar charts, histograms, and box plots from stored data.

Installing packages

RStudio is installed with a wide variety of built-in functions that are contained within tried and tested binary code "packages". Installed packages appear as a library listed in alphabetical order on the Packages tab in the Notebook pane, together with a brief description of the functionality they provide:

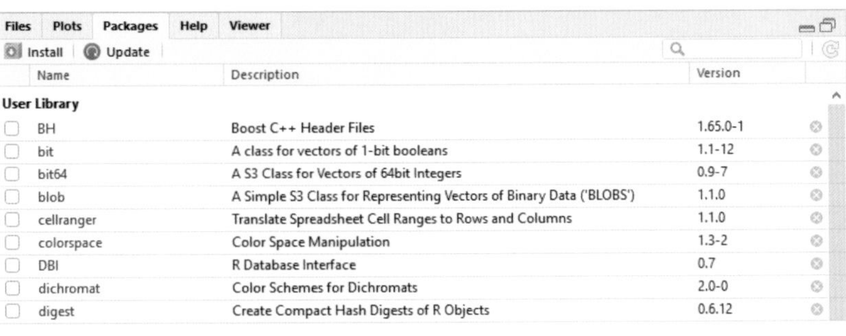

Files | Plots | Packages | Help | Viewer

Install | Update

Name	Description	Version
User Library		
BH	Boost C++ Header Files	1.65.0-1
bit	A class for vectors of 1-bit booleans	1.1-12
bit64	A S3 Class for Vectors of 64bit Integers	0.9-7
blob	A Simple S3 Class for Representing Vectors of Binary Data ('BLOBS')	1.1.0
cellranger	Translate Spreadsheet Cell Ranges to Rows and Columns	1.1.0
colorspace	Color Space Manipulation	1.3-2
DBI	R Database Interface	0.7
dichromat	Color Schemes for Dichromats	2.0-0
digest	Create Compact Hash Digests of R Objects	0.6.12

Packages in the library list are installed but not accessible until they have been loaded by the **library( )** function.

Additional packages can be installed by specifying a package name within quotes as the argument to the **install.packages( )** function. Optionally, a second **dependencies=TRUE** argument can be included to also install any packages required by the specified package. One of the most useful additional packages for the creation of elegant data visualizations is the "ggplot2" package:

InstallPackage.R

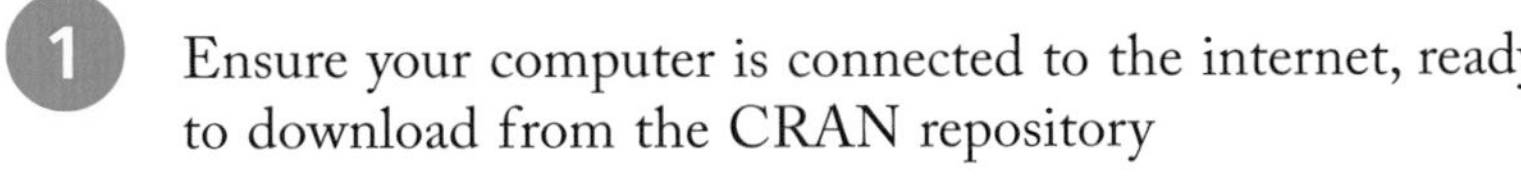

1. Ensure your computer is connected to the internet, ready to download from the CRAN repository

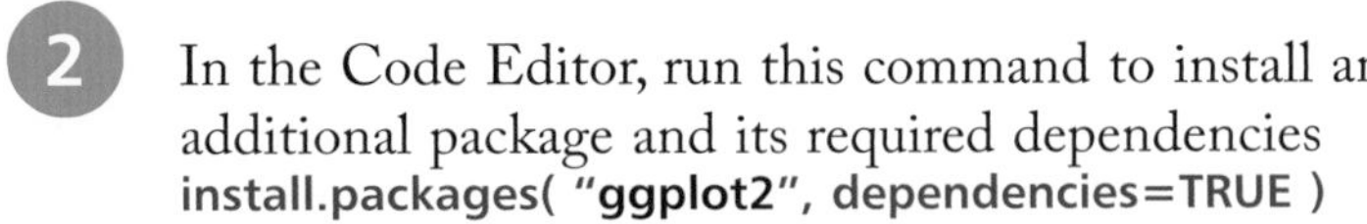

2. In the Code Editor, run this command to install an additional package and its required dependencies
install.packages("ggplot2", dependencies=TRUE)

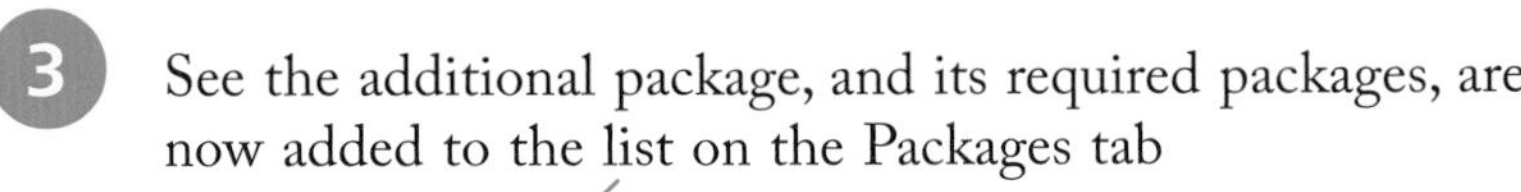

3. See the additional package, and its required packages, are now added to the list on the Packages tab

Files | Plots | Packages | Help | Viewer

Install | Update

Name	Description	Version
digest	Create Compact Hash Digests of R Objects	0.6.12
dplyr	A Grammar of Data Manipulation	0.7.4
evaluate	Parsing and Evaluation Tools that Provide More Details than the Default	0.10.1
Formula	Extended Model Formulas	1.2-2
gdtools	Utilities for Graphical Rendering	0.1.6
ggplot2	Create Elegant Data Visualisations Using the Grammar of Graphics	2.2.1
ggplot2movies	Movies Data	0.0.1
glue	Interpreted String Literals	1.2.0

As the list of installed packages is so extensive, RStudio does not load them all at the start of each session in order to save time and system memory. This means that you must specifically load an additional installed package before you can access its functionality. An installed package can be loaded by specifying its name as an argument to the built-in **library( )** function:

4. In the Code Editor, run this command to load a specific package
library(ggplot2)

You can also load an installed package by checking its checkbox in the library list.

5. See the specified package gain a check mark in the list on the Packages tab – indicating that it is now loaded

Files | Plots | Packages | Help | Viewer

Install | Update

	Name	Description	Version
☐	digest	Create Compact Hash Digests of R Objects	0.6.12
☐	dplyr	A Grammar of Data Manipulation	0.7.4
☐	evaluate	Parsing and Evaluation Tools that Provide More Details than the Default	0.10.1
☐	Formula	Extended Model Formulas	1.2-2
☐	gdtools	Utilities for Graphical Rendering	0.1.6
☑	ggplot2	Create Elegant Data Visualisations Using the Grammar of Graphics	2.2.1
☐	ggplot2movies	Movies Data	0.0.1
☐	glue	Interpreted String Literals	1.2.0

The "ggplot2" package provides a **qplot( )** Quick Plot function that allows you to quickly create a number of different types of plots using consistent parameters:

The **qplot( )** function is used throughout this chapter to demonstrate various types of data visualization.

6. In the Code Editor, run this command to open the Help page and explore the possible function arguments
help(qplot)

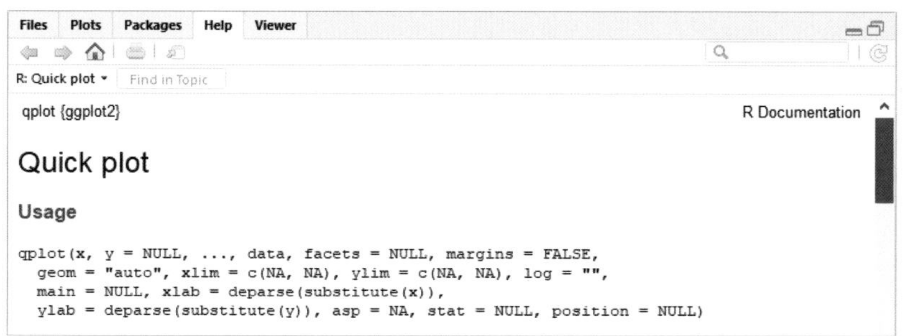

Files
Plots
Packages
Help
Viewer
R: Quick plot
Find in Topic
qplot {ggplot2}
R Documentation
Quick plot
Usage
qplot(x, y = NULL, ..., data, facets = NULL, margins = FALSE,
geom = "auto", xlim = c(NA, NA), ylim = c(NA, NA), log = "",
main = NULL, xlab = deparse(substitute(x)),
ylab = deparse(substitute(y)), asp = NA, stat = NULL, position = NULL)

Scattering points

The **qplot( )** Quick Plot function in the ggplot2 package can produce a simple scatter plot by supplying two vector arguments of equal length to represent X-axis and Y-axis coordinates:

ScatterPlot.R

1. Begin an R Script by creating two vectors of equal length

```
x <- 1:10
y <- x^2
```

2. Next, load the ggplot2 library

```
library( ggplot2 )
```

3. Now, call the Quick Plot function to plot the coordinates

```
qplot( x, y )
```

4. Click the **Run** button, or press **Ctrl** + **Enter**, to execute the code and see the graph appear on the Plots tab

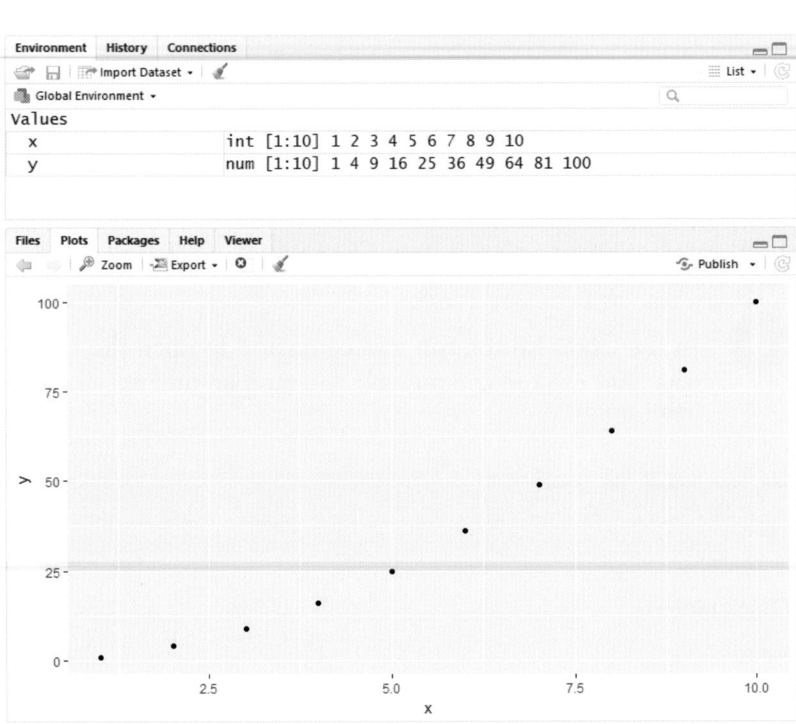

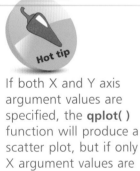

If both X and Y axis argument values are specified, the **qplot( )** function will produce a scatter plot, but if only X argument values are specified, the function will produce a histogram (see page 142).

Optionally, a **geom=** argument can be included in the function call to specify the type of graph to produce. This can be assigned a "point" value to draw a scatter plot, as shown above.

Lines can be added between points by assigning both "point" and "line" values to the **geom=** argument:

5. Edit the function call to add lines between the points, then execute the code again to see the change
qplot(x, y, geom=c("point", "line"))

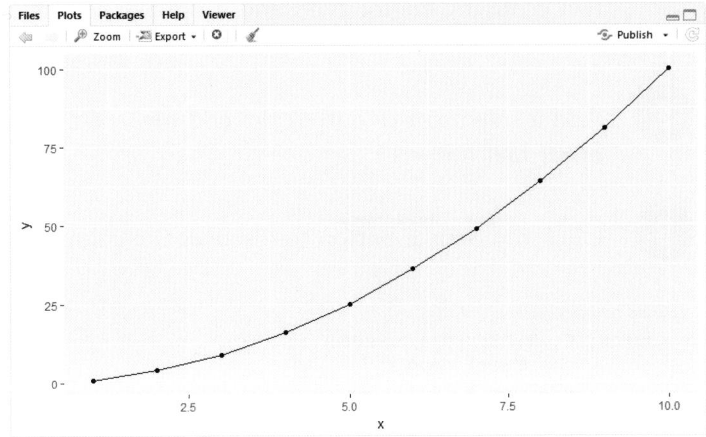

Specify only a "line" value if points are not required to be visible.

The color of plotted points and lines can be specified by including a **color=** argument in the function call, and the value specified as an argument to the built-in **I( )** function to inhibit interpretation:

6. Edit the function call to specify a point and line color, then execute the code once more to see the change
qplot(x, y, geom=c("point", "line"), color=I("Red"))

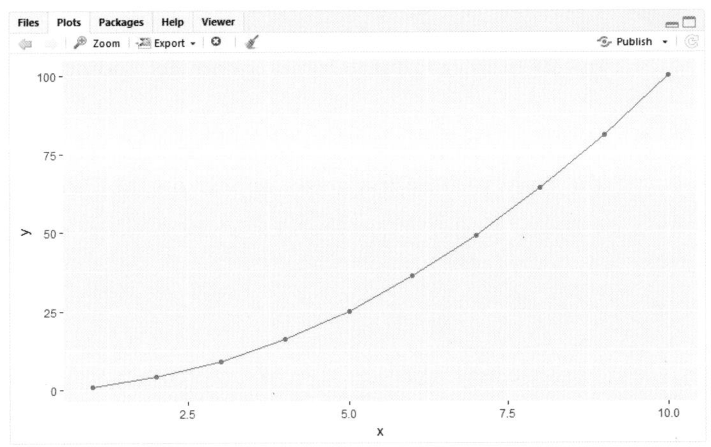

Colors can be specified by name or by hexadecimal value, such as "#FF0000" for "red".

Smoothing lines

The **qplot( )** Quick Plot function can be used to produce visualizations from data frames by specifying the data frame name to a **data=** argument. Column values can then be assigned as X-axis and Y-axis coordinates simply by stating the column names as arguments in the function call:

SmoothPlot.R

1. Begin an R Script by importing a dataset describing the fuel economy, engine type, and weight of several cars
   frame <- read.csv("DataSet-Autos.csv")

2. Add a statement to output the end rows of the data frame
   print(tail(frame))

3. Click the Source button to discover the column names

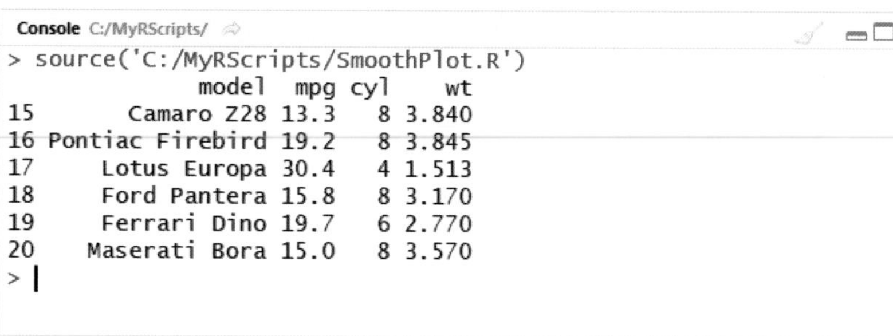

```
Console C:/MyRScripts/
> source('C:/MyRScripts/SmoothPlot.R')
              model  mpg cyl    wt
15       Camaro Z28 13.3   8 3.840
16 Pontiac Firebird 19.2   8 3.845
17     Lotus Europa 30.4   4 1.513
18     Ford Pantera 15.8   8 3.170
19     Ferrari Dino 19.7   6 2.770
20    Maserati Bora 15.0   8 3.570
> |
```

Notice that there are cars with engines that have 4, 6, or 8 cylinders which might be classified as three distinct groups.

4. Next, load the ggplot2 library
   library(ggplot2)

5. Now, call the Quick Plot function to plot the coordinates of fuel economy and car weight
   qplot(mpg, wt, data=frame, geom=c("point", "line"))

6. Click the **Run** button, or press **Ctrl** + **Enter**, to execute the code and see the graph appear on the Plots tab

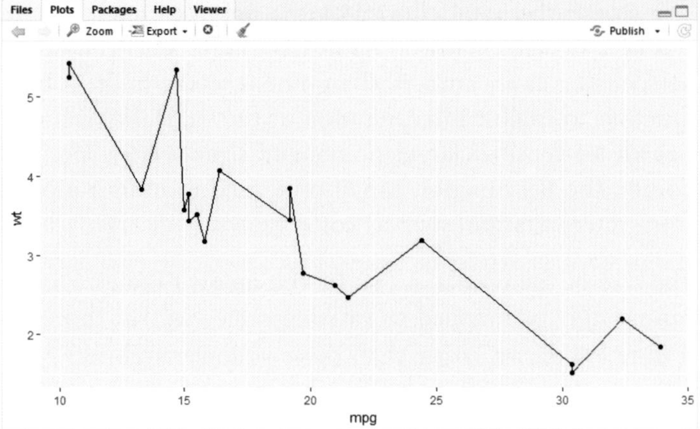

As the points on a scatter plot may contain wide variations it is often helpful to create a smoothed line to better visualize a pattern. The **qplot( )** function can add a smoothed line if you simply assign a "smooth" value to the **geom=** argument:

7. Edit the function call in step five to replace the lines between each point with a smoothed line
qplot(mpg, wt, data=frame, geom=c("point", "smooth"))

8. Execute the code once more to see how the change more clearly illustrates a pattern

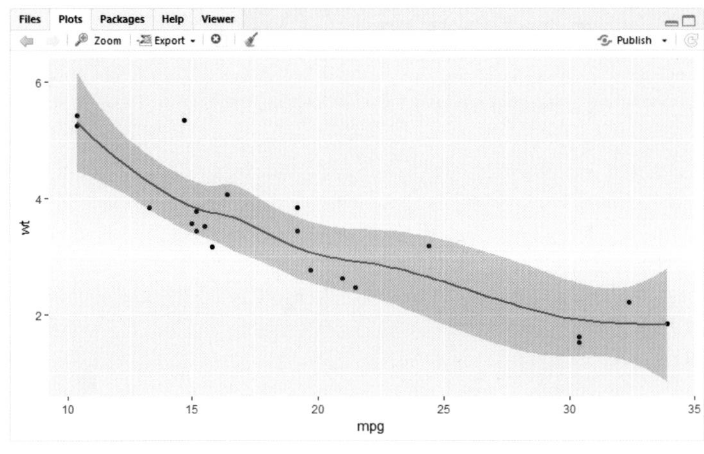

The insight here indicates that lighter cars are more fuel efficient.

Portraying stature

The size of the points drawn by the **qplot( )** Quick Plot function can be specified by including a **size=** argument. The value should be specified as an numerical argument to the built-in **I( )** function to inhibit interpretation of the value. For example, **size=I(5)** specifies larger points and **size=I(0.5)** specifies smaller points. The **I( )** function can also be used to inhibit other values from interpretation, such as color values.

The size of the points drawn by the **qplot( )** Quick Plot function can usefully be mapped to variable values so that those of higher stature are drawn larger than those of lower stature:

StaturePlot.R

1. Begin an R Script by importing a dataset describing the fuel economy, engine type, and weight of several cars
```
frame <- read.csv( "DataSet-Autos.csv" )
```

2. Next, load the ggplot2 library
```
library( ggplot2 )
```

3. Now, call the Quick Plot function to plot the coordinates of fuel economy, giving prominence to greatest efficiency
```
qplot( mpg, wt, data=frame, size=mpg, color=I( "Green" ) )
```

4. Click the **Run** button, or press **Ctrl** + **Enter**, to execute the code and see the graph appear on the Plots tab

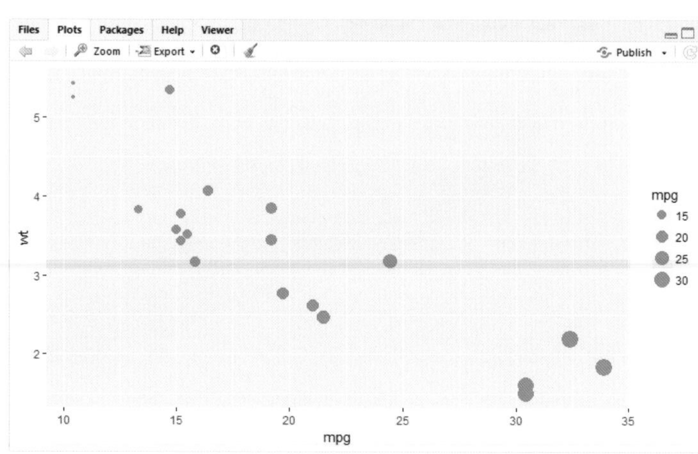

Notice that a legend is automatically created for mapped data.

Depicting groups

The shape of the points drawn by the **qplot( )** Quick Plot function can be specified by including a **shape=** argument. The value should be specified as an numerical argument to the built-in **I( )** function within the range 0-25. For example, **shape=I(17)** specifies triangular filled points.

The shape of the points drawn by the **qplot( )** Quick Plot function can usefully be mapped to variable values so that different groups are denoted by the shape of their points. The vector must first be encoded as a factor using the **factor( )** function. Similarly, the color of the points drawn by the **qplot( )** Quick Plot function can be mapped to variable values using the **factor( )** function:

Multiple shapes can be specified as a range that must match the data length. For example, **shapes=I(15:18)** for four different points.

1. Begin an R Script by importing a dataset describing the fuel economy, engine type, and weight of several cars

```
frame <- read.csv( "DataSet-Autos.csv" )
```

GroupPlot.R

2. Next, load the ggplot2 library and encode variable values

```
library( ggplot2 )
Cylinders <- factor( frame$cyl )
```

3. Now, call the Quick Plot function to plot the coordinates of fuel economy and weight, differentiating engine types

```
qplot( mpg, wt, data=frame, size=I( 5 ),
          shape=Cylinders, color=Cylinders )
```

4. Click the **Run** button, or press **Ctrl** + **Enter**, to execute the code and see the graph appear on the Plots tab

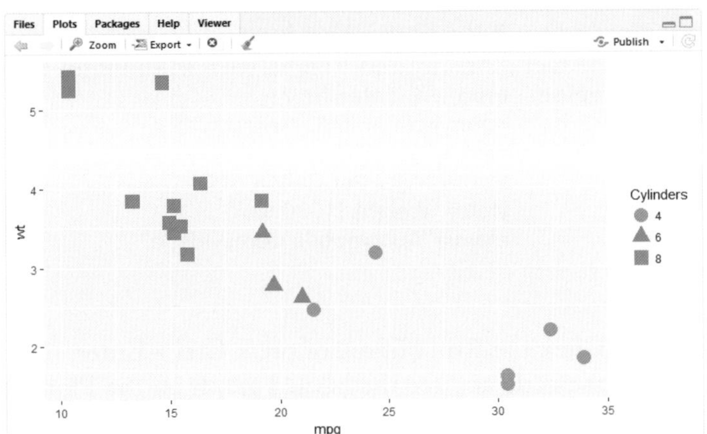

The insight here indicates that cars whose engines have fewer cylinders are more fuel efficient.

Adding labels

The default labels drawn by the **qplot( )** Quick Plot function on the X-axis and Y-axis are the column names of the data set supplying the values. Typically, you will want to provide more meaningful labels by including **xlab=** and **ylab=** arguments to specify text strings to display on each axis.

A plot title label can be added by including a **main=** argument in the call to the **qplot( )** function to specify a text strings to display above the graph.

Individual points on the plot can also be labeled by assigning a "text" value to the **geom=** argument and by including a **label=** argument in the call to the **qplot( )** function to specify text to display beside each point. This can be a single string or can be mapped to the data set. For example, each point can be labeled using the **rownames( )** function or with values from a column.

The limit of each axis can be specified by including **xlim=** and **ylim=** arguments in the call to the **qplot( )** function. This can be useful when adding point labels to ensure the text does not exceed the boundaries of the graph:

LabelPlot.R

1. Begin an R Script by importing a dataset describing the fuel economy, engine type, and weight of several cars

```
frame <- read.csv( "DataSet-Autos.csv" )
```

2. Next, load the ggplot2 library and encode variable values

```
library( ggplot2 )
Cylinders <- factor( frame$cyl )
```

3. Now, call the Quick Plot function to plot the coordinates of fuel economy and weight, with meaningful labels

```
qplot(  mpg, wt, data=frame,
        geom=c( "point", "smooth" ) ,
        color=Cylinders ,
        xlab="Miles Per Gallon (US)" ,
        ylab="Weight (1000 lbs)" ,
        main="Automobile Comparison"
)
```

4. Click the **Run** button, or press **Ctrl** + **Enter**, to execute the code and see the labeled graph on the Plots tab

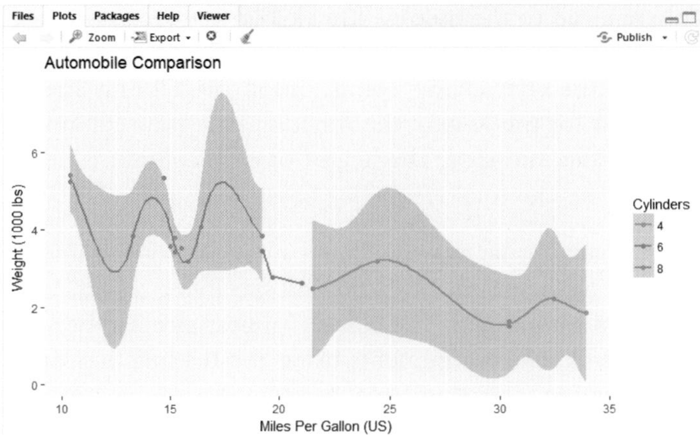

The colors are mapped to the engine types.

5 Edit the call to the Quick Plot function to add point labels and to extend the limit of each axis

```
qplot(  mpg, wt, data=frame ,
        geom=c( "point", "smooth", "text" ) ,
        color=Cylinders ,
        xlab="Miles Per Gallon (US)" ,
        ylab="Weight (1000 lbs)" ,
        main="Automobile Comparison",
        label=frame$model ,
        xlim=c( 8, 35 ) ,
        ylim=c( 0, 6 )
)
```

6 Click the **Run** button, or press **Ctrl** + **Enter**, to execute the code once more to see the changes

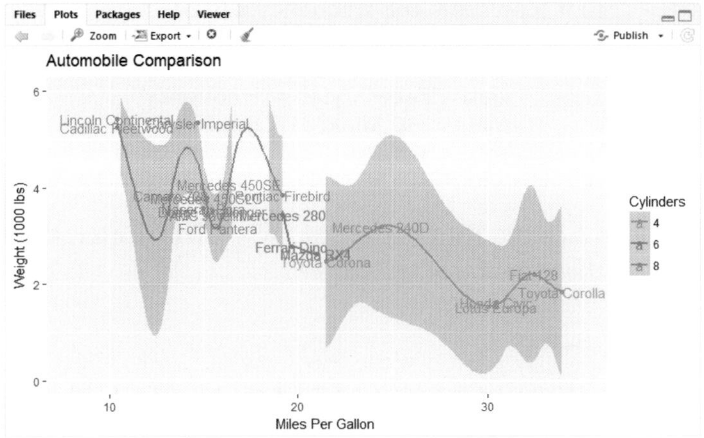

Point labels may overlap, making them difficult to read easily.

Drawing columns

Where a call to the **qplot( )** Quick Plot function specifies arguments for both X-axis and Y-axis coordinates, the function will plot the intersecting points, but if the call only specifies an argument for the X-axis, the function will draw columns for each unique value supplied. The height of each column is determined by counting the total frequency of each unique value.

A bar chart can be drawn when a single X-axis argument is supplied to the **qplot( )** function by specifying a "bar" value to the **geom=** argument. The column appearance can be specified to **fill=** and **color=** arguments using the **I( )** function to inhibit interpretation.

The built-in **sample( )** function could be used to produce a randomly distributed sequence of integers for a bar chart. This function requires three arguments to specify a range from which to choose, the quantity of items to choose, and whether to replace a selected item back in the range so it can be selected again:

BarPlot.R

1. Begin an R Script by assigning a random sequence of thirty integers to a vector variable, in the range 1-6

```
nums <- sample( 1:6, 30 , replace=TRUE )
```

2. Output the selected sequence in the Console to discover the frequency pattern, then load the ggplot2 library

```
print( nums )
library( ggplot2 )
```

3. Now, call the Quick Plot function to draw a bar chart that represents the frequency pattern

```
qplot( nums, geom="bar" ,
        color=I( "Blue" ) , fill=I( "Lightblue" ) ,
        xlab="Face" , ylab="Frequency" ,
        main="30 Shakes of the Dice"
)
```

4. Click the **Run** button, or press **Ctrl** + **Enter**, to execute the code to see the pattern

```
Console C:/MyRScripts/
> print( nums )
 [1] 1 1 4 4 5 2 4 3 3 4 6 4 4 6 4 3 4 2 3 2 6 4 5 4 3 4 2 1 2 6
```

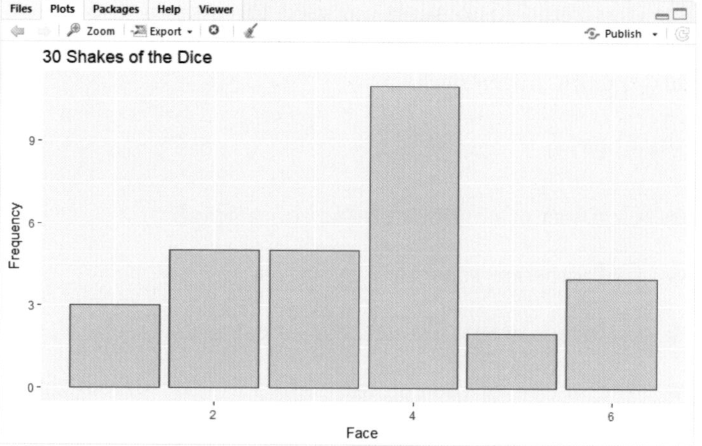

The tick marks on the bar chart are automatically created by R, but do not adequately represent each column. This can be remedied using the snappily-named **scale_x_continuous( )** function – to specify the number of required ticks to a **breaks=** argument, and category labels to a **labels=** argument:

There is also a similar **scale_y_continuous( )** function that can be used to specify ticks along the Y-axis.

5. Append the tick requirements immediately after the closing parenthesis of the call to the Quick Plot function
+ scale_x_continuous(breaks=1:6,
labels=c("One", "Two", "Three", "Four", "Five", "Six"))

6. Click the **Run** button, or press **Ctrl** + **Enter**, to execute the code once more and see another sequence appear

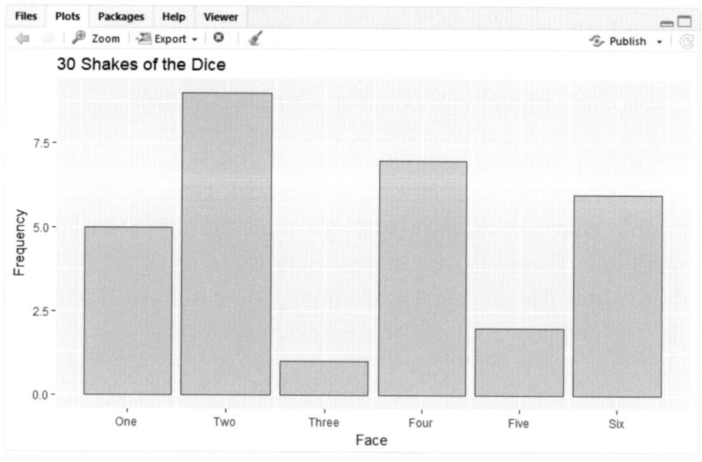

Understanding histograms

Bar charts and histograms are used to compare the sizes of different groups. Although these appear similar, there are some very specific differences:

Bar chart

- Consists of columns plotted on a graph
- Columns are separated by spaces
- Columns are positioned over a category label
- The height of the column represents the size of the group defined by the category label

Hot tip

Bar charts are also known as bar graphs.

The bar chart below depicts the average per capita income for four states. Each state is a category, defined on a column label, and the height of each column represents the size of that group.

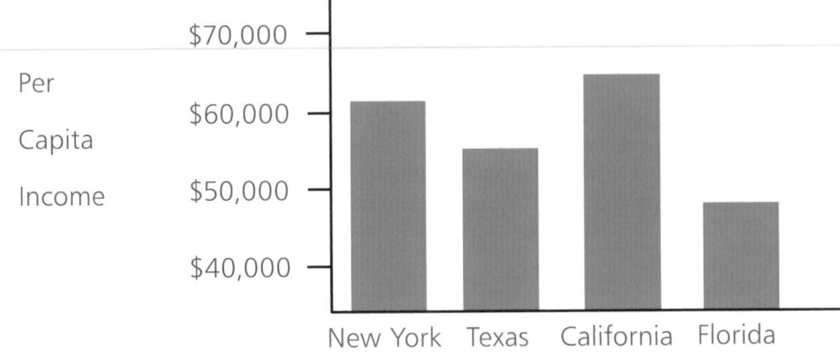

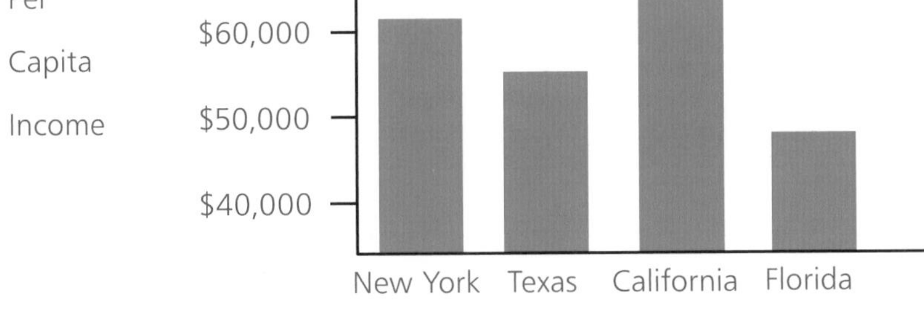

Bar charts are used to compare variables.

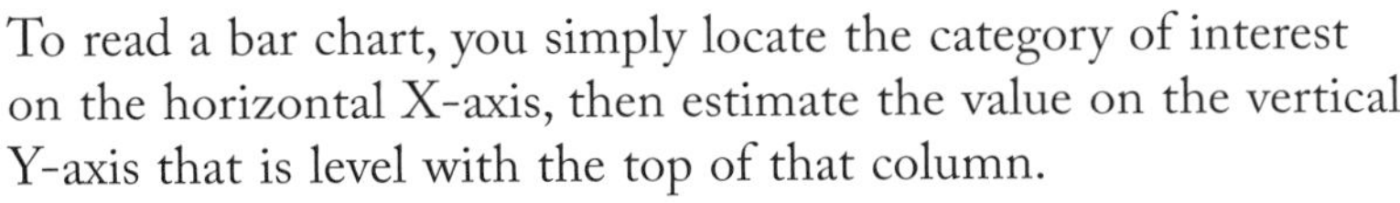

To read a bar chart, you simply locate the category of interest on the horizontal X-axis, then estimate the value on the vertical Y-axis that is level with the top of that column.

It is important to recognize that bar charts have columns that represent a group defined by a “categorical variable”. This is a variable that can take only values that are names or labels. For example, a Blood Group categorical variable of A, B, AB, or O label values. In the bar chart above, the categorical variables can take only values that are the name of a state.

Histogram

- Consists of columns plotted on a graph
- Columns are not generally separated by spaces
- Columns are positioned over a numerical range label
- The height of the column represents the size of the group defined by the range label

The histogram below depicts the average per capita income for five age ranges. Each range is defined on a column label, and the height of each column represents the size of that group.

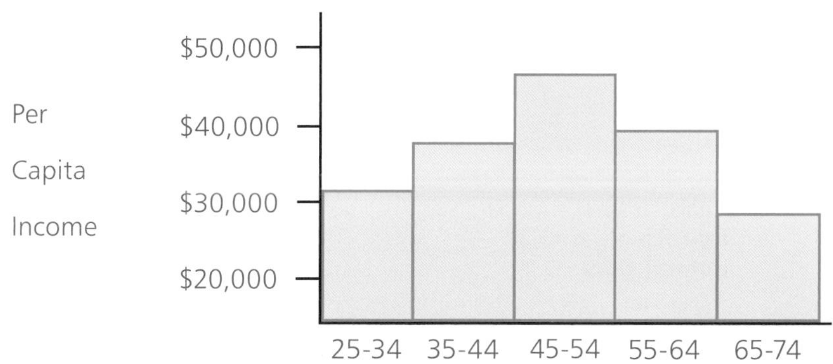

The ranges are also known as "bins". Choose the best bin size (range) to illustrate underlying patterns in the data.

To read a histogram you simply locate the range of interest on the horizontal X-axis, then estimate the value on the vertical Y-axis that is level with the top of that column.

It is important to recognize that histograms have columns that represent a group defined by a "quantitative variable". This is a variable that can take only numerical values that represent a measureable quantity. For example, a City Population quantitative variable of the number of people in a city represents a measureable quantity of residents. In the histogram above, the quantitative variables accept continuous numerical values for each age group.

Histograms are used to show the distribution of variables.

It can be useful to consider the "skewness" of a histogram where the height of the columns fall more on the low end or the high end of the horizontal X-axis to indicate a trend. This technique cannot be applied to a bar chart, as its X-axis does not have a low end or a high end.

Producing histograms

The **qplot( )** Quick Plot function can be made to draw a histogram by specifying only an X-axis argument in the function call and assigning a "histogram" value to its **geom=** argument. Additionally, it is recommended that you specify how many bins (columns) to draw by assigning an integer to a **bins=** argument. The color of the bins can be specified using the **fill=** argument and can usefully be mapped to variable values:

Histogram.R

1. Begin an R Script by creating a vector containing 1000 gender labels and a vector containing 1000 random numbers around different mean values

```
Sex <- rep( c( "Female", "Male" ), each=500 )
height <- c( rnorm( 500, 65 ), rnorm( 500, 69 ) )
```

2. Now, combine the two vectors in a data frame

```
frame <- data.frame( Sex, height )
```

3. Output the first and last three rows in the Console to see the data, then load the ggplot2 library

```
head( frame, n=3 )
tail( frame, n=3 )
library( ggplot2 )
```


4. Now, call the Quick Plot function to draw a histogram that displays the frequency in 40 bins – colored according to gender

```
qplot( height, data=frame, geom="histogram" , fill=Sex,
bins=40,
        ylab="Frequency" , xlab="Height in Inches" ,
        main="Average Adult Height (USA)"
)
```

If you omit a **bins=** argument, R will provide a default number of bins, but it is better to specify how many bins you want, to display the information most clearly.

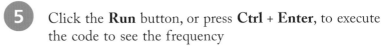

5. Click the **Run** button, or press **Ctrl** + **Enter**, to execute the code to see the frequency

```
Console C:/MyRScripts/
> head( frame, n=3 )
     Sex   height
1 Female 67.54316
2 Female 65.30378
3 Female 64.86170
> tail( frame, n=3 )
      Sex   height
998  Male 70.30887
999  Male 68.75543
1000 Male 69.51117
> 
```

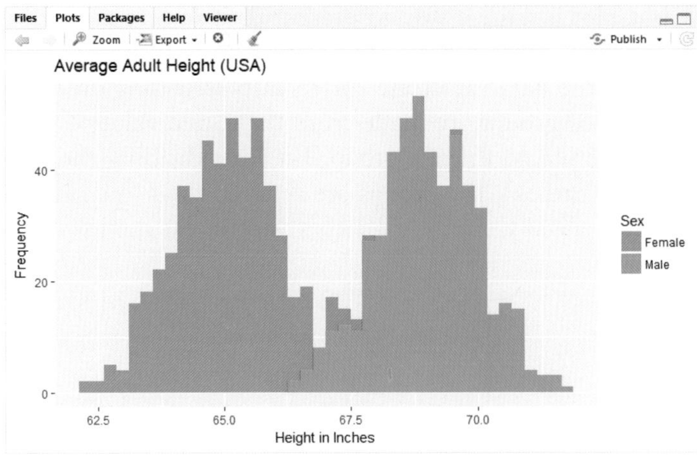

In the USA, average female height is 65 inches and average male height is 69 inches – the mean values specified to **rnorm( )** function calls.

To examine the area where the bins overlap, the same data can be redrawn as lines in a density plot by assigning a "density" value to the **geom=** argument. The width of line can be specified as a numerical argument to the **size=** argument, using the built-in **I( )** function to inhibit interpretation of the value. Color and type of lines can be specified to the **color=** and **linetype=** arguments, and can usefully be mapped to variable values:

6. Edit the call to the Quick Plot function to plot density, then execute the code once more to see the overlap

```
qplot( height, data=frame, geom="density" ,
        size=I( 2 ), color=Sex, linetype=Sex,
        ylab="Density" , xlab="Height in Inches" ,
        main="Average Adult Height (USA)"
)
```

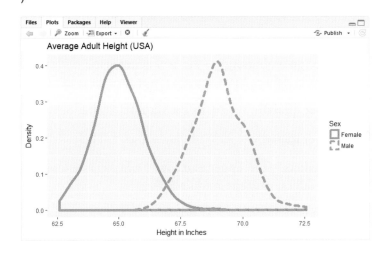

The insight here indicates that both female and male averages occur between 66-68 inches.

Understanding box plots

Box plots are also known as box-and-whisker plots.

A box plot is a great way to present data so that numerical distribution characteristics and levels can be easily visualized. Initially, the data values are sorted into ascending order, then four equal-sized groups are made from the sorted values – 25% of all values are placed in each group. The lines dividing the groups are called "quartiles". The groups are referred to as "quartile groups" and are typically numbered 1 to 4, starting at the lowest level.

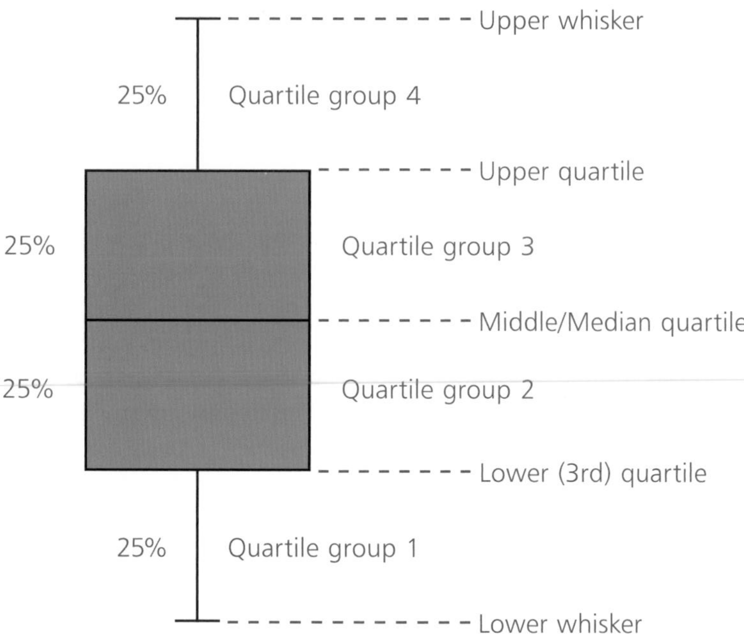

The quartiles are alternatively referred to numerically, where the Upper quartile is 1st, Media quartile is 2nd, and the Lower quartile is 3rd.

- **Median** – the middle quartile line denotes the mid-point of the data, where half the values are greater than or equal to this point and half are less.
- **Inter-quartile range** – the box denotes the middle 50% of the data values, between the lower quartile and upper quartile.
- **Upper quartile** – 75% of the data values fall below this line.
- **Lower quartile** – 25% of data values fall below this line.
- **Whiskers** – the upper and lower whiskers denote data values that fall outside the middle 50%.

Box plots are especially useful for comparing distributions between several groups of data. For example, the box plots below might represent student responses on a variety of topics.

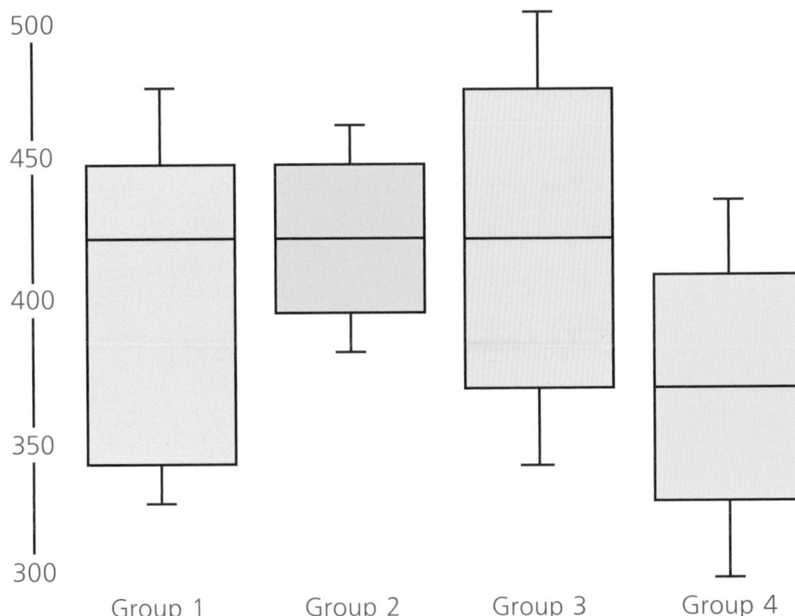

Observations

- **Group 1** – the four sections of the box plot are uneven in size, suggesting the students have similar views on some aspects of this topic but their views differ in other aspects.
- **Group 2** – the box plot is relatively short, suggesting the students hold similar views on this topic.
- **Groups 1 & 3** – the box plots are relatively tall, suggesting that the students hold quite differing views on these topics.
- **Groups 1, 2 & 3** – the box plots all have the same median, suggesting the same average level of response but the box plots show a different distribution of views.
- **Group 4** – the box plot is lower than the others, suggesting a poor level of response on this topic.

Whiskers often stretch over a wider range of values than those in the inter-quartile range.

Producing box plots

The **qplot( )** Quick Plot function can be made to draw a box plot by specifying X-axis and Y-axis arguments in the function call, and assigning a "boxplot" value to its **geom=** argument. The name of a data frame can be specified to the **data=** argument so its column names can be used to supply the coordinate values. The color of the boxes can be specified using the **fill=** argument and can usefully be mapped to variable values.

To ensure a trend is not missed, it is useful to make the data points visible on a box plot by also assigning a "jitter" value to the **geom=** argument in the call to the **qplot( )** function:

BoxPlot.R

1. Begin an R Script by importing a dataset describing three sets of weight results from an experiment
```
frame <- read.csv( "DataSet-Experiment.csv" )
```

2. Next, output the first three rows of data in the Console to see the column names and row values
```
print( head( frame, n=3 ) )
```

3. Now, load the ggplot2 library
```
library( ggplot2 )
```

4. Call the Quick Plot function to draw a box plot that displays the distribution of results and data points
```
qplot( Group, Weight, data=frame,
       geom=c( "boxplot", "jitter" ),
       fill=Group,
       main="Experiment Results"
)
```

5. Click the **Run** button, or press **Ctrl** + **Enter**, to execute the code to see the results

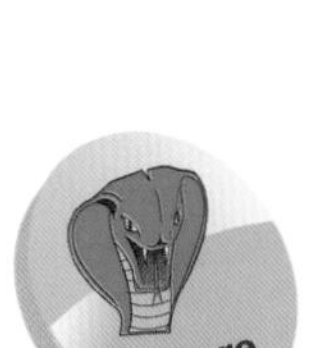

The order in the assignment to the **geom=** argument is important – the boxes will be drawn over the points if the order is reversed from that listed.

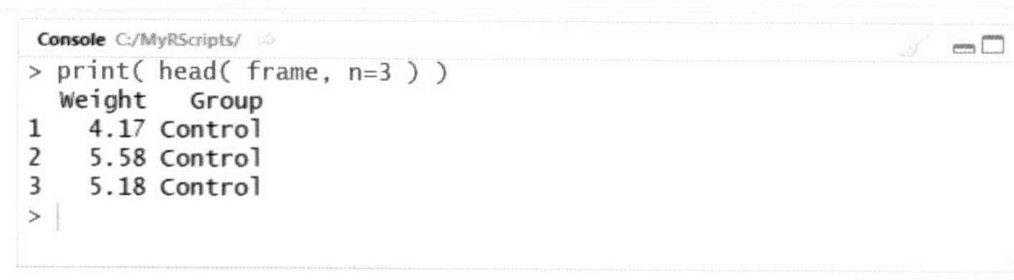
```
Console C:/MyRScripts/
> print( head( frame, n=3 ) )
  Weight   Group
1   4.17 Control
2   5.58 Control
3   5.18 Control
>
```

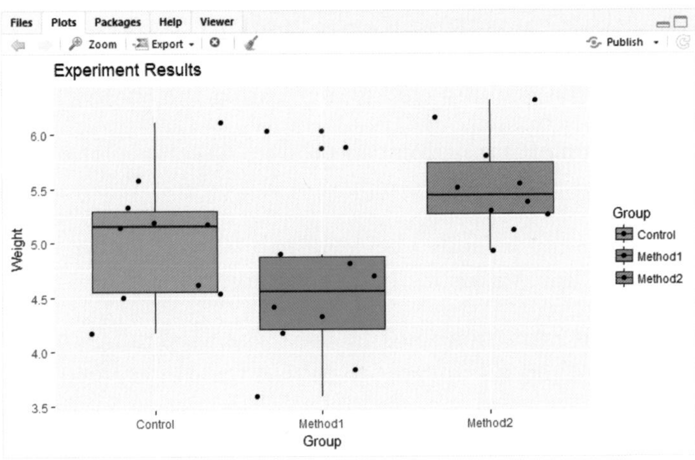

Do not use jitter for large data sets so that the box plot will not display data points.

If you prefer to demonstrate the distribution without displaying individual data points, you can produce a violin plot that indicates density by the width of the plot. This requires a "violin" value to be assigned to the **geom=** argument in the call to the **qplot( )** function. The plot will be truncated, however, unless you also include a **trim=** argument and assign it a **FALSE** value:

6. Edit the call to the Quick Plot function, then execute the code again to see the results once more

```
qplot( Group, Weight, data=frame,
        geom="violin", trim=FALSE,
        fill=Group,
        main="Experiment Results"
)
```

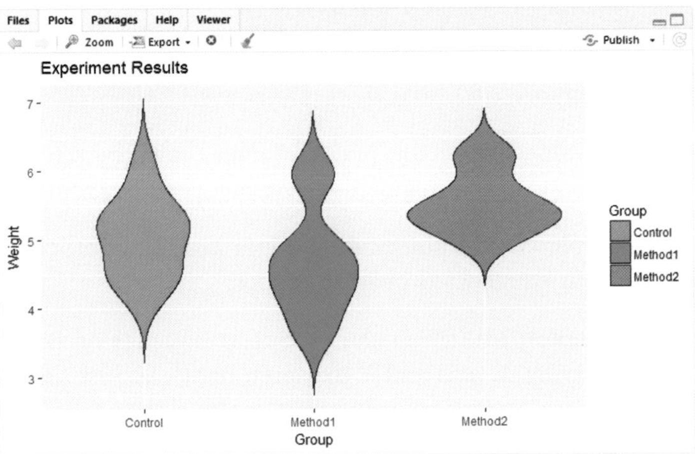

Summary

- Additional packages can be downloaded from the CRAN repository using the **install.packages( )** function and loaded into the RStudio environment using the **library( )** function.
- The **qplot( )** function can produce a scatter plot by supplying vector arguments to represent X-axis and Y-axis coordinates.
- Lines can be added between points by assigning both "point" and "line" values to the **geom=** argument.
- The **I( )** function must be used when assigning color, size, shape, and fill values – to inhibit their interpretation.
- The **qplot( )** function can produce a visualization from a data frame by specifying column names for X-axis and Y-axis coordinates, and its name to the **data=** argument.
- The **qplot( )** function can add a smoothed line by assigning a "smooth" value to the **geom=** argument.
- The size and shape of the points drawn by the **qplot( )** function can be specified to the **size=** and **shape=** arguments.
- Labels can be added by including **main=**, **xlab=**, and **ylab=** arguments in the call to the **qplot( )** function.
- Bar chart columns represent a categorical variable, but histogram columns represent a quantitative variable.
- The **qplot( )** function can produce a bar chart or histogram by supplying an X-axis argument and a "bar" value or "histogram" value to the **geom=** argument.
- The **scale_x_continuous( )** function can be used to control the appearance of X-axis ticks and labels.
- The color, size, shape, and fill values drawn by the **qplot( )** function can be mapped to variables for distinction.
- Box plots sort numerical data into ascending order separated in four equal sized quartile groups.
- The **qplot( )** function can produce a box plot or violin plot by specifying X-axis and Y-axis arguments, and by assigning a "boxplot" or "violin" value to its **geom=** argument.

9 Storytelling with data

This chapter demonstrates how to produce data visualizations that most effectively convey the messages within data.

Presenting data

The visual representation of data in a graphical format enhances the human ability to see patterns and trends. Data visualization is closely related to information graphics ("infographics") that can clearly and efficiently communicate data visually. The popularity of infographics has increased recently – but they're not a new idea.

A French civil engineer, named Charles Minard (1781-1870), was noted for his representation of numerical data on geographic maps. In 1869, Minard created an influential infographic on the subject of Napoleon's disastrous march on Moscow:

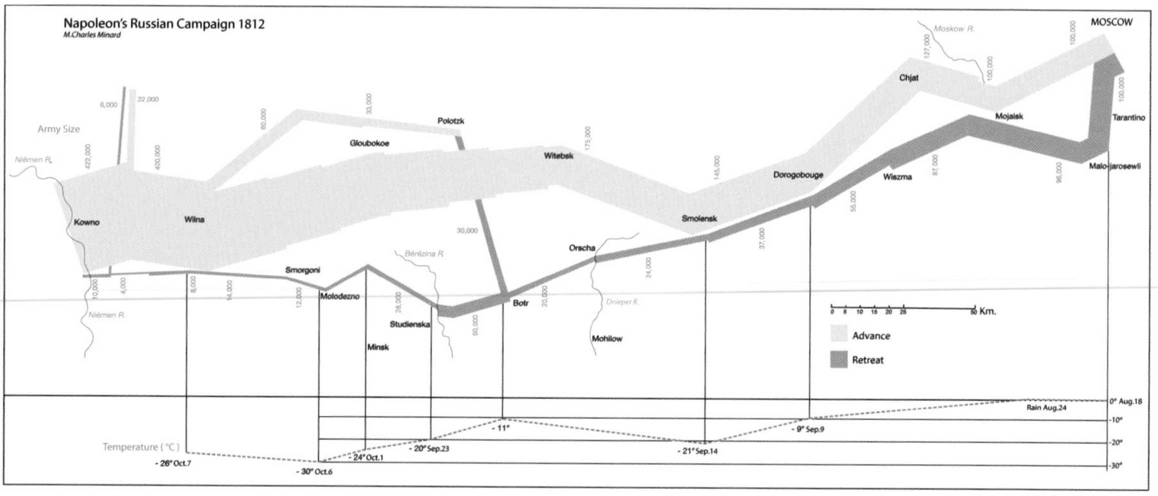

Charles Minard worked throughout Europe on large construction projects. Modern information scientists say his illustration may be the best statistical graphic ever drawn.

This infographic captures six changing variables that contributed to Napoleon's downfall in a single two-dimensional image:

- **Army size** – the dwindling number as troops died from hunger and wounds (422,000 down to 10,000).
- **Direction** – the army's direction as they advanced from the Polish border and retreated back from Moscow.
- **Distance** – the scaled length of the advance and retreat.
- **Temperature** – the freezing cold experienced by the troops as they retreated (0° Celsius down to -30° Celsius).
- **Location** – the cities that the army passed through during its advance and retreat.
- **Time** – the duration of the retreat (August 18-October 7).

The grammar of graphics

Plots and charts created for data visualization share many components – data is represented by graphical elements, and labels help to make the meaning clear. Just as the grammar of a language provides a structure in which words of a language can be combined into meaningful sentences, the grammar of graphics provides a structure in which graphical elements can be combined into meaningful visualizations.

The grammar of graphics was introduced by Leland Wilkinson in the late 1990s, and popularized by Hadley Wickham with the ggplot plotting library for R programming. The latest version is the ggplot2 package.

In the grammar of graphics, visualizations are comprised of seven vertically stacked layers containing graphical elements and labels that can be arranged and combined in different ways:

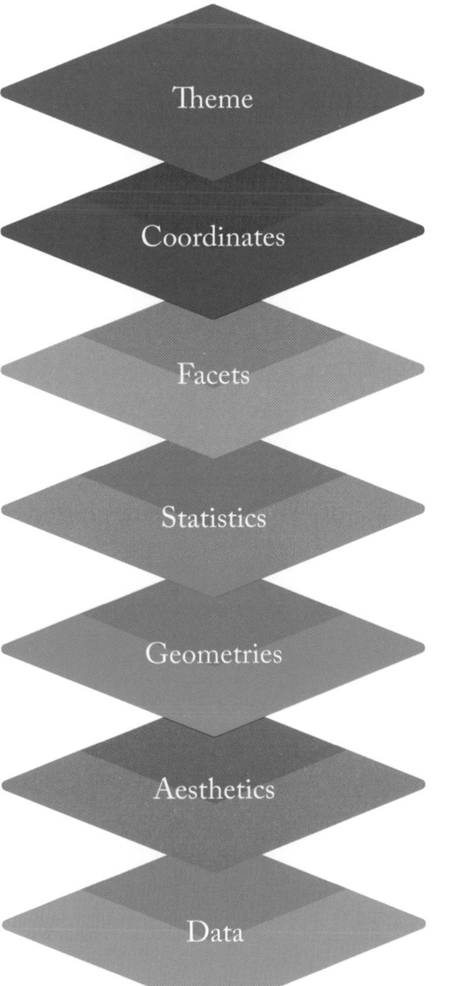

Theme – axes labels, title color and size, plus legend position.

Coordinates – focus and zoom of the plot area.

Facets – multiple plots of data subsets in individual panels.

Statistics – data transformation for computed plots.

Geometries – graphical points, lines, bars, boxes, axes labels and title text.

Aesthetics – map or set axes, plus plot color, fill, shape, and size.

Data – tidy rows of individual source values.

Each grammar of graphics layer is described in detail on the ensuing pages.

Considering aesthetics

The **qplot( )** function is great for producing quick visualizations, but more complex graphics require the power of the **ggplot( )** function from within the ggplot2 package. This requires the name of a data frame to be specified to a **data=** argument to satisfy the fundamental Data layer of the grammar of graphics.

Variables in the data can be mapped to the X-axis and Y-axis by including an **aes( )** argument in the call to the **ggplot( )** function. The variable names can be specified to **x=** and **y=** arguments in the call to the **aes( )** function, but the argument for the Y-axis can be omitted if a bar chart or histogram is required. Calling the **ggplot( )** function creates a ggplot object and satisfies the basic requirements of the Aesthetics layer of the grammar of graphics:

Aesthetics.R

1. Begin an R Script by importing a dataset describing the salaries of a number of college professors
```
frame <- read.csv( "DataSet-ProfSalaries.csv" )
```

2. Next, output the first 10 rows in the Console to see the column names, then load the ggplot2 library
```
head( frame, n=10 )
library( ggplot2 )
```

3. Now, call the function to create a ggplot object
```
ggplot( data=frame, aes( x=yrs.since.phd, y=salary ) )
```

4. Click the **Run** button, or press **Ctrl** + **Enter**, to execute the code and see the axes are drawn, but no data plotted

Optionally, variable names alone can be specified as comma-separated arguments to the **aes( )** function – omitting the **x=** and **y=** assignments. For example, in this case **aes(rank, salary)**.

This data set is used throughout this chapter to demonstrate data presentation adhering to the grammar of graphics.

Console C:/MyRScripts/
```
> frame <- read.csv( "DataSet-ProfSalaries.csv" )
>
> head( frame, n=10 )
        rank discipline yrs.since.phd yrs.service sex salary
1       Prof    Applied            19          18   M 139750
2       Prof    Applied            20          16   M 173200
3   AsstProf    Applied             4           3   M  79750
4       Prof    Applied            45          39   M 115000
5       Prof    Applied            40          41   M 141500
6  AssocProf    Applied             6           6   M  97000
7       Prof    Applied            30          23   M 175000
8       Prof    Applied            45          45   M 147765
9       Prof    Applied            21          20   M 119250
10      Prof    Applied            18          18   F 129000
>
```

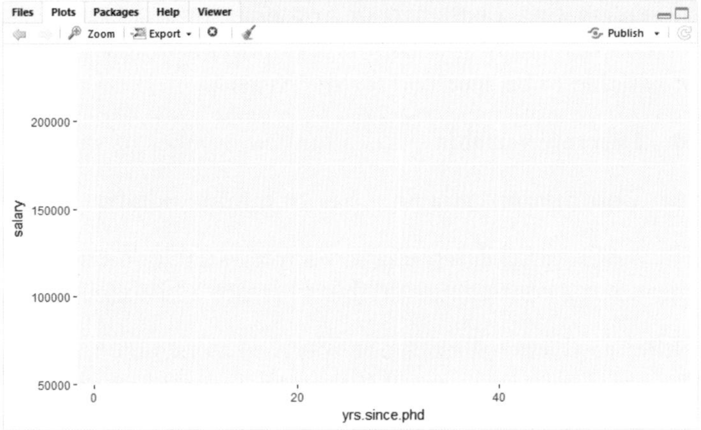

What's happening here? No data has been plotted because the code does not yet specify how to plot the mapped variable values. It is necessary to add a function call to also satisfy the Geometries layer of the grammar of graphics. The ggplot2 library provides functions for many geometry types, and these can be appended after the call to the **ggplot( )** function using the **+** operator:

5. Append a function call to specify a point geometry
```
ggplot( data=frame, aes( x=yrs.since.phd, y=salary ) ) +
  geom_point( )
```

6. Run the code once more to see the axes drawn and now also see the data plotted as points

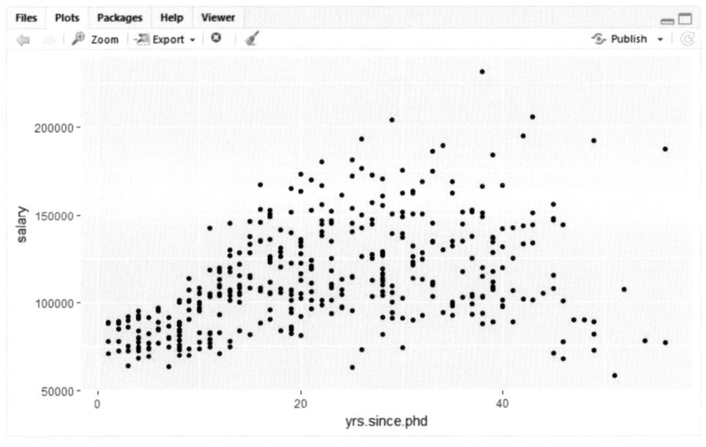

Multiple functions can be appended, so it is convenient to place the **+** operator on the same line as the previous function call, then place the appended function call on the next line – as listed in this example.

The minimum layers required to create a visualization adhering to the grammar of graphics are the Data, Aesthetics, and Geometries layers.

Using geometries

Geometries

When creating a bar chart or histogram on the Geometries layer of the grammar of graphics, it is important to recognize the type of variable to be specified for the X-axis:

- **Discrete variable** – has a limited number of values
- **Continuous variable** – has an infinite number of values

The **aes( )** function requires a discrete variable to create a bar chart, but a continuous variable to create a histogram.

Other aesthetic values can be specified as arguments directly in the geometry function call if they are assigned an absolute value, such as **color="Red"**. To map an aesthetic value to a variable, the assignment must instead be made as an argument to the **aes( )** function in the geometry function call, such as **aes(color=var)**:

Geometries.R

1. Begin an R Script by importing the dataset describing professors' salaries, then load the ggplot2 library

```
frame <- read.csv( "DataSet-ProfSalaries.csv" )
library( ggplot2 )
```

2. Next, create a ggplot object using a discrete variable, then append a function to specify a bar chart geometry – with other aesthetics assigned absolute values

```
ggplot( data=frame, aes( x=rank ) ) +
  geom_bar( fill="Yellow", color="Red" )
```

3. Click the **Run** button, or press **Ctrl** + **Enter**, to execute the code and see the bar chart appear

The **fill=** argument specifies the bar color, whereas the **color=** argument specifies only the bar's border color.

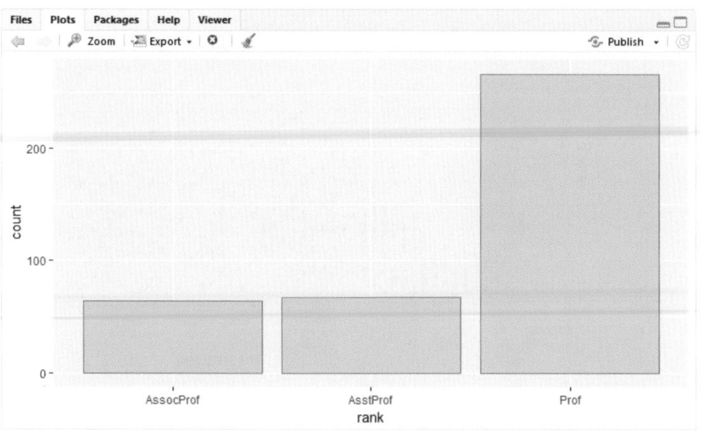

4. Edit the code to create a ggplot object using a continuous variable, then append a function to specify a histogram geometry – with other aesthetics assigned absolute values

```
ggplot( data=frame, aes( x=salary ) ) +
  geom_histogram( fill="Purple", color="White", bins=20 )
```

Remember to include a **bins=** argument to specify the number of columns to display on a histogram.

5. Run the code once more to see the histogram appear

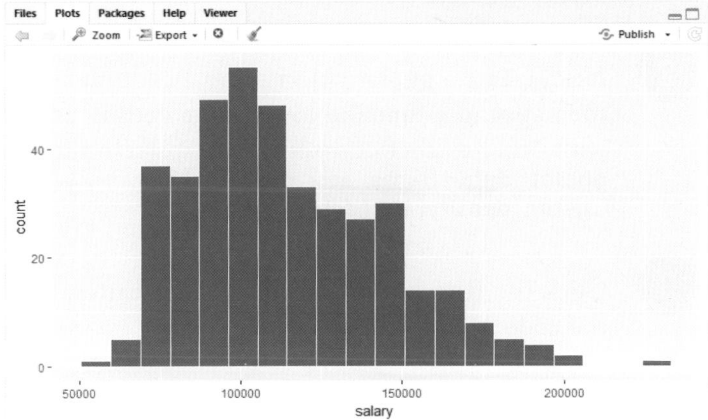

6. Further edit the code to specify a histogram geometry – with other aesthetics mapped to a discrete variable

```
ggplot( data=frame, aes( x=salary ) ) +
  geom_histogram( aes( fill=rank) , color="Black", bins=20 )
```

7. Run the code again see the modified histogram appear

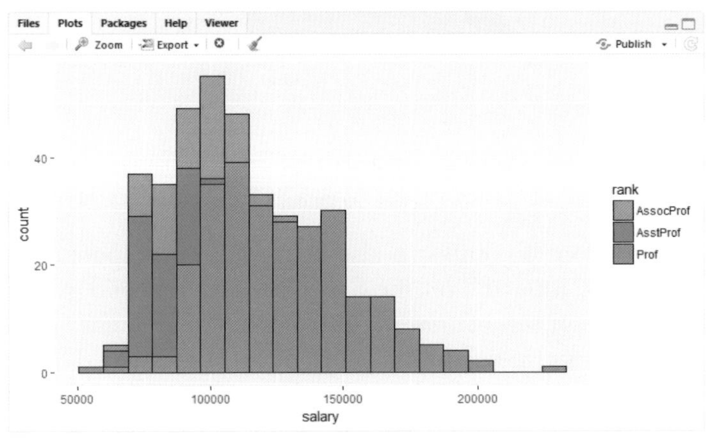

All the geometry function names in gggplot2 begin with "geom_". Type this in the Code Editor to see a popup list appear of all these functions.

```
geom_
geom_hex          {ggplot2}
geom_histogram    {ggplot2}
geom_hline        {ggplot2}
geom_jitter       {ggplot2}
geom_label        {ggplot2}
geom_line         {ggplot2}
geom_linerange    {ggplot2}
```

Showing statistics

Statistics.R

The Statistics layer of the grammar of graphics allows for data transformation so that computed statistics can be drawn to summarize the raw source data. For example, to draw a smoothed version of a histogram displaying computed density estimates:

1. Begin an R Script by importing the dataset describing professors' salaries, then load the ggplot2 library

```
frame <- read.csv( "DataSet-ProfSalaries.csv" )
library( ggplot2 )
```

2. Next, create a ggplot object using a continuous variable, then append a function to compute density estimates – with other aesthetics mapped to a discrete variable

```
ggplot( data=frame, aes( x=salary ) ) +
  geom_density( aes( fill=rank) )
```

3. Click the **Run** button, or press **Ctrl** + **Enter**, to execute the code and see the computed density statistics

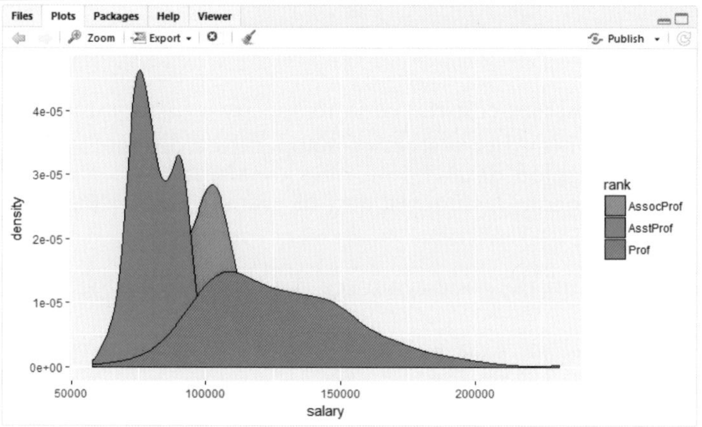

Similarly, the Statistics layer can be used to draw a computed smooth line of mean values over a point geometry layer.

The location of points can also be moved to computed random positions ("jittered") on the Statistics layer, to avoid overplotting one point on top of another, and a box plot geometry can be specified to summarize the distribution of the data. Drawing boxes over points can hide the points unless an **alpha=** argument is included to specify transparency for the fill color of the boxes.

The order of function calls is important as they will be drawn in sequence.

4 Edit the code to create a different ggplot object, then append functions to specify a point geometry and a function to add lines of computed mean values

```
ggplot( data=frame, aes( x=yrs.since.phd, y=salary ) ) +
  geom_point( aes( color=rank ) ) +
  geom_smooth( aes( color=rank ) , fill=NA )
```

Include a **fill=NA** argument to hide the broad backgrounds that are drawn beneath computed smooth lines by default.

5 Run the code again to see the computed mean statistics

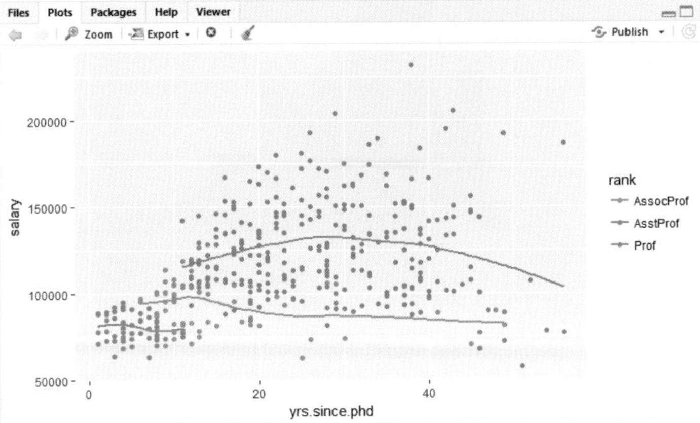

6 Edit the code to create another ggplot object, then append functions to compute point locations and to specify a computed box plot geometry – run the code

```
ggplot( data=frame, aes( x=rank, y=salary ) ) +
  geom_jitter( aes( color=rank ) ) +
  geom_boxplot( aes( fill=rank ) , alpha=0.5 )
```

Possible values for the **alpha=** argument range from 0 (fully transparent) to 1 (fully opaque).

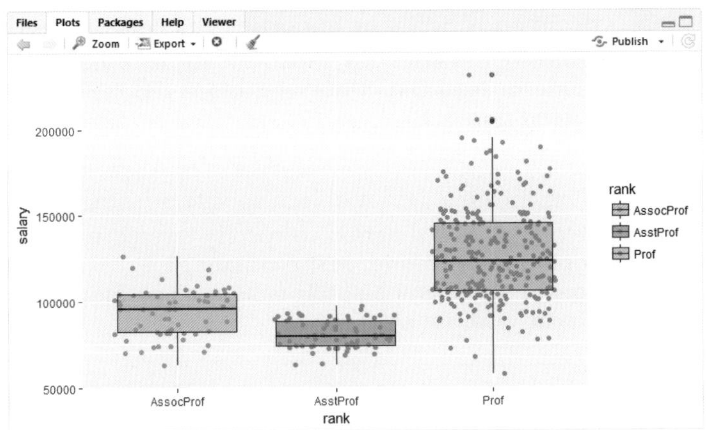

Illustrating facets

A data visualization may sometimes overplot points, rows, or columns, so that some information is hidden. For example, the histogram below (repeated from page 155) overplots some columns for the Assistant Professor and Associate Professor ranks:

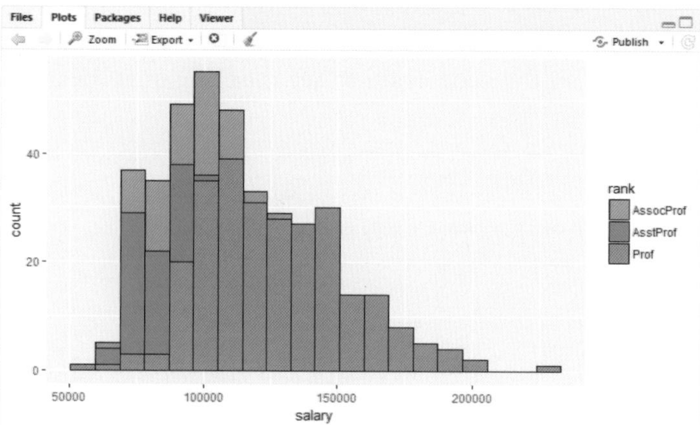

For clarity, it would be better to illustrate the information for each rank individually as separate "facets". The Facets layer of the grammar of graphics allows you to create a matrix of panels to display separate variables by appending a **facet_grid( )** function. This has an unusual argument requirement where a variable name or . period character is specified around a ~ tilde character. Placing the variable name before the tilde maps the values to rows, whereas placing the variable name after the tilde maps the values to columns. The period character on the side opposite the variable name indicates that no faceting is required in that dimension:

Facets.R

1. Begin an R Script by importing the dataset describing professors' salaries, then load the ggplot2 library

```
frame <- read.csv( "DataSet-ProfSalaries.csv" )
library( ggplot2 )
```

2. Next, create a ggplot object, specify a histogram geometry, then append a function to specify faceted rows

```
ggplot( data=frame, aes( x=salary ) ) +
  geom_histogram( aes( fill=rank ), color="Black", bins=20 ) +
  facet_grid( rank~. )
```

3 Click the **Run** button, or press **Ctrl** + **Enter**, to execute the code and see the rank information in separate panels

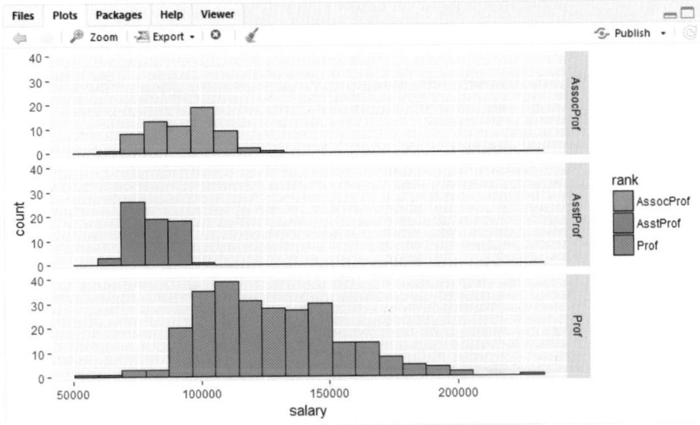

The count scale on the Y-axis is uniform for all three panels, automatically calculated to accommodate the tallest column in the bottom panel. This perhaps illustrates information in the other panels less clearly, but you can have each panel's scale calculated individually by specifying a "free" value to a **scales=** argument in the call to the **facet_grid( )** function:

4 Edit the code to allow maximum column height in each panel, then run the code again to see the improvement

```
ggplot( data=frame, aes( x=salary ) ) +
  geom_histogram( aes( fill=rank ), color="Black", bins=20 ) +
  facet_grid( rank~. , scales="free" )
```

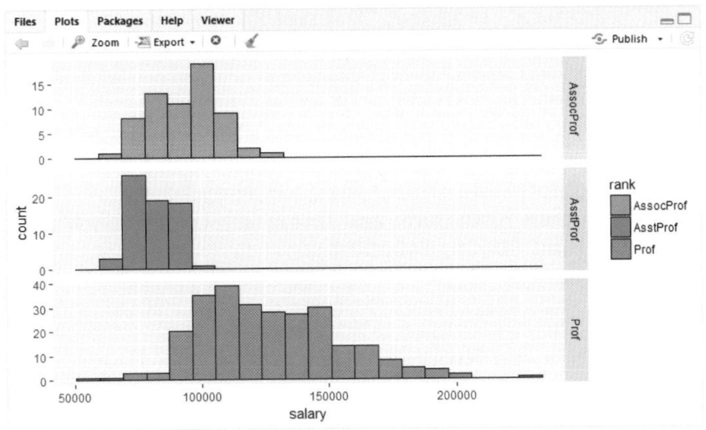

Switch the argument to **facet_grid(.~rank)** then run the code to see the data now displayed in columnar panels.

Controlling coordinates

Coordinates

It is often useful to refine a data visualization to focus on a particular area of interest. For example, in the histogram below (repeated from page 155) it might be of interest to focus on Professor salaries between $80,000-$140,000:

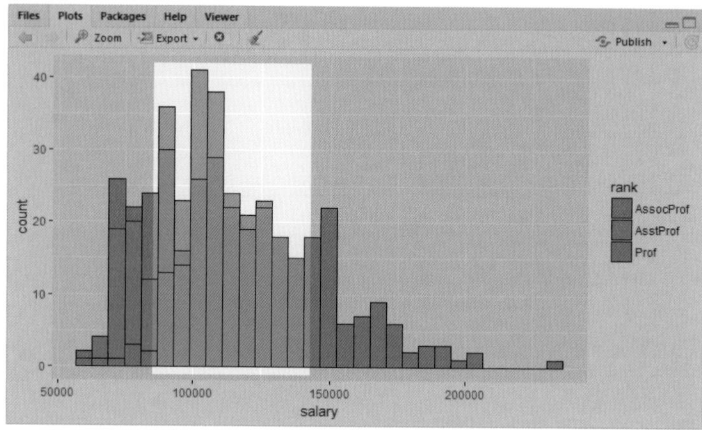

The Coordinates layer of the grammar of graphics allows you to focus on a particular area of interest in two ways. You can specify the start and end coordinates of the area as arguments to appended **xlim( )** and **ylim( )** functions, to limit the axes range.

Alternatively, you can specify the start and end coordinates of the area as vectors to **xlim=** and **ylim=** arguments in an appended **coord_cartesian( )** function, to zoom into a particular area:

Coordinates.R

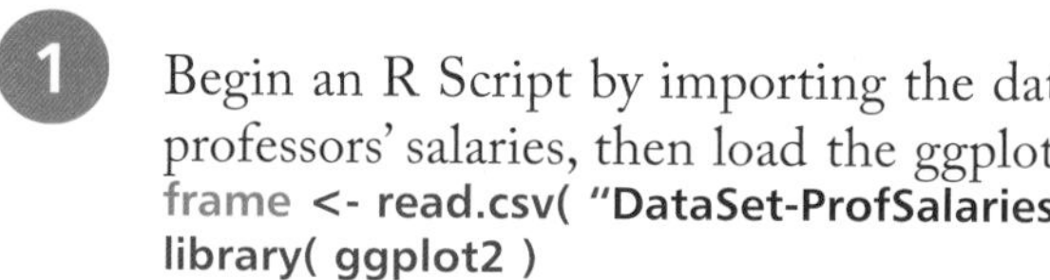

1. Begin an R Script by importing the dataset describing professors' salaries, then load the ggplot2 library

```
frame <- read.csv( "DataSet-ProfSalaries.csv" )
library( ggplot2 )
```

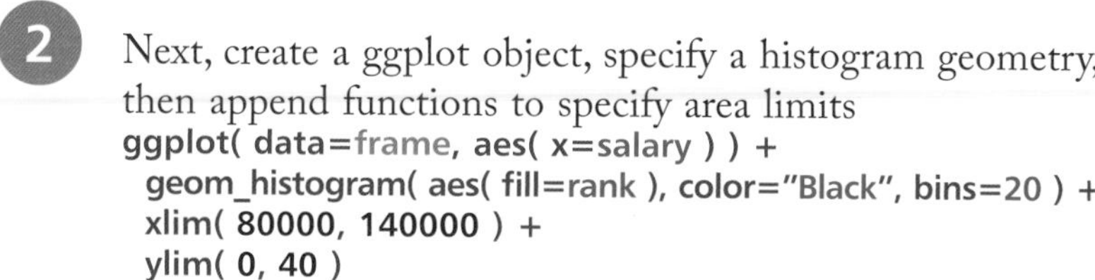

2. Next, create a ggplot object, specify a histogram geometry, then append functions to specify area limits

```
ggplot( data=frame, aes( x=salary ) ) +
  geom_histogram( aes( fill=rank ), color="Black", bins=20 ) +
  xlim( 80000, 140000 ) +
  ylim( 0, 40 )
```

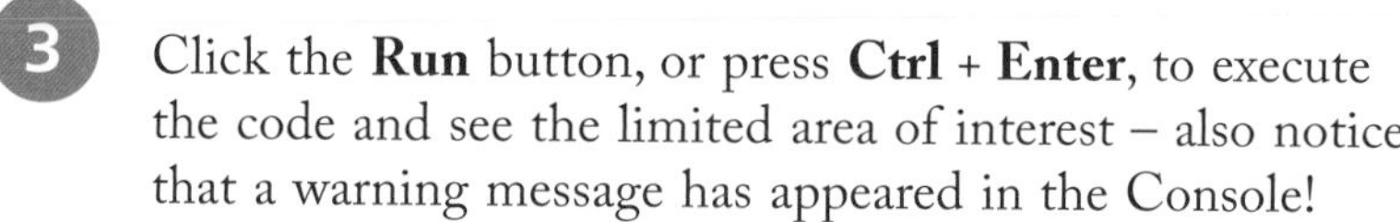

3. Click the **Run** button, or press **Ctrl** + **Enter**, to execute the code and see the limited area of interest – also notice that a warning message has appeared in the Console!

...cont'd

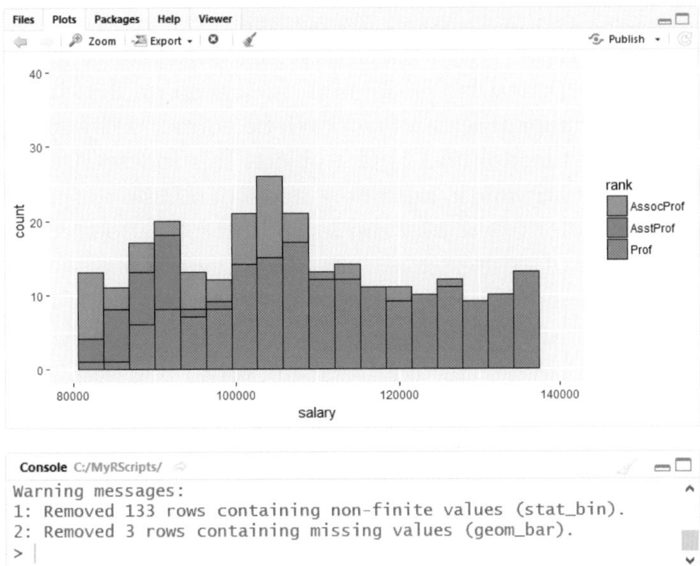

By removing rows of data, the plot may not accurately reflect the actual distribution.

The warning message indicates that R has removed some of the data in preparing the visualization – this is probably undesirable:

4. Replace the functions that specify area limits with a function to specify an area on which to focus
ggplot(data=frame, aes(x=salary)) +
geom_histogram(aes(fill=rank),color="Black", bins=20) +
coord_cartesian(xlim=c(80000, 140000), ylim=c(0, 40))

5. Run the code again to zoom into the area of interest – without any warning message appearing in the Console

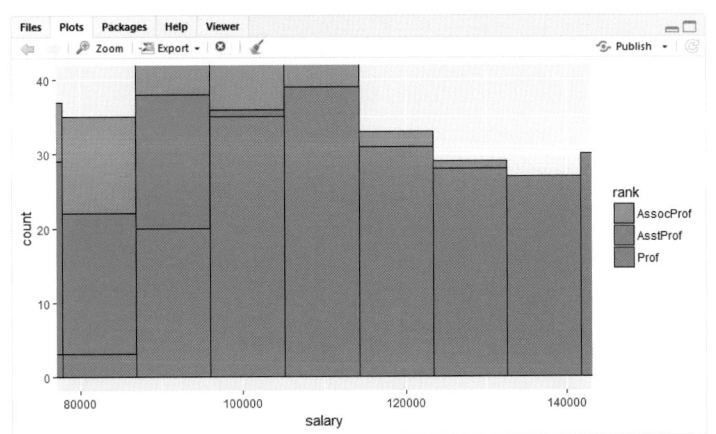

The zoomed area reveals that a number of Assistant Professors have salaries in excess of $100,000 – information not visible on the other views of this histogram.

Designing themes

The final top-level layer of the grammar of graphics is the Theme layer that allows you to specify the size and color of the axes and legend labels, and the position of the legend on the visualization. These component features can each be controlled by appending a **theme( )** function to a ggplot object. This function can accept arguments **axis.title.x, axis.title.y**, and **legend.title** to specify the size and color of the axes and legend titles. It also accepts similar arguments of **axis.text.x, axis.text.y**, and **legend.text** to specify the size and color of the tick mark text and legend item's text. The assignment to each of these is made by specifying values to **size=** and **color=** arguments of an **element_text( )** function.

Hot tip

The **theme( )** function can accept many arguments. Enter **?theme** to open its Help page and read through the list of available arguments.

The position of the legend is specified to **legend.justification** and **legend.position** arguments as a vector of X,Y coordinates where 0 and 1 represent the start and end point of each axis respectively.

For example, specifying coordinates of 1,1 to both arguments positions the legend at the top-right corner of the plotting area.

Specifying slightly different values to the **legend.position** argument allows the legend to be inset from the edges of the plotting area. For example, in the box plot below (repeated from page 157) it might be desirable to position the legend inset at the top-left empty corner on the plotting area.

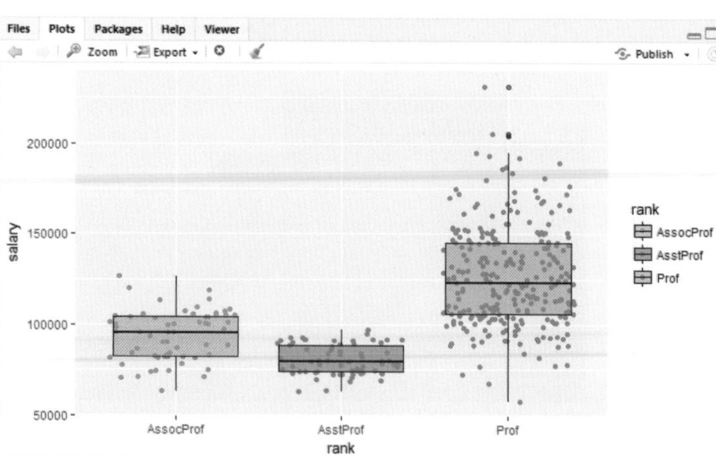

Don't forget

You should specify both **legend.justification** and **legend.position** arguments to anchor the legend position.

Themes.R

1. Begin an R Script by importing the dataset describing professors' salaries, then load the ggplot2 library

```
frame <- read.csv( "DataSet-ProfSalaries.csv" )
library( ggplot2 )
```

2. Next, create a ggplot object, specify a jitter and box plot geometry, then append a function to specify a theme

```
ggplot( data=frame, aes( x=rank, y=salary ) ) +
geom_jitter( aes( color=rank ) ) +
  geom_boxplot( aes( color=rank ), alpha=0.5 ) +
  theme(
        # Assignments to be inserted here (Steps 3-4).
      )
```

3. Now, insert these assignments to specify titles and text values for axes and legend

```
axis.title.x=element_text( size=15, color="Red" )
axis.title.y=element_text( size=15, color="Blue" )
legend.title=element_text( size=15 )
axis.text.x=element_text( size=15, color="Red" )
axis.text.y=element_text( size=15, color="Blue" )
legend.text=element_text( size=15 )
```

4. Insert these assignments to specify the legend position

```
legend.justification=c( 0, 1 )
legend.position=c( 0.02, 0.97 )
```

5. Click the **Run** button, or press **Ctrl** + **Enter**, to execute the code and see the theme

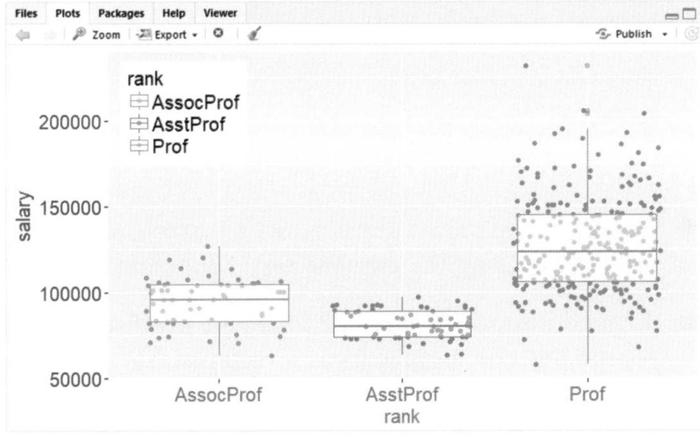

Here, the **legend.position** values inset the legend by .02 from the X-axis starting edge at 0, and by .03 from the Y-axis finishing edge at 1.0. Experiment by changing these values to see how the position is affected.

Summary

- The grammar of graphics defines seven vertically stacked layers for Data, Aesthetics, Geometries, Statistics, Facets, Coordinates, and Theme.
- The **ggplot( )** function requires the name of a data frame to be specified to a **data=** argument – for the Data layer.
- Variables can be mapped to axes by an **aes( )** argument in the call to the **ggplot( )** function – for the Aesthetics layer.
- It is necessary to append a function call after the call to the **ggplot( )** function – for the Geometries layer.
- Functions for many geometry types can be appended after the **ggplot( )** function call using the **+** operator.
- A discrete variable has a limited number of values, whereas a continuous variable has an infinite number of values.
- The **aes( )** function requires a discrete variable to create a bar chart but a continuous variable to create a histogram.
- Data transformation can provide computed statistics to summarize the raw source data – for the Statistics layer.
- A data visualization can display separate variables on a matrix of individual panels – for the Facets layer.
- The **facet_grid( )** function requires an argument where a variable name or . is specified around a ~ tilde character.
- The axes range can be limited to an area of particular interest using **xlim( )** and **ylim( )** functions – for the Coordinates layer.
- The **coord_cartesian( )** function can be used to zoom into an area of particular interest.
- Plot component features can each be controlled by appending a **theme( )** function to a ggplot object – for the Theme layer.
- Title and text values are assigned for axes and legend arguments using the **element_text( )** function.
- Legend position is specified to **legend.justification** and **legend.position** arguments as a vector of X,Y coordinates.

10 Plotting perfection

This chapter demonstrates how to produce multiple visualizations from one data set for insightful analysis of various aspects of the data.

Loading the data

When you create an object in RStudio, it is usually retained in the Environment, so further code in the R Script can instantly recall any object for additional use. This means you can easily produce multiple visualizations to illustrate different aspects of the data by reusing objects.

Objects created by an R Script are listed on the Environment tab in RStudio's Workspace pane. Each list item provides the object type, name, and a brief description. Beside each object name is a drop-down button that expands the item to reveal its contents. Typically, the first object created will, of course, be a data object:

MultiplePlots.R

1. Begin an R Script by importing a dataset describing historical Atlantic hurricane events
   frame <- read.csv("DataSet-Hurricanes.csv")

2. Run the line of code to create a data frame object and see it on the Environment tab in the Workspace pane

3. Click the drop-down button beside the object name to reveal its contents

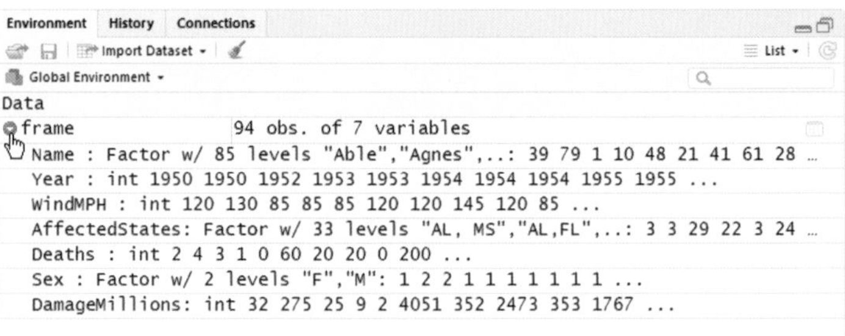

Notice that the contents of the object, revealed by clicking the drop-down button, describe its structure – just like calling **str(frame)** in the R Script code.

Examination of the data frame object reveals that it contains the hurricane names, the year they struck, the wind speed when they made landfall, two-letter abbreviations of the states they hit, the number of fatalities that arose, the gender of the name each hurricane was given, and the cost of the damage they caused. Visualizations comparing many aspects of this data could prove interesting, so this data object will be used, and reused throughout this chapter.

4. Next, add a statement to output the first eight rows in the Console to see the columns, then run this line of code
head(frame, n=8)

```
Console C:/MyRScripts/
> head( frame, n=8 )
      Name Year WindMPH AffectedStates Deaths Sex DamageMillions
1     Easy 1950     120             FL      2   F             32
2     King 1950     130             FL      4   M            275
3     Able 1952      85             SC      3   M             25
4  Barbara 1953      85             NC      1   F              9
5 Florence 1953      85             FL      0   F              2
6    Carol 1954     120    NC,NY,CT,RI     60   F           4051
7     Edna 1954     120          MA,ME     20   F            352
8    Hazel 1954     145       SC,NC,MD     20   F           2473
>
```

Notice that some hurricanes affected multiple states that are listed in a single cell.

5. Add a statement to load the ggplot2 library, then run this line of code
library(ggplot2)

6. Now, add function calls to create a ggplot object and specify geometry to simply plot points

```
ggplot( data=frame,
        aes( x=Year,
        y=DamageMillions, size=DamageMillions,
        color=WindMPH ) ) + geom_point( )
```

7. Run the lines of code in the previous step to see the plot – but no object is added to the RStudio Environment as this object is not retained (the next example will fix this)

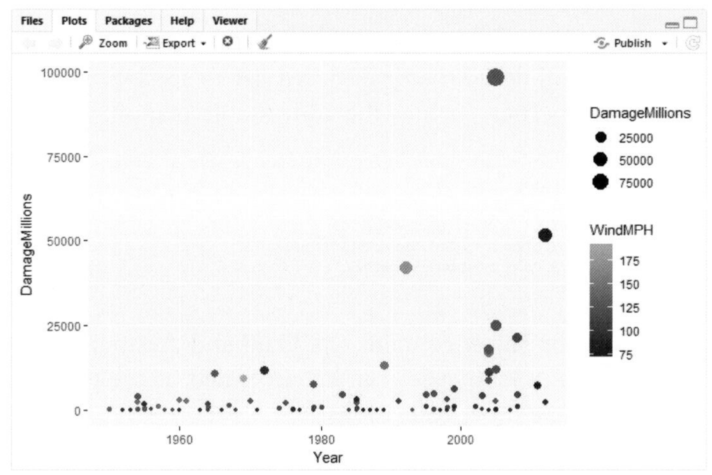

The points illustrate that the cost of damage caused by each hurricane over the years is less than 25 billion – with three notable exceptions.

Retaining objects

In order to retain a ggplot object in RStudio, it is necessary to assign the call to the **ggplot( )** function to a variable name of your choice. This adds the object to the Environment tab in RStudio's Workspace pane. The Data contents appear as in the previous example but each of their rows now begins with ..$ indicating they can be addressed in code using the $ dollar operator:

MultiplePlots.R (continued)

1. Add a statement to create a ggplot object

```
damage_plot <- ggplot( data=frame,
        aes( x=Year,
        y=DamageMillions,
        size= DamageMillions,
        color=WindMPH ) )
```

2. Run the lines of code in the previous step to see the object added to the RStudio Environment

3. Click the drop-down button beside the object name to reveal its contents and see the dollar operators

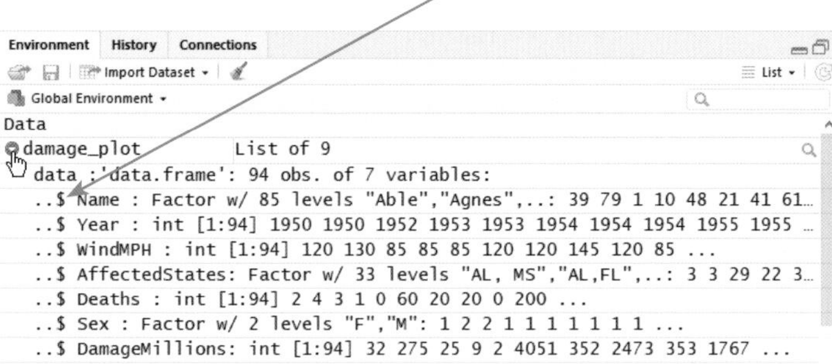

4. Scroll down the drop-down list to see lots of object properties, such as the addressable mapping items

```
mapping :List of 4
..$ x : symbol Year
..$ y : symbol DamageMillions
..$ size : symbol DamageMillions
..$ color: symbol WindMPH
```

You can assign new values to the mapping items in R Script code to change property values of the ggplot object.

As the ggplot object contains the Data and Aesthetics specifications, Geometries can be appended to the ggplot object to create simple data visualizations.

5. Append a geometry specification to simply plot points – recreating the previous plot, but with a re-usable object
damage_plot + geom_point( )

6. Run the line of code to see the plot appear, as before

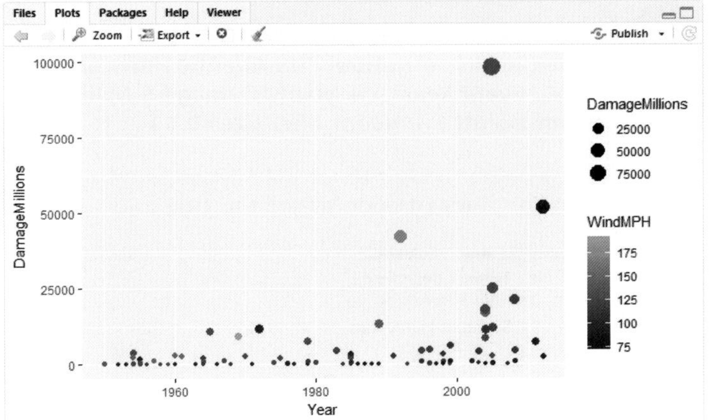

You can confirm that an item is a ggplot object by specifying its name as the argument to the **is.ggplot( )** function.

The ggplot object can be re-used to easily add more layers to the visualization to suit your requirements:

7. Append a second geometry specification to draw lines between the points, to emphasize spikes in the pattern
damage_plot + geom_point( ) + geom_line(size=0.5)

8. Run the line of code to see the revised plot appear

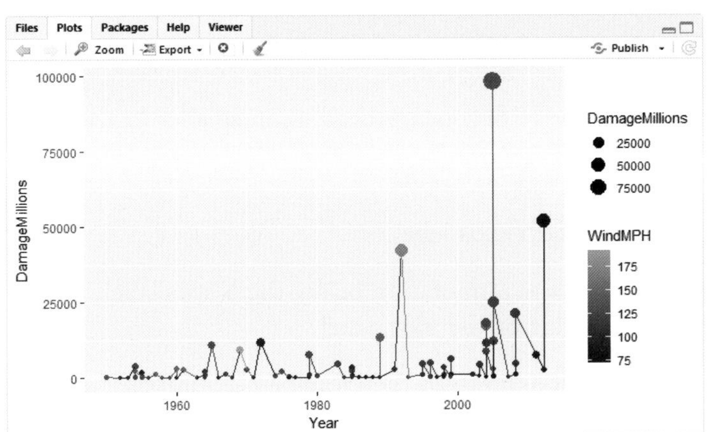

The spikes emphasize that the cost of hurricane damage has generally increased since 2000.

Overriding labels

Typically, the default X-axis and Y-axis labels on a plot are simply the names of the data fields from which the data is taken. You can override these by specifying your own label names as the argument to **xlab( )** and **ylab( )** functions respectively. Additionally, you can specify a plot title as the argument to a **ggtitle( )** function. For example, to override default labels on the previous example:

MultiplePlots.R
(continued)

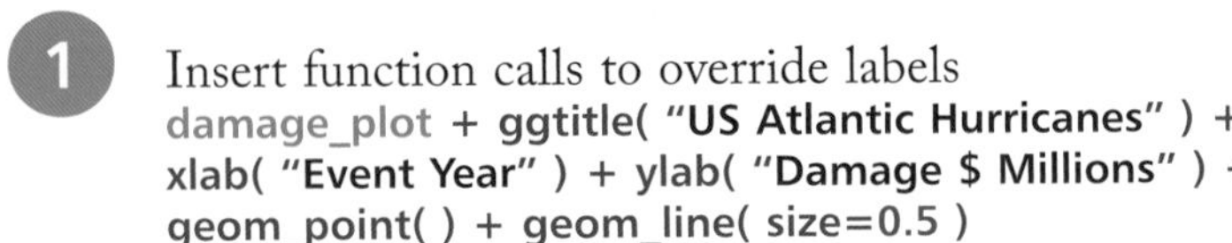

1. Insert function calls to override labels

```
damage_plot + ggtitle( "US Atlantic Hurricanes" ) +
xlab( "Event Year" ) + ylab( "Damage $ Millions" ) +
geom_point( ) + geom_line( size=0.5 )
```

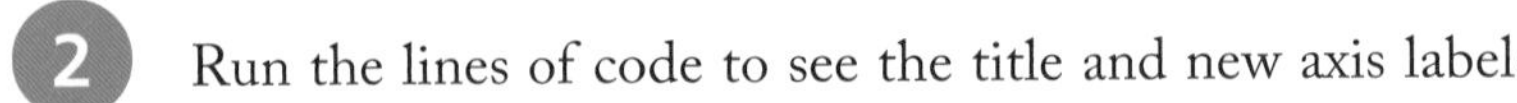

2. Run the lines of code to see the title and new axis labels

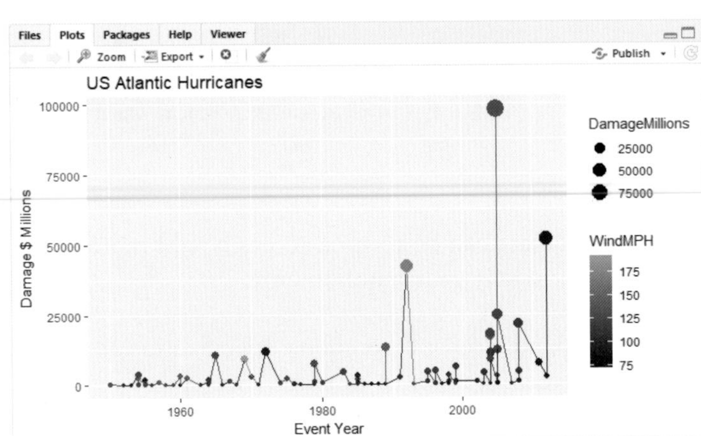

Labels are a part of Aesthetics, so come between the Data layer and Geometry layer in the grammar of graphics.

Alternatively, default plot labels can be overridden by specifying label names to these arguments of the **labs( )** function:

- **title=** – The main title above the top of the plot.
- **subtitle=** – Secondary heading in smaller text below the title.
- **x=** – The X-axis label.
- **y=** – The Y-axis label.
- **caption=** – Annotation below the Y-axis label, aligned to the right edge of the plot panel.

The **labs( )** function can therefore be used in place of **ggtitle( )**, **xlab( )**, and **ylab( )** function calls in the example above.

3. Replace the function calls in the previous example to override labels, then run the code to see new labels
damage_plot + labs(title="US Atlantic Hurricanes", subtitle="1950-2012", x="Event Year", y="Damage $ Millions", caption="Source: Wikipedia") + geom_point( ) + geom_line(size=0.5)

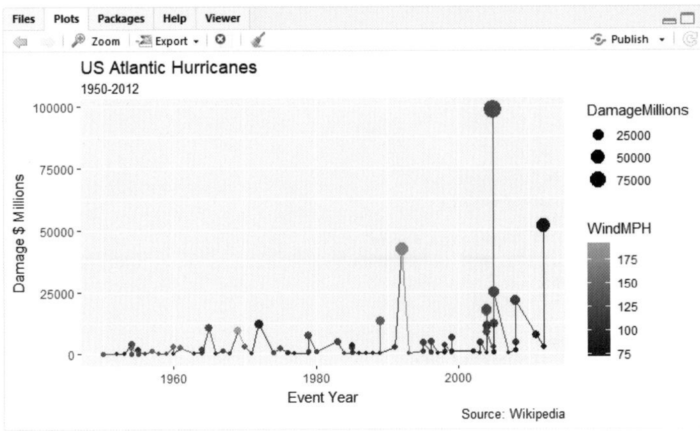

The code above that specifies the labels is becoming unwieldy and is not convenient to type repeatedly when producing multiple visualizations from one set of data. The solution is to create a label object that can be easily reused, just like the ggplot object:

4. Assign all specified labels to a name of your choice
label_object <- labs(title="US Atlantic Hurricanes", subtitle="1950-2012", x="Event Year", y="Damage $ Millions", caption="Source: Wikipedia")

5. Replace the previous function call with the label object
damage_plot + label_object + geom_point( ) + geom_line(size=0.5)

6. Run the code to see the labels appear as illustrated above, and see a reusable label object in the Environment tab

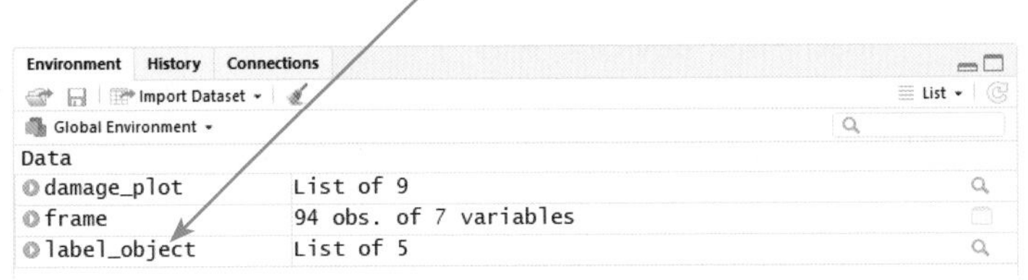

The label object created here is reused by all ensuing examples in this chapter.

Adding a theme

Refer back to page 162 for more on themes.

MultiplePlots.R (continued)

The **theme( )** function allows you to specify the size and color of the axes and legend labels, and the position of the legend on the visualization. Additionally, it can specify a particular font to a **family=** argument of a text element. The assignment must be the name of a font that is installed in RStudio. Initially, the choice of available fonts may be limited, but many more fonts can be made available by installing the "extrafont" package:

1. Call a function to list all (3) currently-installed fonts
windowFonts( )

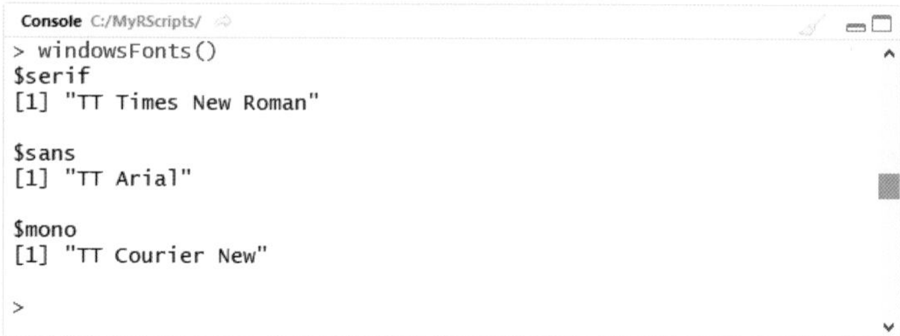

Console C:/MyRScripts/
> windowsFonts()
$serif
[1] "TT Times New Roman"
$sans
[1] "TT Arial"
$mono
[1] "TT Courier New"
>

2. Ensure your computer is connected to the internet, ready to download from the CRAN repository
3. Call a function to install an additional package
install.packages("extrafont", dependencies=TRUE)
4. When the download completes, load the new package into RStudio
library(extrafont)
5. Call a function to import the new fonts into RStudio without being prompted for confirmation
font_import(prompt=FALSE)
6. Call a function to register the fonts with a device for output
loadfonts(device="win")
7. Call a function to see that the list of currently-installed fonts has now increased greatly (presently up to 194)
length(windowFonts( ))

The installation of extra fonts into RStudio can take quite a while.

When producing multiple visualizations from one set of data, it is generally desirable to format each visualization with a common theme. It is therefore convenient to create a theme object that can be easily reused, just like the ggplot object and labels object:

8. Assign all specified theme values to a name of your choice

```
theme_object <- theme(
plot.title=element_text( color="Red", family="Wide Latin" ),
plot.subtitle=element_text( color="Red" ),
axis.title.x=element_text( color="Red", face="bold" ),
axis.title.y=element_text( color="Red", face="bold" ),
plot.caption=element_text( color="Black", face="italic" ),
legend.background=element_rect( color="Gray" ) )
```

9. Run the code to see a reusable theme object now appear on the Environment tab

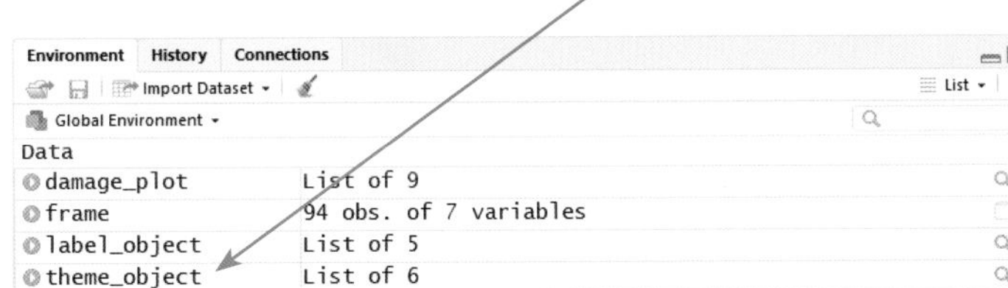

10. Append the theme object to the previous example, then run the code to see the theme applied

```
damage_plot + label_object +
geom_point( ) + geom_line( size=0.5 ) + theme_object
```

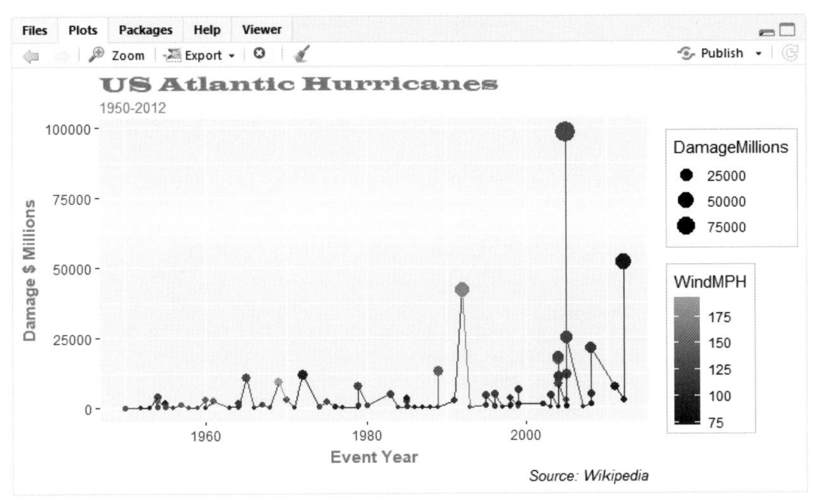

Use a font viewer, such as the drop-down menu in WordPad, to preview the available fonts.

The theme object created here is reused by all ensuing examples in this chapter.

Restoring the Workspace

You can choose the **Save** option on the "Quit R Session" dialog to restart RStudio with Environment objects preserved, so you can continue immediately.

Examples on the preceding pages of this chapter have described how to build up one data visualization using data frame, ggplot, label, and theme objects. Now, other data visualizations can be easily created to illustrate further insights into the same dataset by creating new ggplot objects. The same label and theme objects can be reused and axis labels updated where necessary by appending calls to the **xlab( )** and **ylab( )** functions after the label object.

If you restart RStudio you will have to rerun the lines of code to recreate the data frame, label, and theme objects, and also reload the ggplot2 and extrafont libraries before you can create more data visualizations:

MultiplePlots.R (continued)

1. Exit RStudio by selecting the **File**, **Quit Session** menu

2. Choose the **Don't Save** option to deliberately not save the Workspace

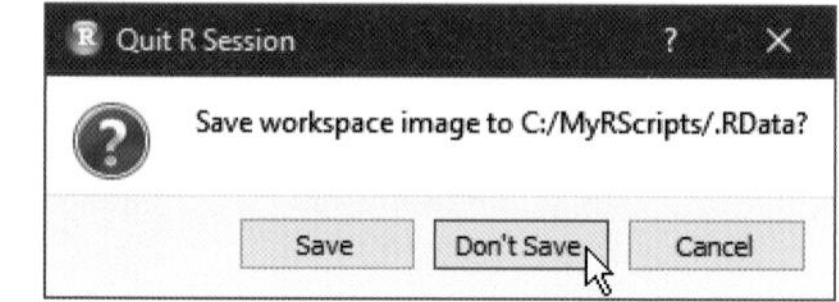

3. Restart RStudio and open the script file – see that the ggplot2 and extrafont libraries are not checked on the Packages tab, and the Environment tab is empty

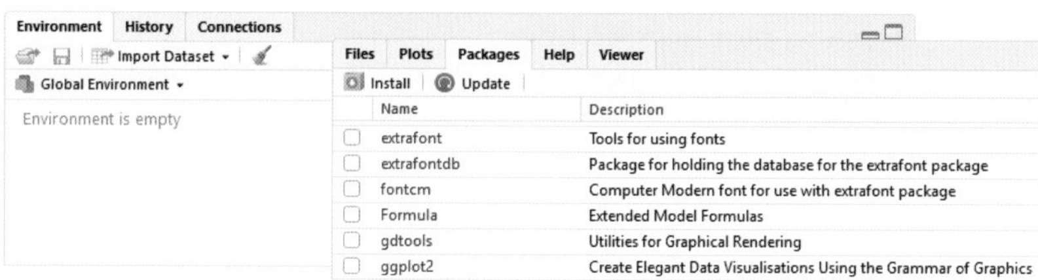

If you close RStudio without saving the Workspace you will need to restore objects and libraries into the Environment as described here for all further plot examples in this chapter.

4. Run the lines of code to recreate the data frame object and load the ggplot2 and extrafont library, then run the code to recreate the label and theme objects

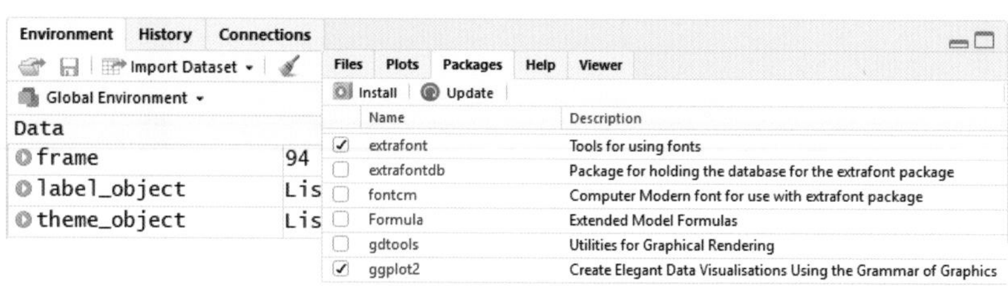

Comparing boxes

With data frame, label, theme objects, plus ggplot2 and extrafont libraries available, a new box plot data visualization can be created:

MultiplePlots.R (continued)

1. Add a statement to output the first eight rows in the Console to see the columns, then run this line of code
head(frame, n=8)

```
Console C:/MyRScripts/
> head( frame, n=8 )
      Name Year WindMPH AffectedStates Deaths Sex DamageMillions
1     Easy 1950     120             FL      2   F             32
2     King 1950     130             FL      4   M            275
3     Able 1952      85             SC      3   M             25
4  Barbara 1953      85             NC      1   F              9
5 Florence 1953      85             FL      0   F              2
6    Carol 1954     120    NC,NY,CT,RI     60   F           4051
7     Edna 1954     120          MA,ME     20   F            352
8    Hazel 1954     145       SC,NC,MD     20   F           2473
> 
```

2. Next, create a new ggplot object from the original data set, to illustrate different insights, then run the code
gender_plot <- ggplot(data=frame,
aes(x=Sex, y=Deaths, color=Sex), size=3)

3. Append labels, geometries, coordinate limit, and theme to the new ggplot object, then run the code to see the plot
gender_plot +
label_object +
xlab("Gender") + ylab("Number of Fatalities") +
geom_jitter( ) + geom_boxplot(alpha=0.5) +
ylim(10, 200) + theme_object

Remember to update the axis labels from those in the label object.

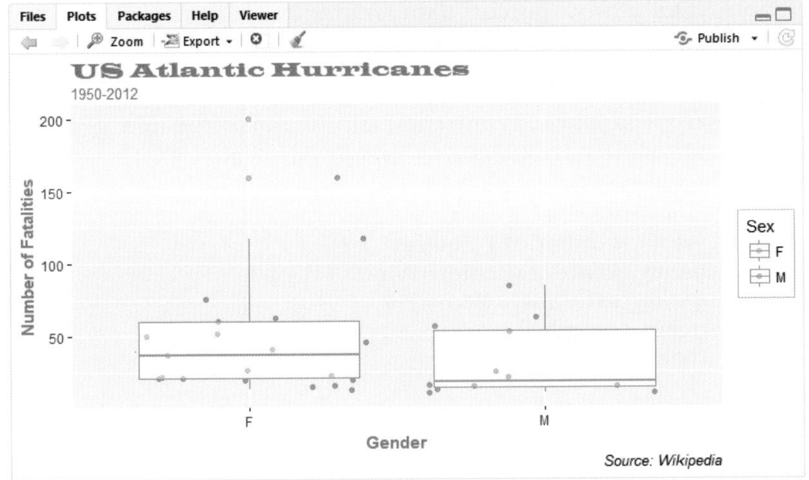

A controversial paper based on an earlier version of this data claimed that hurricanes with female names, presumably taken less seriously, caused more deaths than hurricanes with male names.

Identifying extremes

With data frame, label, theme objects, plus ggplot2 and extrafont libraries available, a new point plot data visualization can be created to illustrate trends.

The average trend can be illustrated by appending a Smooth geometry to the ggplot object so that points outside the average band are instantly apparent.

In order to identify points, they can be labeled by mapping each point label to a data field in the ggplot object in a call to the **geom_text( )** function. As usual, the mapping must be wrapped in an **aes( )** argument to the **geom_text( )** function. The field name can then be assigned to a label= argument to the **aes( )** function:

MultiplePlots.R (continued)

1. Add a statement to output the first eight rows in the Console to see the columns, then run this line of code
head(frame, n=8)

```
Console C:/MyRScripts/
> head( frame, n=8 )
      Name Year WindMPH AffectedStates Deaths Sex DamageMillions
1     Easy 1950     120             FL      2   F             32
2     King 1950     130             FL      4   M            275
3     Able 1952      85             SC      3   M             25
4  Barbara 1953      85             NC      1   F              9
5 Florence 1953      85             FL      0   F              2
6    Carol 1954     120    NC,NY,CT,RI     60   F           4051
7     Edna 1954     120          MA,ME     20   F            352
8    Hazel 1954     145       SC,NC,MD     20   F           2473
> 
```

2. Next, create a new ggplot object from the original data set, to illustrate different insights, then run the code

```
fatal_plot <- ggplot( data=frame,
                      aes( x=Year, y=Deaths ) )
```

3. Append labels, geometries, and theme to the new ggplot object, then run the code to see the plot

```
fatal_plot +
label_object +
ylab( "Number of Fatalities" ) +
geom_point( aes( color=WindMPH ) ) +
geom_text( label=Name ) +
geom_smooth( ) +
theme_object
```

Remember that appended functions inherit access to the field names in the ggplot object.

The labels overlap each other in the average area and overlap the points, so it would be better to label only the extreme points.

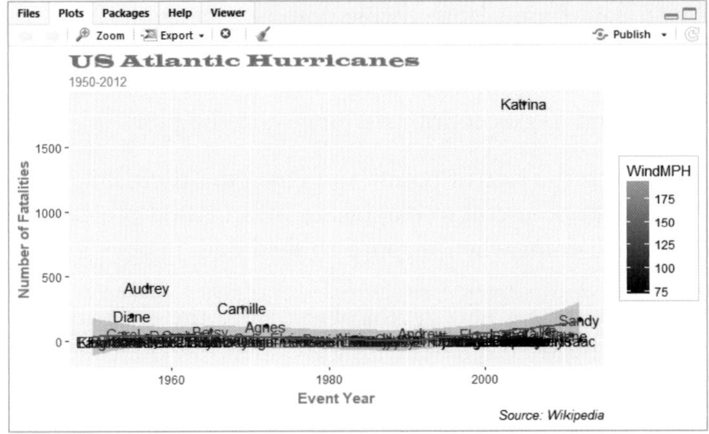

A **hjust=** argument can be included to adjust the horizontal position of the labels, and a conditional **ifelse** test can be included in the **label=** assignment to label selective points. This returns factors, so text must be converted by the **as.character( )** function:

4. Edit the assignment in the previous step to include a conditional test

```
geom_text( aes( label=ifelse( Deaths > 180,
                as.character( Name ), "" ) ,
                hjust=1.1 ) ) +
```

5. Run the code again to see the plot now labels only the extreme points outside the average band

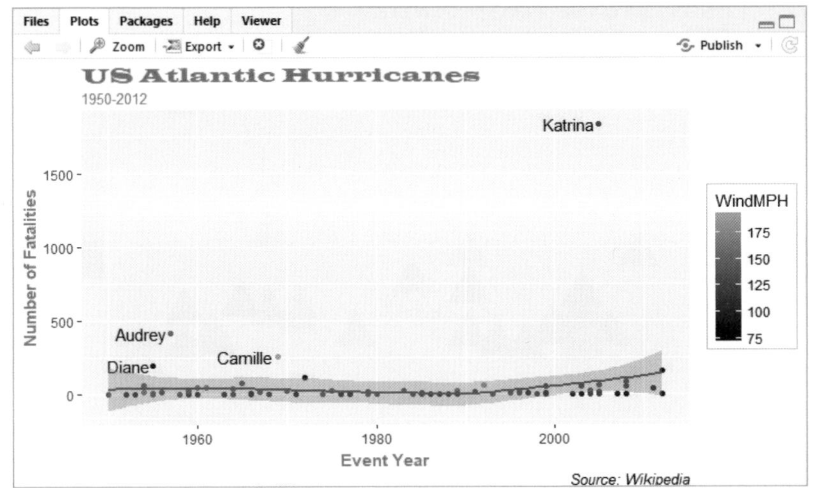

There is also a **vjust=** argument that can be used to adjust the vertical position of labels. Experiment with different values to see how they adjust the label position.

This plot illustrates that hurricane Katrina of 2005 was by far the most devastating, and significantly more deadly than any other hurricane.

Limiting focus

With data frame, label, theme objects, plus ggplot2 and extrafont libraries available, a new point plot data visualization can be created to focus on a particular area of interest by limiting the X-axis and Y-axis coordinate ranges on the plot.

Increasing the size of points and changing their shape can sometimes be useful to emphasize information provided by the points' fill color when mapped to field data in the ggplot object:

MultiplePlots.R (continued)

1. Create a new ggplot object from the original data set, to illustrate different insights, then run the code

```
windspeed_plot <- ggplot( data=frame,
                          aes( x=Year, y=Deaths ) )
```

2. Append labels, a geometry, coordinate limits, and a theme to the ggplot object

```
windspeed_plot +
label_object +
ylab( "Number of Fatalities" ) +
geom_point( aes( color=WindMPH ), size=10, shape=17 ) +
xlim( 1980, 2000 ) +
ylim( 0, 65 ) +
theme_object
```

The possible point shapes are illustrated on page 98.

3. Run the code to see the plot display triangles filled with color mapped to wind speed

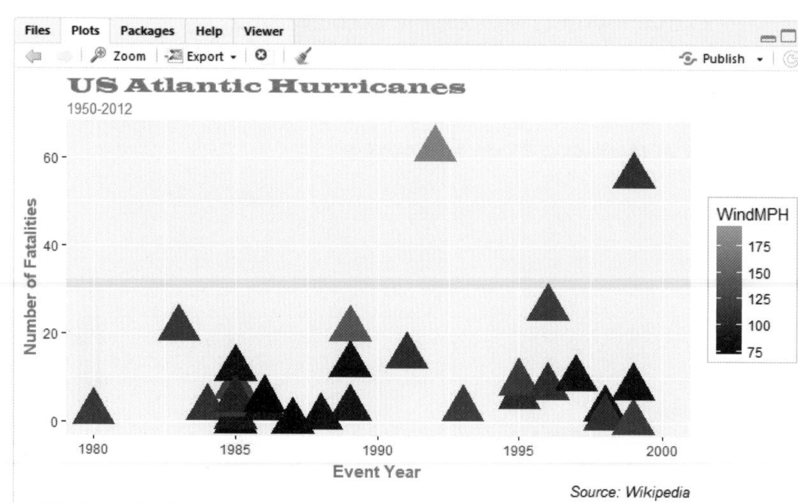

Looking at the top two strikes illustrates that hurricanes with high or low windspeed can both be costly to human life.

Zooming focus

With data frame, label, theme objects, plus ggplot2 and extrafont libraries available, a new bar chart data visualization can be created to focus on an area of interest by zooming into that area.

Remember that limiting the X-axis and Y-axis coordinate ranges on the plot R may remove some of the data in preparing the visualization. This means that the chart may not accurately represent the data. It is, therefore, advisable to zoom into the area of interest for accuracy:

1. Create a new ggplot object from the original data set, to illustrate different insights, then run the code

```
strike_plot <- ggplot( data=frame,
                       aes( x=Year, y=Sex ) )
```

MultiplePlots.R (continued)

2. Append labels, a geometry, coordinate zoom, and a theme to the ggplot object

```
strike_plot +
label_object +
ylab( "Number of Strikes" ) +
geom_bar( ) +
coord_cartesian( xlim=c( 1980, 2000 ) ) +
theme_object
```

The **xlim( )** function requires two numeric arguments, but the **xlim=** argument requires a vector.

3. Run the code to see the chart display bars filled with color mapped to the gender of hurricane names

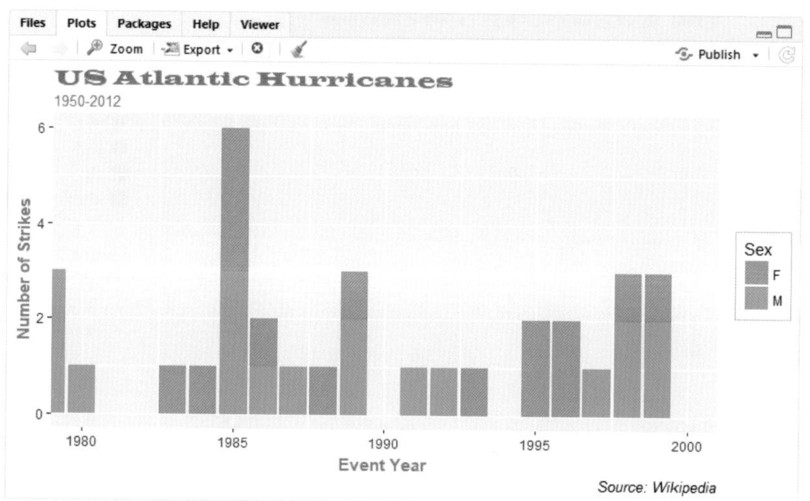

Counting the number of strikes of each gender name reveals an equal number of strikes for male and female names (15 for each).

Displaying facets

The **grep( )** function can be used to retrieve only specific data that is of interest for comparison. For example, to retrieve data only for the state where a hurricane made landfall and adjacent states that were affected only by those hurricanes:

MultiplePlots.R (continued)

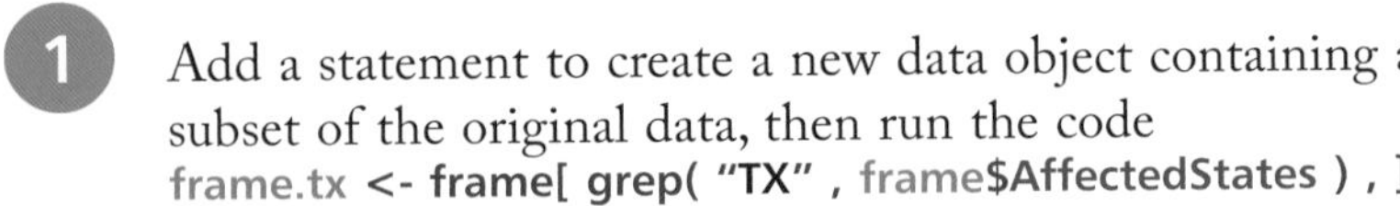

1. Add a statement to create a new data object containing a subset of the original data, then run the code

```
frame.tx <- frame[ grep( "TX" , frame$AffectedStates ) , ]
```

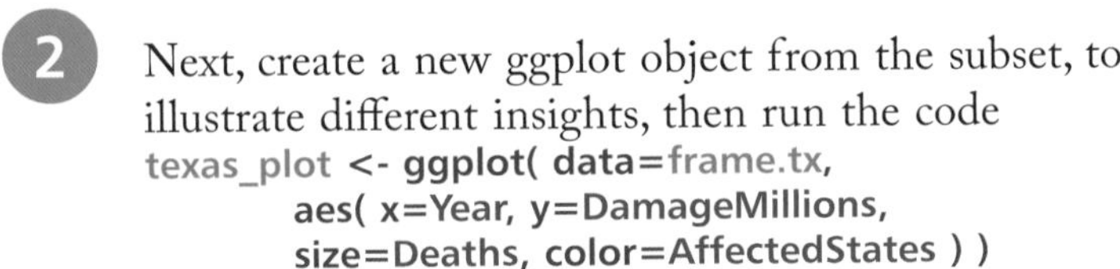

2. Next, create a new ggplot object from the subset, to illustrate different insights, then run the code

```
texas_plot <- ggplot( data=frame.tx,
        aes( x=Year, y=DamageMillions,
        size=Deaths, color=AffectedStates ) )
```

Click the "brush" icon on the Plots tab then rerun if RStudio fails to display all plot components.

Clear all Plots

3. Append labels, a geometry, a facet grid, and a theme to the ggplot object, then run the code to see the plot

```
texas_plot +
label_object +
geom_point( aes( size=Deaths ) ) +
facet_grid( AffectedStates~. )+
theme_object
```

Looking at the facets indicates that only two adjacent states were affected by hurricanes that make landfall in the state of Texas.

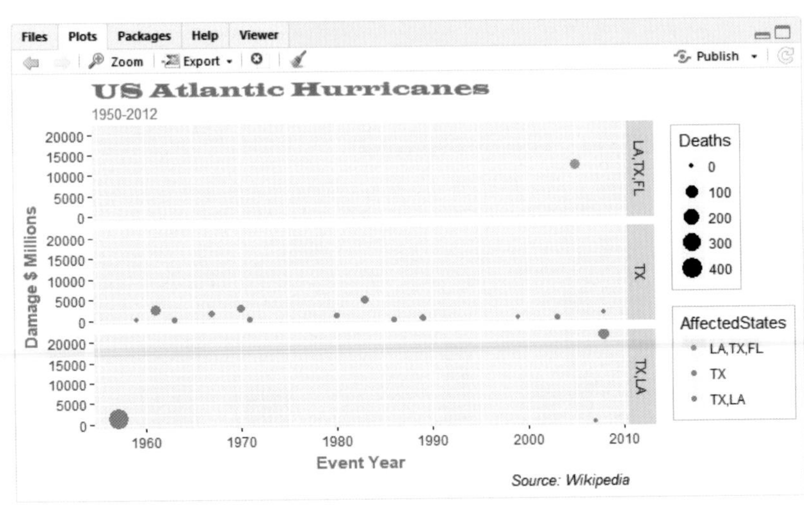

...cont'd

Where a facet grid produces too many facets to be useful, it is often better to produce a histogram chart for comparison of specific data. For example, to retrieve data only for the state where a hurricane made landfall and adjacent states that were affected only by those hurricanes – similar to the example opposite:

MultiplePlots.R (continued)

1. Add a statement to create a new data object containing a subset of the original data, then run the code

```
frame.fl <- frame[ grep( "FL" , frame$AffectedStates ) , ]
```

2. Next, create a new ggplot object from the subset, to illustrate different insights, then run the code

```
florida_plot <- ggplot( data=frame.fl, aes( x=Year  ) )
```

3. Append labels, a geometry, and a theme to the ggplot object

```
florida_plot +
label_object +
ylab( "Number of Strikes in Florida" ) +
geom_histogram( aes( fill=AffectedStates ),
                        color="Black", bins=20 ) +
theme_object
```

4. Run the code to see the various facets of the data mapped to colors on the plot

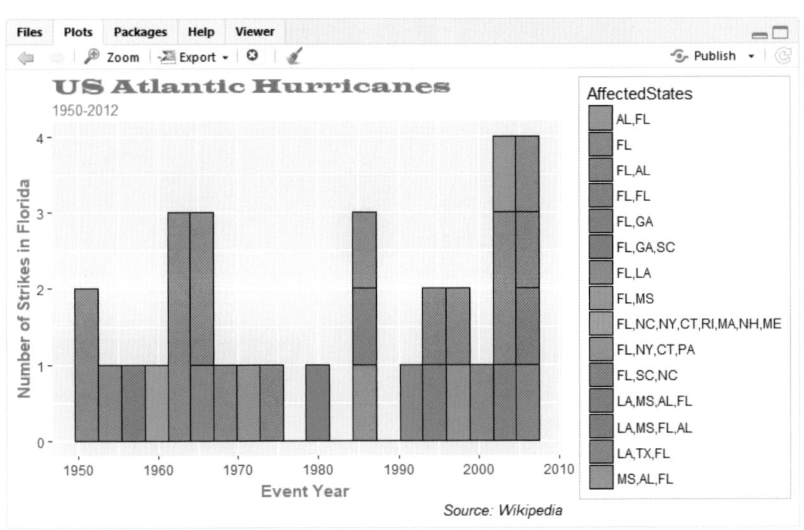

Looking at the stacked columns indicates that many adjacent states were affected by hurricanes that made landfall in the state of Florida.

Exporting graphics

Having created a collection of data visualizations in RStudio, you can export them as graphic images to present your analysis. RStudio supports the export of BMP, JPEG, PNG and TIFF bitmap file formats, plus EPS, EMF, SVG, and PDF formats:

MultiplePlots.R
(continued)

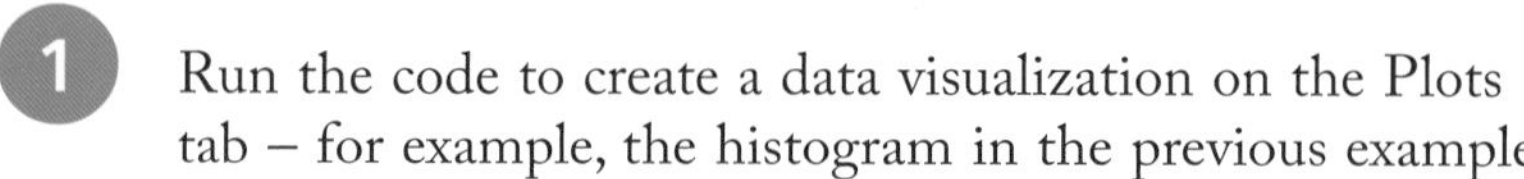

1. Run the code to create a data visualization on the Plots tab – for example, the histogram in the previous example

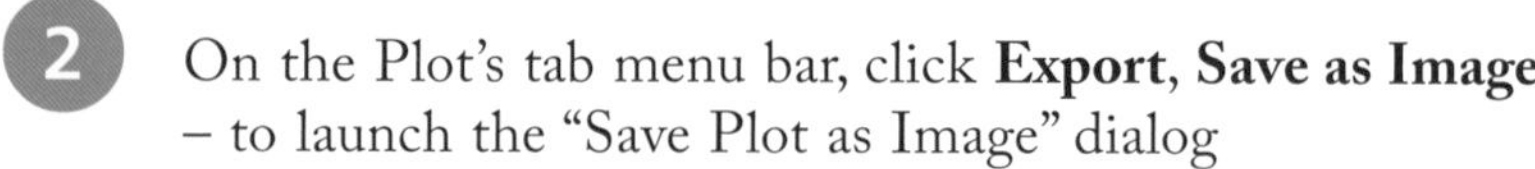

2. On the Plot's tab menu bar, click **Export**, **Save as Image** – to launch the "Save Plot as Image" dialog

3. Choose a format from the drop-down menu
4. Select a directory location, and file name

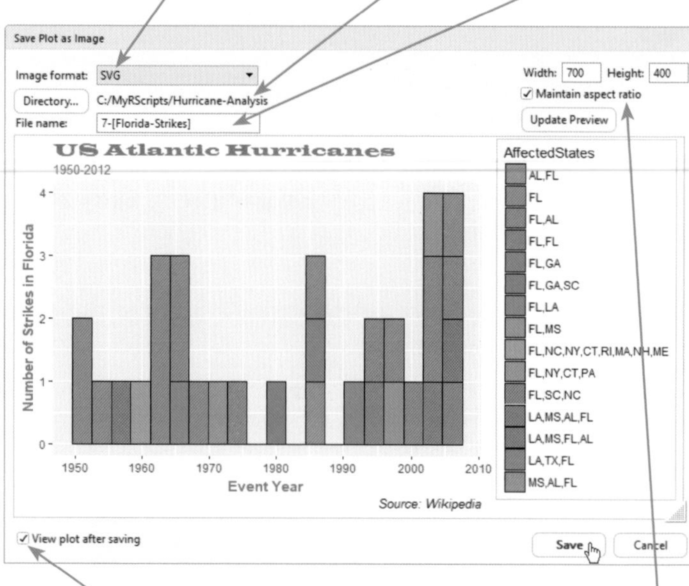

5. Check **View plot after saving** (if required)
6. Check **Maintain aspect ratio** option (if desired)
7. Click the **Save** button to create an image at the selected location, and see the image open in the application associated with the chosen format on your system

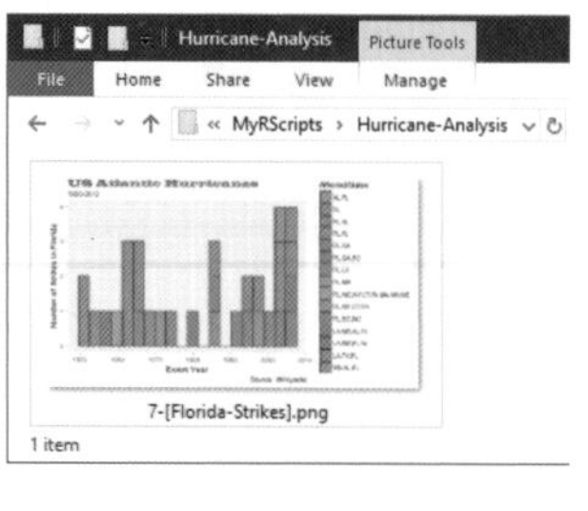

You can edit the values in the **Width** and **Height** boxes, then click the **Update Preview** button to see how it will look before proceeding to create the image.

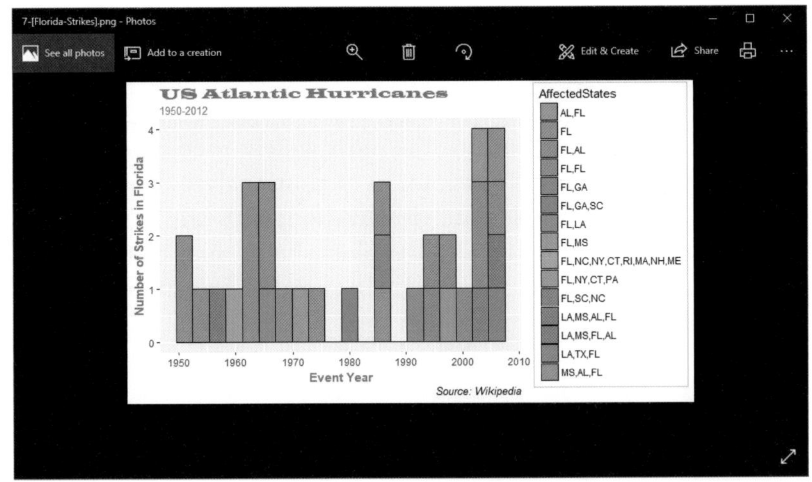

The PDF format does not appear in the drop-down list on the "Save Plot as Image" dialog. Choose **Export**, **Save as PDF...** on the Plot tab instead.

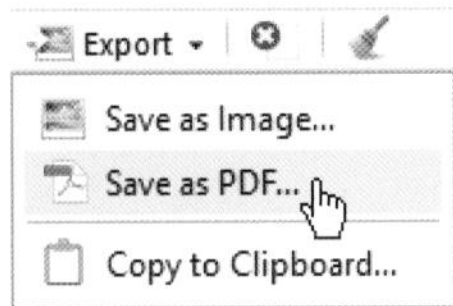

Deciding on an image file format in which to save your data visualizations largely depends on how you want to use them. Simple comparisons are listed in the table below, together with the file size of saving the image illustrated above in each file type:

Format:	Description:	File Size:
BMP	Non-resizable, Windows standard and supported almost everywhere.	275KB
JPEG	Non-resizable, good for use on web pages for older web browsers.	123KB
PNG	Non-resizable, good for use on web pages for modern web browsers.	10KB
TIFF	Non-resizable, uncompressed RGB best choice for color separation for print.	817KB
EPS	Resizable, best choice for color separation for print.	7KB
EMF	Resizable, best choice for use with Microsoft Office applications.	243KB
SVG	Resizable, best choice for use on web pages for modern web browsers.	208KB
PDF	Resizable, best choice for distribution such as email attachments.	7KB

The small file size of the PNG file format shown here demonstrates why this is generally preferred for fixed-size images.

Presenting analyses

The most effective way to communicate and distribute the results of your analyses is to create a slide show presentation to convey insights into the data on each slide.

Microsoft PowerPoint remains the most widely-used presentation application so is best for distribution of your analyses. Each slide may contain a single data visualization, with any insights it reveals annotated on that slide. The plots should first be exported from RStudio as graphics in the EMF metafile format, for best compatibility with the PowerPoint app:

MultiplePlots.R (continued)

1. Run the code in RStudio to create the first data visualization analysis, then click **Export**, **Save as Image** and choose the **Metafile** option

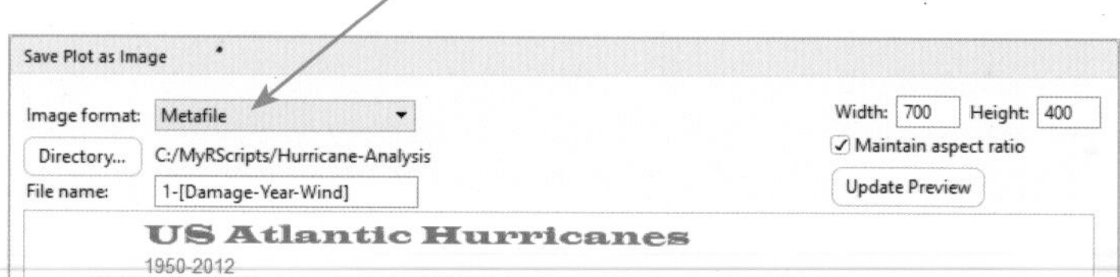

2. Save the image in a unique folder, then repeat for each plot

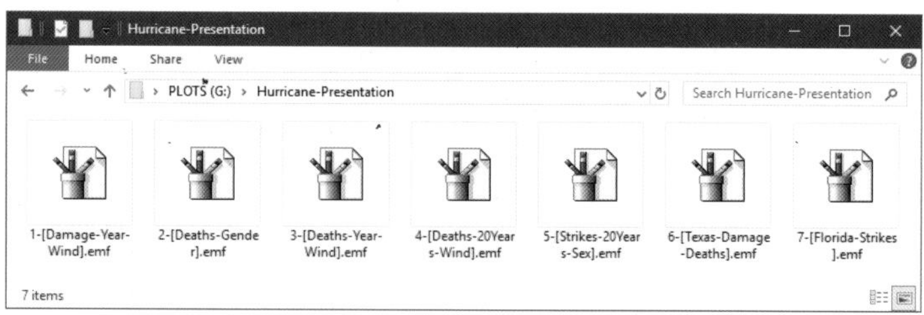

3. Launch the PowerPoint app and start a new presentation with your preferred theme, such as “Ion Boardroom”

4. Complete the title page with your presentation’s title, then click **New Slide**, **Blank** on PowerPoint’s “Home” tab

5. Select the **Insert** tab, then click the **Pictures** icon and choose the first image in your unique folder

Metafile EMF images imported into PowerPoint can be converted to Microsoft Office drawing objects for direct editing.

6. Next, resize the image to your preference, then drag it to your preferred position

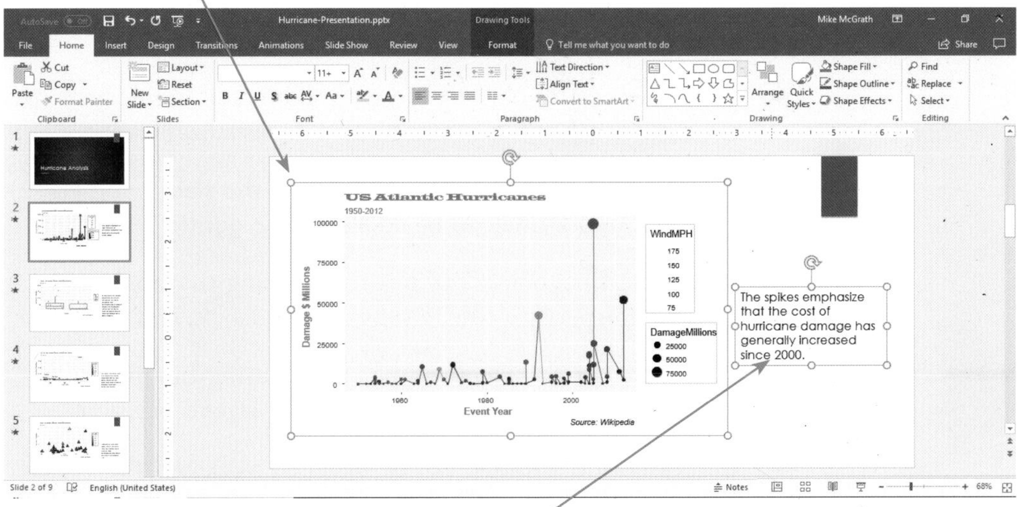

7. To annotate the slide with insights, select the **Text Box** icon on the **Insert** tab, then click the slide and type text

8. Repeat the process for each plot, then select **From Beginning** on the **Slide Show** tab to run the presentation

9. Adjust as required then save the file – you can now freely distribute this as your PowerPoint analyses presentation

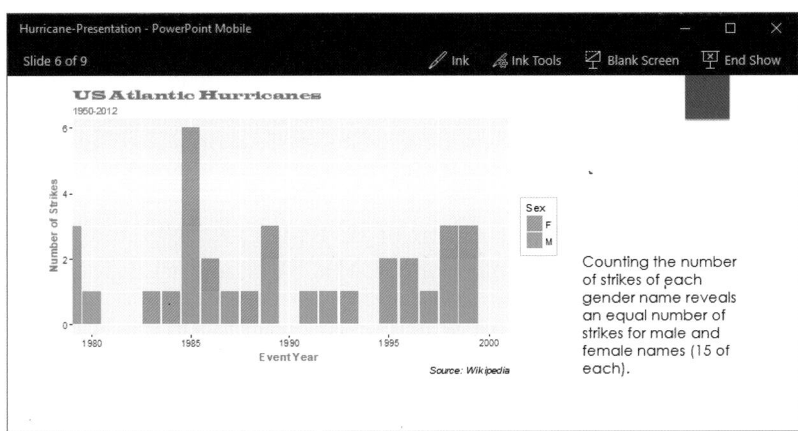

Summary

- Objects created in RStudio are retained in the Environment so they can be reused to create multiple data visualizations.
- A ggplot object must be assigned to a variable name in order to retain the ggplot object within the Environment.
- A retained ggplot object can be reused to add more layers to one data visualization, or multiple data visualizations.
- Default axis labels can be overridden by the **xlab( )** and **ylab( )** functions, and a title can be added by the **ggtitle( )** function.
- A reusable label object can be created using the **labs( )** function to specify a title, a subtitle, axis labels, and a caption.
- A reusable theme object can be created using the **theme( )** function to specify label appearance and legend position.
- The "extrafont" package can be installed to extend the number of fonts available in RStudio.
- Closing RStudio without saving the Workspace will require objects to be recreated before more plots can be created.
- Additional visualizations may require labels to be updated by appending calls to **xlab( )** and **ylab( )** after the label object.
- Plot points can be labeled by mapping each point's label to a data field in the ggplot object in a call to **geom_text( )**.
- Selective points can be labeled by including a conditional **ifelse** test in the **label=** assignment within **geom_text( )**.
- Factors must be converted to strings by the **as.character( )** function before they can be applied as label text.
- The **grep( )** function can be used to retrieve only specific data that is of interest for comparison.
- RStudio supports the export of BMP, JPEG, PNG and TIFF bitmap file formats, plus EPS, EMF, SVG, and PDF formats.
- PowerPoint is the most widely-used presentation application.
- Plots should be exported from RStudio in the EMF metafile format for best compatibility with the PowerPoint app.

Index

A

B

C

D

E

F

G

H

I

K

L

M

N

O

P

Q

R

S

T

U

V

W

X

Y